JN422023

Greening Global Logistics

Greening Global Logistics

Pak Myong-Sop | Hwang Seok-Joon | Shin Soo-Yong | Kim In Sun | Justin Hiraga
Sungkyunkwan University SSK SME Research Division

아카데미프레스

Pak Myong-Sop, Ph.D. (Univ. of Liverpool)
Professor of International Logistics and Trade in the Business School at Sungkyunkwan University. He is also President of Korea Trade Research Association., Sungkyunkwan University. He has published more than 200 books and articles in Korean, English and Japanese. He has also been the recipient of several Korea Research Foundation and Japan Foundation grants to study global logistics.

Hwang Seok-Joon, Ph.D. (Pennsylvania State University)
_ Assistant professor
_ School of Economics and Trade
_ Kyungpook National University, Korea

Shin Soo-Yong, Ph.D. (Sungkyunkwan University)
_ Lecturer at Sungkyunkwan University
_ M.A. Economics (University of Glasgow, U.K.)
_ MSc International Business (Glasgow Caledonian University, U.K)

Kim In Sun
_ Lecturer at Soongsil University
_ University of Illinois at Urbana Champaign – Undergraduate in Economics and Psychology
_ Sungkyunkwan University, International Trade, ABD

Justin Hiraga
_ Assistant Professor, Seokyeong University, Seoul, Korea.
_ BS (Univ. of California, Davis)
_ MS (Business School, Sungkyunkwan University, Seoul, Korea)
_ Ph.D. Candidate (Dept. of International Trade, Sungkyunkwan University, Seoul, Korea)

Preface

First and foremost, I would like to thank everyone who has supported me in completing this book. This book would not have been possible without their support and encouragement.

Also I would like to extend my gratitude to National Research Foundation of Korea Grant. This research was supported by the National Research Foundation of Korea Grant funded by the Korean Government (NRF-2013S1A3A2055150). This book is a product of SSK SME Research Division: A Harmonization of FTA, Energy, Environment and Economy.

The journey to writing this book has been a long one but, I deeply wished to produce a book that would provide comprehensive yet fundamental knowledge in International Logistics and supply chain management (SCM) in an easily approachable manner. International logistics and SCM are basic tools for modern global competition. Firms cannot and will not survive without efficiently managing their logistics and SCM system. Thus, this book serves as an introduction to how logistics and SCM enhance and contribute to cutting costs and building competitive advantage.

Understanding and applying logistics and SCM concepts to build competitiveness are important to all. Therefore key concepts are provided in a way both international logistics majors and non-majors can easily comprehend. It starts with the basics; definition, history and development of international logistics and SCM.

This book consists of four units.

Unit 1 illustrates the evolution of logistics and SCM, how globalization and international trade effected the development of logistics and SCM and finally defines elements of supply chain management. Basic elements of SCM are introduced in Unit 1 but four key elements are further discussed in Unit 2 and Unit 3.

Unit 2 takes a deeper look into distribution and transportation. In this Unit, different types of transportation mode will be discussed and the roles and functions of distribution will also be studied.

Unit 3 focuses on storages and inventory management and identifies key operation strategies for competitiveness. Efforts towards conserving the environment have been the center of attention in the 21st century and lead to "green logistics and SCM" concept.

Unit 4 lays out milestones in green SCM development process and gives real-life examples of how firms are incorporating sustainability in order to maximize profits while behaving environmentally conscious.

In each unit, it contains case studies and recent news articles which will help students to better grasp the concepts and systems of logistics and SCM using real world related topics. Case studies and news articles will provide students with critical thinking ability in addition to traditional theories. Special thanks to Korea JoongAng Daily, Korea Times and Korea Herald for allowing us to reprint articles. I hope this book will provide an opportunity for students to better understand the concepts and themes of international logistics and SCM.

Table of Contents

Unit 3
Elements of Supply Chain Management and its Operation II

Unit 4
Green SCM

UNIT. 1

INTRODUCTION TO LOGISTICS AND SCM

CHAPTER 1

History and Development of Logistics

Learning objectives

- Understand the term of logistics
- Be able to explain the origin and developmental process of logistics
- Be able to explain the major aims and role of logistics

1.1 Definition of Logistics

Before we dive into the fascinating subject of logistics, supply chain management, and international trade, we must first define the term logistics. There are various definitions of logistics and while the majority of them are similar, some differ.

Canadian Association of Logistics Management defines logistics as

> "The process of planning, implementing, and controlling the efficient, cost effective flow and storage of raw materials, in-process inventory, finished goods and related information from point of origin to point of consumption for the purpose of meeting customer requirements."

LogisticsWorld defines logistics as

> "The science of planning, design, and support of business operations of procurement, purchasing, inventory, warehousing, distribution, transportation, customer support, financial and human resources."

As stated above, this book will consider logistics as "the basic concept of managing and implementing efficient flow of resources, products and services". From this definition of logistics, we will derive a definition of supply chain management. To do so, we must study the history and developmental process of logistics.

Logistics dates back to ancient civilization and has existed ever since the history of human race began. Transporting and storing essentials-food-naturally became a priority in the ancient times and they eventually led to the full development of logistics as we know today. Logistics has been the building block of great economic and social development. Thus, we can grasp a basic understanding of the history and developmental process of logistics by examining the development history of human civilization.

1.2 History of Logistics

The first elaborate logistics system can be found around 2700 B.C. when the Great Pyramid of Giza was constructed. Great Pyramid of Giza is 146 meters high and 6 million tons in weight and even today, we still cannot fully understand how stone building blocks were transported and the engineering techniques behind it. But the fact remains, tons of stone building blocks were 'somehow' transported under an elaborate logistics system. How stone building blocks were transported remains controversial but the most accepted view is water transport.

One school of thought pioneered by Polish engineer Andrzej Bocknacki argues that stone building blocks were transported by River Nile. Papyrus boats were attached on top of huge stones and awaited for flood season ready for transport. During the flood season water level reached near the pyramid construction site and the "floating" stones were easily transported to close proximity to the construction site. Then the workers waited for the water level to reduce and transported a short distance to the actual construction site. This gave Egyptians the advantage of constructing and assembling on site rather than struggling with transporting semi-finished or finished products. By transporting stones using water level difference the Egyptians could avoid the hassle of loading and unloading. It also meant Egyptians could overcome scare resource problems by sourcing stones from far away.

Intercontinental trade became possible with the invention of Greek rowing vessels around 300 B.C. which allowed large quantities of army supplies to be rapidly transported over long distance. Alexander the Great used this logistics supply system to travel to India with his troops, war supplies and their families. Systematic procurement logistics developed around 700 A.D. when pillars and raw materials for constructing the Mezquita Mosque was brought in from all over the world. Mezquita Mosque is still the largest Mosque in Europe with 865 pillars holding its arcaded ceiling. Pillars were procured and transported from ruined churches and roman temples under Islamic empire.

How construction were managed;

1. Large stones were scoured and brought to the river bank for transportation.
2. Papyrus boats were attached to the stones for river transportation during low river level.
3. During flood season the water level rises and stones are able to float.
4. Stone building blocks are transported to a river bank nearby the pyramid construction site. By using river transport, stone building blocks were easily transported across a long distance com-

pared to backbreaking and time consuming land transport.

5. When stone building blocks reach the closest river bank to the construction site they await for the water level to fall. Labor intensive loading and unloading process are simplified by attaching and removing papyrus boats.
6. After water level falls, stone building blocks are transported to the final construction site. By using river transportation and clever loading and unloading methods, Egyptians cut labor, cost, and time related to resource transportation and increased its logistics system efficiency.

Hanseatic League

The first international maritime transport alliance that established a system of trade across regional boarders was the Hanseatic League. "Hanse" has the meaning for "guild" or "association" in Germany was found by north German town and merchants in the 1280s for cooperation on transport bundling and to protect mutual trading interests. The Hanseatic League enjoyed its height of power during the 13th and 15th centuries.

Association amongst German merchants existed before the Hanseatic League for securing their cargo from pirates but it was neither systematically organized nor recognized by foreign cities or nations. Association began its history with two German northern towns, Hamburg and Luebeck, located on the opposite side of Danish peninsula. Leubeck had a rich supply of herring which was matched by the abundant demand of fish diet in Europe. Christian Europe's diet consisted largely of fish since there were many fast days and the church prohibited eating meat on Fridays. Luebeck had the resources but had trouble transporting 'fresh' products. With no refrigerators, Luebeck was in desperate need of salt from Hamburg to prevent them from becoming perishable. Trade between Hamburg and Luebeck was essential in transporting and distributing fish and meat safely throughout Europe. It was only natural that trade boomed along the 'salt' road. This association was joined by Cologne in 1201 and other major port cities such as Danzig.

In 1265, "law of Luebeck" was introduced and all northern German towns agreed on common legislation to protect merchants' goods. In the 1270s, Hamburg-Luebeck association gained trading privileges in Flanders and major port cities in Baltic joined as well, thus the Hanseatic League as we know today was found in the 1280s. At its prime, Hanseatic League had over sixty cities as members and cooperation was much more extensive and regularized than 'pre-Hanseatic League' association. Hanseatic League formed its own parliament to govern over inter-city trade and common policies related to trade. Its main objective was to protect its merchants from unfair trading practices since merchants' goods were often confiscated upon arrival in foreign market and denied market entry. It also aimed to monopolize the market they supplied by gaining negotiation rights and trade privileges from foreign nations.

Trade privileges included safe passage of men and goods, equal treatment when compared to local goods making goods of Hanseatic League merchants as 'domestic products', tax exemptions, and establishment of foreign trade centers, residency status, and many other. Trade centers in foreign nations were called 'kontors' and these kontors were normally 3 story building. First floors were retail stores for selling and buying, second floors were warehouses for storage, and third floors were normally office spaces or adjusted to living accommodations. Kontors were located in Bruges in Flanders, Bergen in Norway, Novgorod in Russia, Wisby in the island of Gotland, London in England, and other major cities. Hanseatic League also took on the role of building lighthouses, promoting safe navigation by traveling in convoys, and training pilots. League's main trade commodities included grain, salt, wine, timber, honey, furs, tar, flax, cloth, copper, iron ore, and herring throughout Germany, Russia, Poland, Flanders, England, and Sweden.

Main reason why Hanseatic League is important in maritime transportation history is because it facilitates international trade. Facilitation of international trade was accomplished by two parts; an extensive self-governing international alliance and transporting major volume of cargo throughout Europe by bundling and bulk shipping. Moving large volumes of cargo was possible due to an innovative ship called Baltic cog. Before Baltic cog, Scandinavian design cargo ship could only transport a limited volume of cargo. Plus major trade commodities of Hanseatic League such as grain and salt were suitable for bulk shipping. Baltic cog allowed bulk shipping and could transport large volumes of cargo in a single voyage. Previous ships could only carry around 20 lasts but Baltic cog, on the other hand, could carry up to 200 lasts and 200,000 fur pelts. Hanseatic League is considered as an important mark in logistics history with its well organized international maritime transportation alliance and transporting large volumes of cargo across international borders.

European postal service

European postal service is also an important part of logistics history in the sense of linking foreign nations. Systematic postal service was established for the first time in Europe during the 1500s. It is considered to be the first and progressive postal service since it has had definite delivery schedule and transit times. Destinations included Paris, Ghent, Spain, Vienna and considering unfavorable conditions of that era, delivery reached its destination without much delay considering. Also technological innovations leading to the invention of vehicles, railroads, steam engines, ships, and crude oil set a historical mark in the evolution of transportation. New and fast discovery of transportation led to expansion of logistics systems and opportunities of linking regions.

Military logistics

During the 1940s, the term 'logistics' as we use in the modern days was introduced by the military. It may seem odd since 'logistics' is used in business nowadays but the term 'logistics' originates from the French word 'logistique' and the Greek word 'logistikos'. 'Logistique' has its roots in the French word 'loger' which means to quarter or lodge soldiers and 'logistikos' means logic and skilled in calculation. In combination logistics is to 'logically calculate and lodge soldiers'. The transfer of military logistics to business logistics is traced to the world wars.

As the name speaks for itself, World War I involved many nations across global territories. Troops, weapons, equipment, and war supplies had to be transported globally at a fast pace. British and Germany's existing military logistics system could not possibly supply troops with rations, weapons, and war supplies since it lacked in scale and efficiency. World War I shed light on the harsh reality of military logistics system and how much it needed to be reformed. Learning from experience, nations improved its military logistics system to sustain global supply. During World War II, military logistics system was further refined due to the nature of World War II. World War II was even more global in size and scale than World War I. War sites were greater in distance from home base and ever faster in pace.

Consumption of ammunition, food, water, fuel, war suppliers proved to be greatest throughout history. Rail transportation was indispensable but air and sea transport played a major role in replenishment and maintenance. Through World War II, the concept and expertise of supplying resources efficiently to a far off location were developed. Logistics was originally the science of transporting, supplying and maintain military forces but later on during the 1950s, it was incorporated by the business sector to manage the flow of raw materials and finished products.

Quiz

- What is logistics? How would you interpret the term of "logistics"? What do you understand by the term?
- Can you think of the earliest logistics system in your region/country?
- Can you think of other milestones in the history of logistics?

Notes

- DHL 2008 http://www.dhl-discoverlogistics.com/cms/en/course/origin/ (accessed January 29th 2014)
- Andrzej Bochnacki (2006) "Different Story about Pyramids", World-Mysteries
- World-Mysteries.com http://www.world-mysteries.com/gw_abc_pl.htm (accessed January 29th 2014)
- Antill, P. (22 August 2001), Military Logistics: A Brief History, http://www.historyof-war.org/articles/concepts_logistics.html (accessed January 29th 2014)
- First Freight CRM for Freight & Logistics (Jan 8th 2011) http://www.firstfreight.com/?p=194 (accessed January 29th 2014)

CHAPTER 2

Globalization and International Trade

Learning objectives

- Define globalization and its effects on international trade (developmental process)
- Define international trade and its effects on globalization (developmental process)
- Understand the roles of containerization on globalization and international trade
- Understand the roles of multinational companies in international trade

2.1 Globalization

'Globalization' and 'international trade' are terms essential to the concept of logistics and supply chain management. There is no doubt that everyone who is reading this book knows the meaning of 'globalization' and 'international trade'. The two terms are highly related to logistics/supply chain management and to each other as well. The three concepts are highly inter-correlated that it is almost impossible to explain one concept without the other two. So how do the three concepts -globalization, international trade, logistics/supply chain management-influence each other? Chapter 2 is broken down to two parts in order to answer the question; how are 'globalization' and 'international trade' related and influence one another (question 1), and how are logistics and globalization/international trade related and influence one another? (question 2). To answer both questions, we must briefly go over globalization and international trade.

Globalization is defined as;

> "international exchange of knowledge, views, cultures, capital, goods and services, and ideas leading to economic, industrial, social, environmental, political, market integration. It is normally brought about by trade, communication, transportation, and immigration, strengthening interdependence between one another. Technological advances such as internet and shipping containers foster globalization."

Numerous literatures attempted to determine when globalization began and stages of globalization. How people classify the stages of globalization and the start of globalization depend on their logic since the definition of globalization is fluid and constantly changing. Globalization known in the 13th century is likely to be different from today's. Since the start of globalization depends on how one defines it, it is foolish to say that globalization is a 'new' concept that developed during the 20th century. Globalization can even be found in prehistoric age since territorial expansion existed in all five continents. Globalization existed from the very beginning but failed to flourish to what we consider 'globalization' today due to limited transportation and technology. There are extensive and detailed timetables of globalization but in this book, history of globalization will be classified into three broad periods. The first period which globalization flourished was during the 16th to 18th century.

During this period, Columbus discovered North America, the Caribbean islands were discovered, European trade surged due to Hanseatic League, and colonialism was at its height. International trade increased dramatically from 1500 to 1799 with an average annual growth rate of 1.06%. 19th century was another important period in the history of globalization. The Industrial Revolution was an era of great technological innovations such as steam engines, steamship, railway, telegraph, mechanized labor, and industrial technologies. These technological advances resulted in labor mobilization, fast transportation of goods, accumulation of capital, rapid industry growth, mass production, and decrease in transportation costs. 19th century industrial revolution integrated regions and brought the world together.

Development in transportation and technology formed a basis for 'modern globalization' during the 20th century. 'Modern globalization' as we refer to these days started during the 20th century in the midst of the two world wars. After World War II, globalization was politically motivated by leaders of developed countries to eliminate borders and promote free trade. International institutions such as the United Nations, Bretton Woods institution, World Bank, IMF, and WTO were established to facilitate globalization. Further development in innovative technology and transportation paired with lowered trade barriers dramatically increased international trade and promoted globalization. Also, development in science and the introduction of internet revolutionized lifestyle and the way people communicate around the world. Internet and mass media have advanced globalization never seen before in history.

International trade is defined as "the exchange of capitals, goods and services across national borders, exports (outflow) and imports (intake)."

2.2 International Trade

International trade or any kind of trade between two economic parties is based on 'comparative advantage' theory. Comparative advantage states that regardless of a nation's developmental status, a nation always has a good which it can produce at a cheaper cost (lower marginal and opportunity costs) compared to the other nation. Trade is specializing in a product and concentrating on what a nation makes best. The exchange of each nation's best product is time, cost, and labor saving and efficient. But in reality, international trade is much more complicated and most often

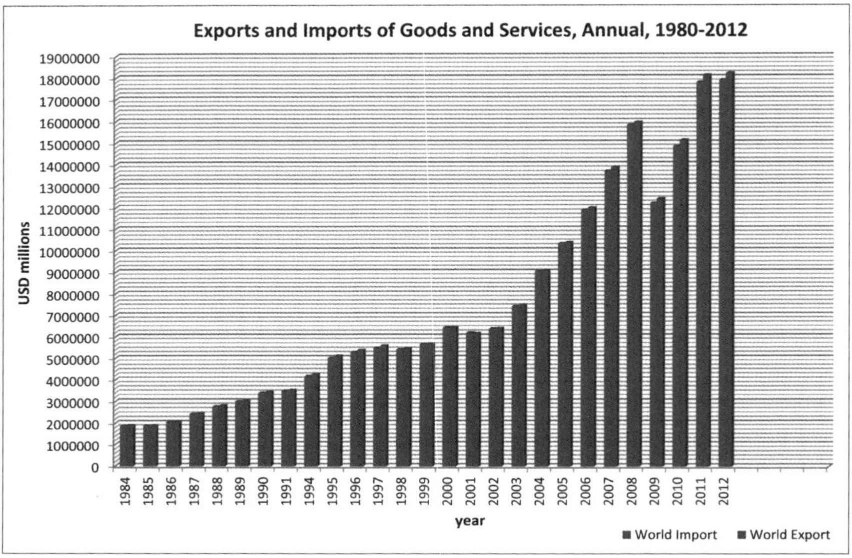

Source: UNCTAD Statistics

Figure 1-1 Exports and imports of goods and services between 1980 and 2012

depends on resource availability. Trade leads to increased competition and results in lower prices for the customers. International trade provides global products to the international market, thus providing goods and services that were otherwise unavailable to the customers in the domestic market. Economic integration and interdependence strengthen as goods and services are transported throughout the world and consumed by global customers.

Merchandise such as industrial equipment, consumer goods, agriculture goods are responsible for over 3/4 of world trade and services such as insurance and banking is responsible for the rest. World War II marked a sharp increase in trade across national borders. After World War II (since the 1950s) transportation costs gradually declined due to cheap price of oil. Even more drastic increase in international trade was recorded in the 1990s and international trade has been increasing at a fast pace ever since. World Merchandise exports reached $5.3 trillion in 1997, $3.5 trillion in 1990, and $58 billion in 1950. This pattern of dramatic and continuous increase in international trade can be also seen in figure 1-1. The figure shows world export and imports of goods (merchandise) and services from 1980 to 2012. Other than the steep decline in world trade in 2009-2010 due to spillover of the 2008 financial crisis, notable increase can be observed starting from 1995 and drastically increasing from 2000 and after.

It is worthwhile to note that while explaining globalization, international trade keeps coming up and the same goes for when explaining international trade. So which comes first? Did international trade occur because of globalization? Or did international trade lead to globalization? It seems unfitting to determine a causal relationship since globalization and international trade are highly interactive and promotes one another.

Trade across national borders and cultures may initiate globalization but globalization occurs alongside with international trade. Also surge of globalization increases trade across borders and this international trade increase may in turn leads to further globalization, thus developing alongside and promoting one another. Putting question one aside, question two (how are logistics and globalization/international trade related and influence each other?) must be explained. Since logistics is transporting goods to the final customer across a distance, it is fair to say the events in logistics history are movements towards globalization and international trade. Containerization and intermodal transportation are one of the milestones in logistics history that fueled international trade and globalization by improving efficiency.

Trade and transportation have existed alongside each other throughout history. They come hand in hand and one cannot be explained without the other. Whether it is domestic or international trade, the objective of transportation to move goods to where it is needed has not changed. Volume, capacity, speed, infrastructure, and efficiency have changed over time to support and enhance international trade and globalization.

2.3 Containerization

The invention of containers in 1956 was a game changer for all; transportation, international trade and globalization. Malcolm McLean's invention revolutionized how freight was moved along the supply chain and facilitated international cargo flow boom.

Container is a reusable standardized box made out of weathering steel for the purpose of carrying freight. Its reference size is 20 feet long, 8 feet high and 8 feet wide. This reference container is called Twenty-foot Equivalent Unit (TEU) and this unit is used to express capacity. Standard container sizes are 20 feet, 40 feet, 45 feet, and 53 feet but the 40 feet container is most commonly used since it carries more than 20 feet while maximizing stacking space on international vessels. Containers are stacked on top of each other-20 feet containers are stacked up to 7 stories- in order to maximize space usage and efficiency. Containerization is an intermodal freight transport system that uses containers to efficiently transport large volume of goods over a long distance. Containers can be loaded and unloaded, stacked, and transferred from one mode to another mode of transportation without ever being opened. Container handling is fully mechanized and moved by cranes and forklift trucks. Container management such as tracking and numbering are all managed by computer system.

Freight of international trade travels a long distance and normally two or more transportation modes are involved in delivering freight to its final destination. The majority of international freight is transported by sea since maritime transportation cost is cheap and moves large volume of freight and once. Once freight arrives at port it is transferred to a different transportation mode, truck or rail, for further transport. Before containers, freight was put in individual sacks or boxes when transferred to ship.

Loading and unloading process of freight between land transport and ships were labor intensive and time consuming. Sacks had to be carried one by one from rail to the dock and once again handled from dock to ship. Loading and unloading freight in separate pieces is called break bulk and it required extensive labor. Accidents and theft were common during the loading and unloading process. Ships had to spend more time on dock than sea due to time consumption during transfer. This inefficient and painstaking transportation system had to be used until several years after World War II. Container invention and implementation to international trade completely changed the operations of transportation system.

Container construction

When new designs are drawn for containers they have to be prototype tested in order to secure their strength. Once the tests prove to be satisfactory certification may be issued by the classification society for the designed container. If any changes are made in the method of construction this may nullify the certification if the changes have not been approved by the classification society. Figure 1-2 shows container design.

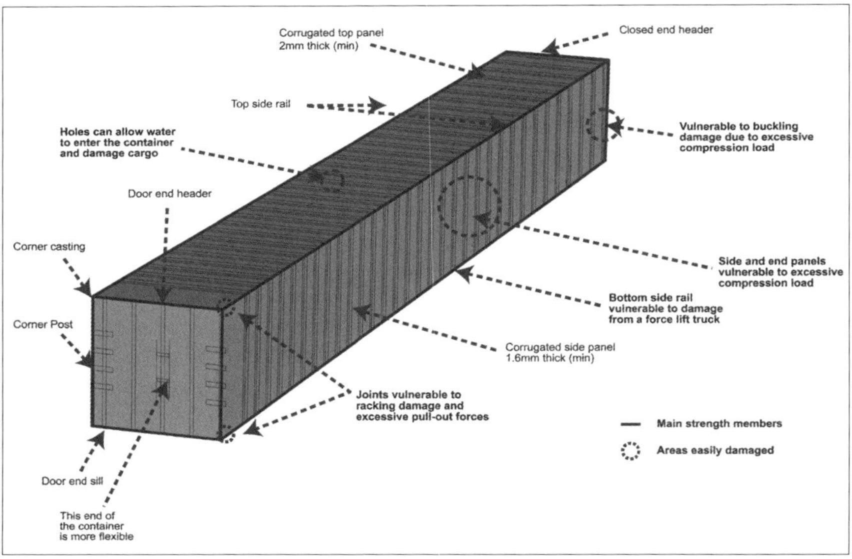

Source: The Standard

Figure 1-2 container construction

Advantages of containerization

Containerization has many advantages over break bulk cargo and improved transportation operations in a numerous ways. First, because containers are standardized in structure, only minimal handling is required. There was no need to sort freight and break bulk. This drastically reduced labor, cost and time and displaced thousands of workers who used to manhandle freight. Efficient loading and unloading sped up operations and reduced congestions in ports which resulted in significant decrease in shipping time. It also allowed smooth operations along the supply chain since transportation bottleneck was removed and freight could pass through the supply chain at a faster pace. Second, containers provided safe transportation of freight since containers were sealed and undisturbed until upon arrival to final destination. Loss from damages and theft were minimized and maritime transportation gained reliability.

Third, containers are flexible in their accommodations of various types of products. A wide range of products can be transported and since products are safely locked and stored away in containers, separate warehousing costs is unnecessary. The container itself acts as its own warehouse and storage unit. Forth, invention of containers revolutionized not only maritime transportation but also rail and road transportation through the development of Intermodal transportation system.

2.4 Intermodal Transportation

Definition of intermodal transportation

Intermodal transportation is increasing the economic performance of transportation system by using two or more modes of transportation in the most productive manner. Intermodal transportation existed before containerization such as piggyback transportation, but flourished with the implementation of containers. Since containers can be easily loaded to maritime, rail, and road transportation modes, transshipment costs and delays were significantly reduced embedding great flexibility to freight transportation.

Transporting freight by maritime and rail for long distances and utilizing efficiencies of trucks for local distribution allows transportation providers to offer door to door service to the customers at a lower cost. Customers can also enjoy the benefit of intermodal transportation by receiving freight at a reasonable price and expected time. Last, containerization brought major infrastructure renovations to efficiently accommodate containers and improve transshipment process. Major ports around the world went under construction to build infrastructure that could support ships built solely for carrying stacked containers. New rail facilities were built in order to handle containers and these efforts paid off when container double stacking railways led to doubled capacity. Road has also made adjustment for container transportation (Jean-Paul Rodrigue).

Nowadays, over 90% of non-bulk freight is transported by containers. Containers with intermodal transportation improve efficiencies and promote international distribution of goods. Through containers, products from all over the world can be enjoyed by customers at affordable prices. In this sense, containers have significantly contributed to the growth and expansion of international trade and globalization. To answer question 2 (how are logistics and globalization/international trade related and influence one another), containerization and logistics act as a catalyst for development of international trade and globalization. International trade and globalization cannot exist without logistics and its transport system such as containerization is a step closer to global integration.

Examples of intermodal transportation

Sea and air transport

Sea-Air combines the transport speed of air freight with the cost efficiency of sea freight and this combination provides huge advantages for the logistics industry.

1) North America sea and air route

This route was established by an airline company and is the eldest in the world. It has the most transportation traffic as well. Recently, forwarders have taken their positions in this route in providing services and the routes used have been diversified. The general route is from South Korea or Japan to North America (Seattle, Vancouver, Los Angeles) by sea and then transferred to air transport to European countries and elsewhere in the world.

2) Busan - Vladivostok – Nakhodka route

This mode offers a maritime transport and delivery of cargos into Busan - Vladivostok - Nakhodka. Busan - Nakhodka line is connecting the Busan port on the East coast of the South Korea and the Nakodka port on the North -West coast of the Sea of Japan.

Busan is the biggest port and industrial center of South Korea. Busan connects with the territory of South Korea with roads and railways. The biggest navigation lines go through Busan. Nakhodka is the Russian Federal Marine Port in Nakhodka bay and on north-west coast of the Sea of Japan. Nakhodka fishing port is one of the basic transport hubs in the Far East region.

3) Hong Kong sea and air route

This route is used to deliver cargos from South Korea or Japan to Singapore, Bangkok or Hong Kong. Sea transport is used for deliveries to these three countries and air transport to Europe.

Other intermodal transportation may include;

1) Intermodal transportation between South Korea, Japan and North America
- Mini Land Bridge (MLB)
- Interior Point Intermodal (IPI)
- Reversed Interior Point Intermodal (RIPI)

2) Intermodal transportation between South Korea, Japan and Europe
- Siberia Land Bridge (SLB)
- America Land Bridge (ALB)
- Canadian Land Bridge (CLB)

In the following you will find some actual activities of logistics concepts:

Customer service

More and more companies have a customer service department to handle complaints, returns, billing problems and other after-sales-services.

Demand forecasting

To meet the customers' requirements it is essential to have the right products and services available where and when they are needed. If a company is not able to serve the customers, they might buy their goods from a competitor.

Information management

This department links all information of the whole supply chain together. As a mistake might cause major problems, this part of the logistics management often operates automatically.

Quiz

- What is globalization? Can you think of any real-life examples of globalization?
- Is globalization a new and recent phenomenon?
- What are the benefits and costs of globalization for the majority of average person?
- What are the benefits and costs of free trade?
- Does globalization create logistics jobs? Does it affect business logistics and SCM? How has globalization impacted SCM?

Notes

- Center for Economic Conversion http://www1.umn.edu/humanrts/edumat/sustecon/lessons/lesson8.html (accessed January 29th 2014), University of Minnesota Human Rights Resource Center
- Nayef Al-Rodhan, Gerard Stoudmann (2006) "Definitions of Globalization: A Comprehensive Overview and a Proposed Definition", Program on the Geopolitical Implications of Globalization and Transnational Security
- Martin Albrow, Elizabeth King (1990) "Globalization, Knowledge and Society: Readings from International Sociology", SAGE Publications
- World Shipping Council http://www.worldshipping.org/about-the-industry/history-of-containerization/before-container-shipping (accessed January 29th 2014), 2014 World Shipping Council
- Jean-Paul Rodrigue (2006) "Transportation and Globalization", Encyclopedia of Globalization, London: Routledge
- Tolga Bektas, Teodor Crainic (2007) "A Brief Overview of Intermodal Transporation", CIRRELT
- The Standard, a master's guide to container securing, in the 5th publication in the master's guide series, Lloyd's Register.

ARTICLE

Interconnectd economies

Global value chains (GVCs) have become an important feature of the world economy in recent years, and increasingly challenge the way we look at the global economy. Today, a good produced in Korea and exported to the United States may include intermediate inputs from China, Japan, or Malaysia, and use raw materials and services from Australia, Brazil, Russia or India. Increasingly, goods and services are "made in the world", although they may be designed or assembled in one single country.

For a long time, it has been difficult to measure and understand what was happening in these GVCs, despite well-known examples of complex products produced across the world such as the Samsung Galaxy or the Apple iPhone.

The OECD-WTO Database on Trade in Value Added, which was launched in January this year, has begun to move beyond case studies and is starting to revolutionize our understanding of what is happening in these global value chains. For example, services account for less than one-quarter of total trade when measured in gross terms. But when the value added by services in the production of goods is accounted for, then the service sector contributes over 50% of total exports in countries like France, Germany, the United Kingdom and the United States, though still less than 40% in Korea.

The data also tell us that Korea is an important player in these GVCs. In 2009, 41% of the value of Korea's exports was derived from imported intermediate inputs, rising to 76% in electrical equipment. And downstream links are important too, in particular in the electrical equipment industry where Korean exports feed into exports by countries further down the value chain. For example, Korean firms provide many of the key components for the Apple products that are assembled in China.

Another important finding of this database is that bilateral trade relations can change significantly when measured in value added terms. Looking at gross trade flows, the United States and China are clearly Korea's major trading partners, with China being the major trading partner. However, in value added terms, the United

States was Korea's main trading partner in 2009. This is because the share of exports to China in value-added terms is about half that in gross terms.

This reflects significant exports from Korea that are further processed by China before being exported to final consumers, notably in the U.S. A similar picture emerges when we look at imports, where again, in value-added terms, the United States displaces China as Korea's major trading partner. This partly reflects Korean processing of Chinese goods for export but it also reflects the relatively low domestic value-added content of Chinese exports compared to the U.S.

These new data help us in better understanding what is really happening in the increasingly interconnected world economy. They also have important implications for policy. Just to mention a few.

First, imports are essential for exports, especially in complex value chains such as transport and electronics. Today, success in international markets depends as much on the capacity to import high-quality inputs as on the capacity to export. This also implies that tariffs and non-tariff barriers on imports are effectively a tax on exports. These negative effects are compounded further in complex GVCs where parts and components may cross borders many times.

Secondly, services, such as business services, transport and logistics, account for over half of value creation in GVCs in many OECD countries. This implies that services matter for the success of countries in international trade. Regulatory reforms and liberalization of services trade are essential to enhance competition in services sectors and increase the productivity and quality of services.

Finally, as economies become more interconnected, they are increasingly specialized in specific activities and stages of value chains rather than in entire industries.

As the example of the iPhone so well illustrates, today, "what you do" (the activities a firm or country is involved in) often matter more than "what you sell" (the products that make up final sales or exports).

Source : The Korea Times, October 6, 2013

Review

Linked economies

Global value chains are of growing importance in the world-wide economy and give us new perspectives on how we look at the economy as a whole. Nowadays products that are produced in Korea and exported to the USA may include parts from China, Japan, or Malaysia, and use resources from places like Australia, Brazil, Russia, or India. Instead of products made in one specific country of origin, they are essentially, "made in the world".

GVCs are complex chains with complex products produced across the world. Measurement and full understanding of these GVCs are difficult to quantify and grasp. The newly formed OECD-WTO Database on Trade in Value Added, has moved on from just analyzing case-studies and has begun to unfold the complexities of GVCs to make it more easily understood and accessible. For example, services make up for less than 25% of total trade in gross terms, but after factoring in the value added by services in the production of goods, it becomes clear that the service sector contributes over 50% of total exports in many developed countries like France, Germany, the UK, and the USA. In Korea, services still only account for less than 40%.

Within this database, an analysis of information leads us to the idea that Korea is an important player in GVCs. In 2009, 41% of Korean export value came from intermediate imported inputs. The number rises to 76% when pertaining to electrical equipment. Furthermore, electrical equipment from Korea flows downstream and feeds exports by other countries further down the value chain. An example of this would be that Korean firms provide many specific key components for large multi-national companies and products like those of Apple, which use these components in their Chinese factories.

Other discoveries made from the database are that bilateral trade relations can notably change when value added is factored in. China is Korea's main trading partner with the US being the second. Yet, when value-added is factored in, the US becomes the clear leader in terms of trade in 2009. In addition, some Korean exports and processed in China before eventual export to the USA. Similarly, the USA displaces China as Korea's top trading partner in terms of imports due to Korean processing of Chinese Goods for export and the low domestic value-added from Chinese exports in relation to the US.

This data shows that high quality inputs (imports) are just as important as the capacity to export. Thus, tariffs and non-tariff barriers on imports ultimately become a tax on exports, too. Additionally, services account for a large chunk of GVC's in many OECD countries. Reforms in regulations and liberalization of services trade are key factors in raising overall productivity and quality. As the world becomes more connected economically, the trend toward specialization becomes more prevalent than being involved in all stages of value chains.

Question

- Describe the complexities of a GVC using a real-world example. Explain how each link (country) within the chain adds value.

CHAPTER 3

Global Supply Chain Management

- Understand what is meant by supply chain management
- Be able to explain main objectives, elements, process of SCM
- Be able to distinguish between logistics and SCM
- Be able to identify major concepts developed throughout the evolution of supply chain management.

3.1 Definition of SCM

During World War II, the term logistics became widely used and after the war, firms adopted the term for business use. After adopting logistics, firms started to look for additional ways to improve the production process and reduce cost, time and increase efficiency. Due to globalization, customers had multiple sources to choose from and firms needed to improve their competitiveness beyond cutting costs in logistics. They soon realized they would have to move away from maximizing profit or efficiency from the focal firm's point of view but to cooperate with 'others' in the supply chain. Emphasizing functional performance and silo mentality were not enough to improve firm's competitiveness in the global level, thus optimizing overall performance of 'product flow' became a new objective.

Numerous definitions of supply chain and its management have been offered by others.

"The network of entities through which material flows. Those entities may include suppliers, carriers, manufacturing sites, distribution centers, retailers, and customers" Lummus and Alber (1997)

"The supply chain - a term increasingly used by logistics professionals - encompasses every effort involved in producing and delivering a final product, from the supplier's supplier to the customer's customer. Four basic processes - plan, source, make, deliver - broadly define these efforts, which include managing supply and demand, sourcing raw materials and parts, manufacturing and assembly, warehousing and inventory tracking, order entry and order management, distribution across all channels, and delivery to the customer." The Supply Chain Council (1997)

"All of those activities associated with moving goods from the raw-materials stage through to the end user. This includes sourcing and procurement, production scheduling, order processing, inventory management, transportation, warehousing, and customer service. Importantly, it also embodies the information systems so necessary to monitor all of those activities." Quinn (1997)

"Supply chain management is an integrating philosophy to manage the total flow of a distribution channel from supplier to ultimate customer" Ellram and Cooper (1993)

"Supply chain is all the activities involved in delivering a product from raw material through to the customer including sourcing raw materials and parts, manufacturing and assembly, warehousing and inventory tracking, order entry and order management, distribution across all channels, delivery to the customer, and the information and technology systems necessary to monitor all of these activities. Supply chain management coordinates and integrates all of these activities into a seamless process. It links all of the partners in the chain including departments within an organization and the external partners including suppliers, carriers, third-party companies, and information systems providers."

(Lummus and Vokurka (1999)

Supply chain management is views the process involved in producing a single product or service as a holistic process and gaining competitiveness through generating synergies across entities or functional processes.

3.2 Evolution of SCM

By studying the evolution process of supply chain and its management, one can easily learn key concepts that became the building blocks of today's supply chain management.

In 1913, Henry Ford developed the first moving assembly line for automobile manufacturing thus, starting the era of mass production. Ford Motor Company's goal was "to create a motor car for the great multitude". Model T automobile was first produced in 1908 and it was produced as an affordable automobile for the middle class Americans. Although Model T was less expensive than other models it was still expensive and was not affordable for the 'multitude'. It took 12 man hours to build a single car since workers moved from work station to work station. Henry Ford, searching for a new efficient production system that would dramatically lower production costs, was inspired by the conveyor belt of meat-packing houses of Chicago which brought the work to the workers. In order to improve productivity while cutting costs, four elements had to be integrated as a whole seamless process; interchangeable parts, continuous work flow, division of labor and reduction of waste. Interchangeable parts were produced by machines which performed standardized operations to produce a part that would fit to any other part. By adopting standardized machines, it eliminated the need for skilled craftsman leading to labor cost reduction. After establishing interchangeable parts, Ford developed a moving assembly line that moved along the workers to ensure seamless production flow. Model T production process was divided into 84 distinctive steps and each worker specialized in one manufacturing step. This reduced the set up time and eliminated wasted efforts (movement of workers). Moving assembly line optimized production operations and maximized efficiency and allowed mass production. Within a year after them implementation of moving assembly line, 12 man hours to build a car was reduced to one and half man hours. Huge reduction in production costs led to reduction in price and automobiles became affordable to the middle class working men. Price of Model T fell from $850 to $360 in 1916 and eventually one Model T was produced every 24 seconds with a price of $300.

Containers were developed by Malcom McLean and implemented in 1956 which led to a boom in international trade and intermodal transportation systems.

In 1952, barcode was invented by Normand Woodland and Bernard Silver which in later years was adopted to identify and track products throughout the supply chain. Barcodes are representation of data that are machine readable. It includes information about the product and can be easily read by unattached scanning thus reducing handling. It is fast and accurate collection of data that increases efficiency and reduces inventory level and costs. Barcodes increase the visibility of the product flow from manufacturer to retail stores.

During the 1960s, innovation in technology led to the development of software which helped integration of business along the supply chain, increase visibility and increase production efficiency. Invention of electronic data interchange (EDI) in the 1960s improved exchange of data and information among businesses. EDI will be explained in detail in unit 3. In 1961, Josef Orlicky developed a software based production planning and inventory control system called Material Resource Planning (MRP). It increased the efficiency of manufacturing process by optimizing production scheduling and inventory control. Its main objective was ensuring the availability of necessary materials for production to meet customer demand, control inventory to maintain lowest inventory level as possible and coordinate manufacturing, delivery and purchasing schedules.

In 1971, William Zikmund and William Stanton conceptualized reverse logistics. Logistics is the flow of product from raw material to the point of consumption but what is not normally considered is the backward flow. Reverse logistics is the backward flow from final destination for recapturing value, proper disposal, remanufacturing, refurbishing and recycling. Reverse logistics can also be the movement process of returned goods, left over inventory and damaged products. Later on, reverse logistics was further developed due to growing consumer awareness in environment and conservation of resources.

In 1985, Kurt Salmon Associates conducted the first supply chain analysis. When Kurt Salmon Associates analyzed the textile and apparel industry's supply chain, they found out that the delivery time from raw material to final customers was 66 weeks long. But products spent around 40 weeks in warehouses or transit process. Due to long and inefficient supply chain, products had to sit in inventory missing opportunities of being at the right place at the right time. In order to correct these mistakes, quick response (QR) strategy was developed. QR is partnership between suppliers and retailers to respond more quickly to customer's demands. Its main objective was to reduce order response time, accurately ship the correct products in correct quantities and reduce inventory costs by UPC code adoption and utilizing technologies such as EDI, barcodes, point of sale scanning system. It was to increase accurate and unblocked information flow between supply chain actors. Further analysis of the grocery industry's supply chain in 1992 by Kurt Salmon Associates developed the concept of efficient consumer response (ECR). Kurt Salmon Associates concluded "by expediting the quick and accurate flow of information up the supply chain, ECR enables distributors and suppliers to anticipate future demand far more accurately than the current system allows". They also included that grocery industry can reduce its inventory by 37% and costs by $24 to $30 billion by practicing efficient consumer response. Further development of ECR led to continuous replenishment (CRP) concept which was put into best practices by Procter & Gamble and Campbell soup in 1987.

Ken Ackermand and Dean Wise developed an early concept of third party logistics in 1985. Later on, third party logistics provider concept was further refined. Third party logistics provider (3PL) is a firm that provides an outsourced integrated logistics services (warehousing, transportation, inventory management, cross-docking, packaging, freight forwarding, etc.) to another firm. When firms outsource or subcontract out logistics activities to 3PL, 3PL firms takes into account customer's needs and provides specialized logistics services that are tailored to specific needs. Fourth party logistics provider (4PL) was developed from the concept of 3PL by Andersen Consulting group. 4PL providers are non-asset based non-operators that specialize in logistics and supply chain management consulting. Using their expertise, 4PL organizes, assembles, contracts out, and manages other 3PL provider's activity to build a comprehensive supply chain network. Examples of 4PL include consulting firms such as SCMO, CPCS, Deloitte, Accenture, BMT, Capgemini, Morpheus, and 3t Europe.

ARTICLE

Samsung-Apple competition comes down to supply chains

Samsung Electronics and Apple are locked in a bitter fight for supremacy in the exploding smartphone and tablet market. But the fight is about more than just introducing cooler touch-screen gadgets and could be determined by innovations in supply chain management, according to a senior official at technology industry researcher Gartner.

According to Gartner's table on supply chain management, Samsung is 13th among the global technology firms, while Apple retained its top status for the fifth consecutive year. However, Jane Barrett, Gartner's vice president of supply chain research, said that Samsung has been making leaps and bounds in improving its inventory of control and distribution strategies and carved its own edge in a number of areas.

"The standing doesn't necessarily mean that Apple is better than Samsung in all aspects. It's how the results of methodology stack up. Apple and Samsung have very different business models, therefore, it's tough to make a direct comparison," she said in an interview with The Korea Times at the Shilla Hotel in Seoul, Tuesday.

"Especially, we consider Samsung as best in terms of class and planning capacities. Samsung is recognized by Gartner as a leader in SCM practices and processes. Samsung is catching up to Apple in some products as we see strong market share in their Galaxy products."

Supply chain management is critical for large corporations that create most of their revenue outside their domestic base because they must find a balance between getting their products out to market quickly and keeping a low inventory. It's about more than just effectively running warehouses and distribution networks, but is also about the ability to detect and measure the impact of potential risks and being flexible and agile in cutting costs, Barrett said.

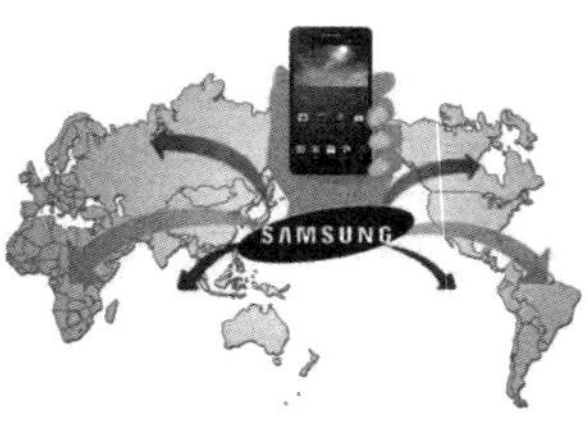

This has always been Apple's strength since its iSomethings became globally popular. New Apple CEO Tim Cook has been putting even more emphasis on improving the company's supply chain management as the company increasingly relies on partners in China, Taiwan and other developing nations to manufacture its products.

Companies in Asia-Pacific ranked lower than their Western counterparts on the Gartner list, but Barrett pointed out that Samsung was rated as the top firm in the region.

''The analysis is based on companies' financial performances such as revenue, inventory turns and return on assets (ROA) and opinion, which is gathered through a voting process in which our analysts and peers globally vote for companies they feel demonstrate the best SCM leadership," she said, adding that more than half of its voters were Asia-based.

Barrett was in Seoul as part of her research trip to China and Korea. While here, Barrett said the research firm met with its key clients such as LG Electronics, Hankook Tire and Doosan Infracore over a host of issues.

''It will be interesting to look forward three to five years and see where these technology companies are, given the passing of Steve Jobs and some of the recent senior management chances at Apple," Barrett said.

''Apple has a simple set of products and do very well in terms of orchestrating the launch of new products across a very outsourced model but maintaining tight control."

Barrett wasn't too concerned too about the shipment problems Apple has been facing as it moves its new iPhone 5 to world markets.

''It hasn't impacted their overall results. However, it would be interesting to see how much better they could do if they did have better availability at launch," she said.

''Also, as their competition catches up and in some instances actually has better features than Apple, we have to question whether they need to take a hard look at their planning capabilities and supply flexibility and realize that consumers will be more likely to switch to another product if the Apple product isn't on the shelf."

Source : The Korea Times, November 6, 2012

Review

Supply chains key to Samsung-Apple competition

The top leaders of the smartphone and tablet market are both Samsung and Apple. Each company is renowned for innovating new technology and constantly one-upping each other. In this fierce competition, supply chain management would be the key determining factor in who wins this battle. Experts place Samsung as the 13th highest ranked global technology firm, while Apple has remained at the top of the pack for the past 5 years. In order to catch up to Apple, Samsung has been significantly improving its inventory control and distribution strategies in various areas of its business. Though Apple is ranked higher, it is important to know that each run on different business models and cannot be directly compared to one another. It's like comparing apples and oranges. Even though Apple is at the top of the pack, it does not mean that Apple is the highest performer in all areas of its business. In actuality, Samsung was rated the highest in terms of class and planning capabilities. They are the leader in supply chain management practices and processes.

Supply chain management is a key issue for businesses that export most of its inventories to other countries because margins depend on quick delivery and low inventory. However, SCM is not only about warehousing and distribution, it's about the ability to foresee and assess potential risks and being able to address them quickly. This is something that Apple has excelled at due to their reliance on partners in China and Taiwan to manufacture their products. Though Western companies rank much higher in SCM as compared to Asia-Pacific companies, Samsung ranked the highest in its region.

Experts are predicting that companies like LG Electronics, Hankook Tire, and Doosan Infracore will be exciting to watch as they are in position to threaten Apple's dominance, especially with Steve Jobs' passing away. Apple's dominance lies in its simple product line and its well-planned launches of its products across an outsourced model with tight control.

Question

1) What are the biggest challenges in SCM when dealing with a business model highly dependent on global outsourcing?
2) In the continuing competition between Samsung and Apple, who do you foresee as the eventual champion in the long run? Why?

ARTICLE

Supply chain management critical amid uncertainty

Barrett believes big Korean companies will show more interest in improving their supply chain management systems as the bad global economy takes a bite out of their export prowess. It appears there will be no quick fix to the heady mix of negatives affecting the global economy, highlighted by the financial troubles in Europe, compounded by predictions that global demand is expected to be sluggish for the foreseeable future.

"When we look back at the crisis we had from 2009 to 2010 in the United States, there is no doubt the companies that were more mature in SCM were not only able to better manage the downturn, they were also better able to predict the upturn and ensure they had the capacity and inventory to gain market share," she said.

According to Barrett, companies that have strong sales and operations planning process, good alignment across supply chain management functions within their departments and trading partners are best positioned to navigate out of troubled waters.

"We also cannot forget about the need to have the right talent and skills for more advanced SCM, and this means the need to have people become more strategically focused, having strong analytical skills, and the right mix of depth in functional excellence and people with broad capabilities across the business," she said.

"The main issues for the companies I met with in Korea as well as China were similar. Due to economic uncertainty in many parts of the world, customer demand has become more difficult to predict and in many cases dropping. This means companies need to improve their capabilities to predict demand and the question normally starts with 'how can I improve my ability to forecast'," according to Barrett.

"Consumer electronics companies need to manage short product lifecycles and ever decreasing costs. So this is why we talk about the need for companies to become excellent in demand management as it is related to their specific environment. We also had several discussions about how to elevate the role of SCM in the company and have the senior executives realize the value of SCM as a strategic enabler to business."

Samsung and Apple's consistent and extensive investment in SCM have helped them retain market share and credibility. But according to Barrett, Korean companies need to keep building a strong SCM foundation regarding their organizational structure, people skills, process and enabling technology as they progress.

"So depending on their maturity level they will need a strategy and roadmap of initiatives to continuously transform their SCM capabilities. Being able to understand end to end cost data by product and customer is something many companies cannot do," she said.

Source : The Korea Times, November 6, 2012

Review

Supply chain management plays a key role in uncertain times

As the world economy slows down, big Korean companies turn to supply chain management to even the score. The financial troubles of Europe are compounded by poor forecasts while no quick fix is in sight. Historically, during 2009-2010 U.S.

companies that had more established SCM increased their survivability among difficult times. Furthermore, they were more capable of predicting the upturns while taking advantage of them due to their better prepared capacities and inventory control to gain more market share. Experts say that such companies that are strong in sales and operations planning with good alignment across the entire supply chain within each of their departments and partners are in a better position to come out of an economic downturn than those which do not.

Recruitment for companies are focusing more on candidates that are skilled in SCM, which means that they need people who are strategically focused and with a balance of functional excellence and broad capabilities across the entire business.

Korean and Chinese companies face similar difficulties due to global economic uncertainty. Customer demand has become unpredictable and generally decreasing. Demand prediction is key in such a situation as forecasting is an integral part in solving or alleviating this situation. For example, consumer electronics companies need to better manage their short product lifecycles and decrease costs. Demand management becomes necessary for success and needs to become part of the larger discussions in business strategy at an executive level. The value of SCM can mean success or failure in many businesses. In order for Korean companies to gain or retain market share and credibility, companies must continue forging new SCM strategies and integrating them throughout their organizational structure. To understand end to end cost data from product to customer is a difficult goal to achieve, but the rewards could give companies the competitive edge they need to survive in the global arena.

Question

1) If SCM is such an integral part of business, why haven't more companies established strong SCM within their business model? What are the challenges?
2) In what ways can SCM be better integrated into a company's culture? How can it be elevated to be part of a higher discussion with company executives?

CASE STUDY

Case study - 3PL and 4PL

L'érablière inc. is a Canadian company founded in 1984, who operates in Montréal, Canada. Their mission is to design, sell and distribute sparkling water with maple syrup taste to it. The company has been present on the entire Canadian market from the beginning of its foundation and in the American territory for almost 10 years. Sales are increasing rapidly and so is their company size. They have many sales offices in Canada and the U.S.A. but only one manufacture in Montreal is providing the products available in the market. L'érablière has always taken care of its logistics. They also have been managing all of the aspect its supply chain. Activities like customer services, demand forecasting, transportation, warehousing, inventory management, packaging and more, have always been normal business functions for L'érablière inc.

However, the company has been growing and the problems related to logistics as well. As the clients are diversified and the roadmap is getting more complex, the supply chain management is getting more and more complicated to handle. Besides, the company is planning on expanding its sales to Europe in the near future. Not only will this strategic operation bring more pain to the constant headache that is logistics to them, but L'érablière inc. would also need to free some resources to direct them on the internationalization of the company. Furthermore, with the raise of environmental concerns, the company wants to make its supply chain management more sustainable and at the same time, make them look like good corporate citizens. In the end, the overall purpose is to improve the network efficiency.

3PL

L'érablière inc. now decided to outsource the entire of its supply chain management. The company DHL will now be taking care of transportation, warehousing, cross-docking, inventory management, packaging, and freight forwarding and therefore every service from the supplier to the customer. This new alliance will benefit L'érablière in many ways. First, it will enjoy the experience of DHL in the supply chain management area. One good example of this is the advantage of using highly advanced logistic software programs that wouldn't have been possible otherwise. Another advantage is the cost reduction of transport services due to the buying power of this 3PL and because DHL regularly deal with various carriers they are probably more skilled and experienced with negotiating prices. These new possibilities will allow L'érablière to be more flexible in delivery as much as improving their ability to deliver to customer in time, which should tend to a consumer satisfaction improvement.

4PL

Thanks to its 3PL provider the company kept on growing and decides to expand their activity in the European market with France as a strategic starting location. They will only ship their products there and do not plan to implant production facilities for now. Unfortunately the North American 3PL provider has no activity in Europe. L'érablière decides to hire a new 3PL provider with a real expertise on this new geographical area. Thus the L'érablière Inc. has now two 3PL providers for two distinct markets. In the prospect of growing the company and wishes to outsource all its logistic concerns and focus on designing a new product-an alcoholic drink made of maple syrup-a 4PL provider was hired to manage the overall SCM of L'érablière. A 4PL provider is also better adapted to changes and will know how to handle the distribution of the new beverage as well. This non-asset based partner will have a consulting role to the Canadian company. After a few weeks of working together, the 4PL provider advised L'érablière to change its current 3PL provider in Europe to a more competitive one. Many changes were implemented. Some suppliers have changed, one new strategic main warehouse is chosen and procurement costs were reduced. The employment of 4PL has allowed L'érablière to reduce costs and improve overall supply chain management.

Notes

- Bade and Mueller (1999), "New for the millennium: 4pl", Transportation & Distribution, Feb99 Vol. 40 Issue 2, p78
- Barnes, P. (2010), The Disadvantages of Third Party Logistics Services Versus Logistics Software http://goarticles.com/article/The-Disadvantages-of-Third-Party-Logistics-Services-Versus-L.ogistics-Software/2693891/

- Handfield, R. (2006), A Brief History of Outsourcing http://scm.ncsu.edu/scm-articles/article/a-brief-history-of-outsourcing
- C. John Langley Jr.; Gary R. Allen; Mark J. Colombo (2003), Third-Party Logistics Study Results and Findings of the 2003 Eighth Annual Study http://www.scl.gatech.edu/research/supply-chain/20033PLReport.pdf
- Norall, S. (2013), 3PL vs 4PL What are these PLs, Anyway? Layers of Logistics Explained http://cerasis.com/2013/08/08/3pl-vs-4pl/
- Richardson, H. (2005), What are you willing to give up? http://mhlnews.com/transportation-amp-distribution/what-are-you-willing-give
- Susanne, H ; Alfredsson, M. (2003), "Strategic development of third party logistics providers". Industrial Marketing Management (Elsevier Science) 32 (2): pp. 139–149
- Schary, B. and Skjøtt-Larsen,T. (2001), Managing the global supply chain. Copenhagen Business School Press, Copenhagen
- Sople (2007), Logistics Management, Pearson Education India
- Coppier S. (2013), 1PL, 2PL, 3PL, 4PL, 5PL... KESAKO? http://www.informatique-transport-logistique.com/2012/02/1pl-2pl-3pl-4pl-5pl-kesako.html
- Jordan, D. (2010) Fourth Party Logistics (4PLP); what this means for your Supply Chain http://supplychain.enchange.com/bid/24156/Fourth-Party-Logistics-4PLP-what-this-means-for-your-Supply-Chain

The concept of postponement was developed in 1950 by Alderson but its practical application in supply chain management and managerial implications were highlighted by Dell's direct order system in 1984. The concept of postponement is based on principles of demand forecasting. Forecast demand's accuracy decreases as time passes. Forecast error increases and demand quantities will vary at greater ranges as the time window for which the demand is being forecasted increases. Demand forecast for 6 months will have more errors than for 1 month. Postponement is an inventory management strategy utilized by production companies to delay the final assembly, packaging, delivery and other final operations of the final product as much as possible until the actual demand is known. Postponement leaves room at the end stage of production for customization and varying product mix according to customer's demands. It increases firm's flexibility to customer's changing demands, reduces inventory costs, minimize the risk of producing unsold product, reduces waste due to excessive production, decreases obsolescence of inventory and increases customer satisfaction. Michael Dell built his business by shipping computers to customers from his dorm room. Dell developed a unique build to order model (BTO) using postponement strategy. Computers were built as generic semi-finished product (casing, boards) and awaited customer order. When customer's placed an order specifying customization, dell started the final process of building a computer tailored to customer's needs and shipped directly to customers. The act of postponing final manufacturing activities until customer's order led to low levels inventory which in turn increased competitive advantage since lifecycle for computers are short thus resulting in low level of product obsolescence and high customer satisfaction.

With high interests in effectively managing inventory level, Just-in-Time concept was developed and implemented across businesses during the 1980s to 1990s. JIT was developed from Toyota production system and later on led to the conceptualization of 'lean' and 'agile' supply chain management. Just in time is elimination of waste by maintaining the 'right' inventory level that assures seamless production. The concept of JIT and case study will be further explained in following chapters. Also the invention of Wal-Mart's cross docking system in 1988 added to the efforts of reducing inventory costs which will be further explained.

In 1990, Gartner Group developed a software system that effectively integrated the entire operations within the supply chain. Enterprise Resource Planning (ERP) goes beyond manufacturing management and includes product planning, costs and development of product, inventory management, transportation, payment process, marketing and sales and stores information such as cash flow, raw materials, orders, and so on. It facilitates information exchange between supplier, manufacturer, distributer and retailers. ERP played a huge role in businesses visualizing the whole supply chain and moving away from the 'silo' mentality and thinking at the 'supply chain level'.

During the late 1990s and throughout the 2000s, technological innovations such as RFID helped business speed up lead time from suppliers to final consumption and reduce costs dramatically. Also with rising concerns about the environment, the concept of green supply chain management developed in 2001 and since then, green efforts have become the key issue of today's supply chain management. After 9/11, global supply chain security became a new research field in supply chain management resulting in programs such as C-TPAT and AEO. Today's supply chain management is an holistic approach considering all processes and parties within the supply chain with the main objective of reducing costs while creating economic, social and environmental value. Technology and information are key players in facilitating the process.

Quiz

- What is Supply Chain Management?
- Is there any difference between logistics and SCM?
- How would you distinguish 3pl and 4pl? What is the biggest difference between them?

Notes

- Lummus, R.R., Alber, K.L., 1997, "Supply Chain Management: Balancing the Supply Chain with Customer Demand", The Educational and Resource Foundation of APICS, Falls Church, VA.
- The Supply Chain Council, 1997, http//www.supply-chain.com/info/faq.html
- Quinn, F.J., 1997, "What's the buzz?", Logistics Management, 36, 2, 43-7.
- Ellram, L., Cooper, M., 1993, "Characteristics of supply chain management and the implications for purchasing and logistics strategy", International Journal of Logistics Management, 4, 2, 1-10.
- Lummus, R.R, Vokurka, R, 1999, "Defining supply Chain Management: a Histori-cal perspective and Practical Guidelines", Industrial Management & Data Systems, 99,1,11-17

UNIT. 2

ELEMENTS OF SUPPLY CHAIN MANAGEMENT AND ITS OPERATION I

PART. 1
Transportation

Learning objectives

- Understand the importance of transportation
- Learn types and roles of each transportation mode: rail, road, sea and air
- Understand the advantages and disadvantages of each transportation mode

Movement of goods from one place to another is called either transport or delivery. The term 'transport' usually refers to the movement of goods for a long-distance while the term 'delivery' is used for short-distance movement of goods. Although the terms are usually distinguished based on the length of distance or amount of goods the exact figures of kilograms or kilometers are not clearly stated. However, it would be appropriate to distinguish the two terms based on locations. It may be allowed to call transport for movement from one region to another while delivery would be better suited for movement within one region or city. Nonetheless, the two terms can still be interchangeably used to refer to the same activity.

Transportation plays important roles in carrying out these 'movement' and 'delivery' activities. Goods may be transported by one or combination of the following transportation modes; air, road, rail and sea. Transportation is also vital in enhancing trade between people and nations which in turn establishes good relations amongst them. In other words, transportation allows economic development to happen. This activity is important for many reasons but one of the main importance lies on its costs. Transportation costs take up most of logistics cost and hence, suppliers seek for the cheapest transportation mode for their delivery of goods. Reducing transportation costs could lead to a sharp decrease in the overall costs of goods. Getting goods from point A to point B as cheaply as possible is one of suppliers' priorities.

In the following chapters, each transportation mode will be discussed along with possible advantages and disadvantages they can offer.

CHAPTER 4

Air

Learning objectives

- Understand the term of logistics
- Be able to explain the origin and developmental process of logistics
- Be able to explain the major aims and role of logistics

When compared to other transportation modes air transport is overall relatively a new and more innovative industry. One of the main characteristics of air transportation is that it offers the fastest delivery of goods (or people) and the most efficient means of transport as well. But, the prices still remain as the largest burden for users. Road and rail transportation modes are widely used for cargo movements but air network is still responsible for most of long distance movements. This mode of transportation is characterized by a considerable mix of passenger and cargo transport.

The biggest advantages air transportation can offer are the speed and fewer risks that are accompanied. First of all, air transportation can be used to transport fresh products or livestock. A time management is important for these types of goods and aviation sector can offer the fastest services for transporting them. Moreover, air transport is not affected by any conditions on the ground. The only condition it can be affected is by the weather. Compared to other transportation mode, it offers relatively safe and reliable conditions. Still, a limited amount of airports and road connections may remain as bottlenecks.

More advantages and disadvantages can be listed as follows.

4.1 Advantages and Disadvantages

Advantages

- Provides fastest delivery services
- Provides better and improved service levels such as tracking service
- Suitable for high-valued goods and small quantities
- Suitable for fragile goods
- Safer than other transportation modes
- Reduced lead time

Disadvantages

- Faced with customs and excise restrictions
- High delivery costs
- Not suitable for large quantities
- Limited routes
- Easier access to airports are required
- Weights that can be transported are limited

4.2 Transportation Options

The Air Cargo industry offers three different systems or networks which are used to carry cargo from one place to another. Cargo goods can be carried by one of the three options.

1) Using normal passenger flights.

During these passenger flights, passengers are seated in the top of the airplane and their baggages are placed at the lower part of the plane. Technological developments have made it possible to place cargo goods in these flights as it offered more storage space availability. These types of flights are scheduled for passengers and are therefore performed on a regularly base for their convenience. This option is mainly used for air cargo that has to be delivered during the same day or even within a couple hours where expected arrival time is required.

2) Using dedicated cargo planes

These types of planes are specially designed to carry cargo only, and therefore possess an enormous amount of storage space. It is also possible to make these types of planes suited to carry products that need for example specified safety equipment, such as living animals or dangerous products.

3) Using super cargo planes

The last option contains huge payloads that ride in super cargo planes, specially designed to ship extremely large-sized freight.

CASE STUDY

Schiphol smart gate cargo

Nowadays, there are a lot of challenges for air cargo industries such as the evolving government regulations. Safety and security matter have become one of the main priorities for this sector. Especially, the exports outside the European Union experienced great level of inefficiency due to such strong regulations.

The Dutch Air Cargo industry had an intention to create seamless logistics from shipper, forwarder, and handler to the airline. In the end, this was done to improve efficiency, reliability, speed and after all the security of the cargo supply chain. This led Amsterdam Airport Schiphol, Air Cargo Netherlands and the Dutch Customs Administration to work together in inventing Schiphol Smart Gate Cargo (SGC). This cargo system innovates government inspections, security procedures and logistic processes.

The main components of the SGC systems are the Smart Gate ICT solution and the Customs Control Centre (CCC). The Smart Gate ICT solution integrates already existing systems but, also offers new functionalities. Some of the new functionalities are a truck pre-notification module, an innovative risk analysis system and a traffic management module. The CCC offers a centralized coordination and control of all custom inspections done by government.

The SGC system instantly starts functioning when vehicles approach the airport. License plates of the trucks are identified by camera systems placed at the highways around the airport. Pre-notified vehicles are directly allowed to proceed to the main entrance gate. The cargo list of pre notified trucks is online available at the CCC and is on beforehand sent to the center by the shipper. Matrix signs guide non pre-notified vehicles towards the Trucker/Visitor Service Point (TVSP). The TVSP will help the truckers to get a special day pass or a Smart Gate ID. With this ID, truckers will be always pre-notified in the future. Once all this procedure is finished all trucks are able to move to the main entrance gate. At the main entrance gate, the ID Pass identifies the truck and the driver, the result of the risk analysis from the CCC will be communicated immediately. When everything is accepted the truck can immediately proceed to unload his cargo. When the cargo is brought to the warehouses it is ready to fly to their final destination. When there are certain risks or uncertainties about the cargo inside the truck, the driver will be guided towards the detection lane. This hyper modern detection system scans the complete truck without opening it. Hereby full scope of the security and safety requirements are covered. When the scanner detects certain dangerous goods or is still uncertain, custom control personnel at the joint inspection and security centre will inspect the truck. In the end, the system results in a strong competitive position for the airport with speed, credibility, safety and low costs.

E-freight

E-freight is a project started by the International Air Transport Organization with the main goal to digitalize the Air Cargo Industry. The Schiphol Group was one of the major players who helped IATA realizing their project. Besides that Schiphol is one of the airports that managed to reduce 64% of their paper volume due to this digitalization. Working with the E-freight procedures replaces all the paperwork that normally travels along with the cargo from the forwarder to the airline. Before this system was used, the trucker had to bring these documents when he delivered the cargo to the handler, which acts on behalf of the airline. At a service desk, these documents were checked and signed before he received permission to access the handler's premises. With the new system all the information about the cargo is stored in central IT systems and is easily accessible for all parties who are involved. Paper is replaced throughout the complete supply chain, including all levels from shippers, forwarders and export customs to carriers, import customs, forwarders and receivers. This resulted in the fact that all the paperwork became obsolete and information about the cargo was digitalized. Besides that the E-freight system resulted in a major cost reduction, all the separate paperwork checks were no longer necessary.

4.3 Hub and Spoke

As volume of International trade grows, more goods (even people) are moving across the nations. In order to make these movements more effectively and efficiently, a system that simplifies a network of routes has been designed. This is called the Hub-and-Spoke model. It is simple to understand the concept of the model. The 'hub' is at the center and each of the 'spoke' extends outward from the center.

The aviation sector was the first place to have introduced the model. The name is derived from a bicycle wheel which has a center connecting to multiple spokes. The hub and spoke model is centralized, which means airplanes fly out of the hub to a destination, and then return back to the central spot, where passengers are gathered together and where they can change to another plane to reach their destination. The purpose of the Hub and Spoke system is to enable better routes to destinations, to standardize routes and to save airlines money considerably.

The hub and spoke model is basically cheaper to maintain. Moreover aircraft are more likely to fly at full capacity, which leads to more efficient use of transportation resources, and can usually fly routes more than once a day. One major disadvantage of this system is that routes from A to B take much longer and therefore increase the duration of the journey for passengers to reach their final destination. Furthermore this model is usually inflexible.

There might be unexpected difficulties throughout the system if there are changes at the hub or in single routes.

Advantages and Disadvantages

Advantages

1) Rapid growth in the airline industry

The hub and spoke model has allowed a rapid growth in the aviation industry in terms of size, competition strategy and traffic demand. However, this had resulted in operational inefficiencies when economies are under slow growth since airlines experience poor financial performances. As a result of this, some airlines restructured their business model to return to the original point to point system and move out of the constant need for a large hub, and utilize hubs in a more uniform matter in terms of arrivals and departures. This phenomenon is known as the rolling hubs.

2) Scarce transportation resources are used effectively

The system has fewer routes connecting all spokes enabling a more efficient use of scarce transportation resources. This however had small airports and economies of smaller regions suffering as per the reduced capacity. As a result this encouraged airports to agree with low cost carriers to offer low airport fees and commissions from local businesses to bring in traffic and passenger flow.

The passenger market favored this type of airline business as lower fares were rolled out to the market from these smaller hubs, which caused great competition to full service carriers that were operating with large amounts of airport fees to use large hubs, and can no longer return to these small hub markets as it was not cost efficient and were dominated by low cost carriers.

Disadvantages

1) Congestion and delays at hub airports

To limit waiting times and provide a large variety of possible connections for passengers at the hub airport, it is essential for the hub airline to schedule as many incoming and outgoing flights as possible during a short time frame. This results in high traffic peaks during these times and often causes delays due to scarce airside facilities such as taxi or runways.

As the result of large capacity at large hubs in the hub-and-spoke system, the on carriage of passengers are easily affected by a small delay on any one end. For example a small delay from spoke A airport has caused a delay into the major hub; as a result, the connecting flight at the major hub, with passengers gathered from other flights (from spokes B and C) may be delayed by waiting for the passengers to arrive from spokes A; ultimately the domino effect is that the larger group of passengers are delayed to their next hub destination. Had the hub been one of the many transiting points for a passenger from spoke B, then further flights would have been affected and so forth.

2) Discontinuous use of airport facilities

The merging of traffic in a hub-and-spoke-system implies a traffic structure consisting of high peaks at certain times a day when airport facilities are highly in use. At some airports, costly additional capacity and infrastructure (e.g. runways) are required to cater for the demands at these peaks. During off-peak hours, as traffic is less, terminal and airside facilities are used inefficiently or even idle. The temporal discrepancy between capacity and demand will continuously result in either congestion and delays or underutilization.

3) Airport dependency

Hub airlines and the corresponding alliances have selected a limited number of airports on each continent through which they route their traffic. For these few hub airports in turn, they represent a high share of their business. As airport capacity is limited and usually not sufficient for other extensive networks, and the necessary slots at attractive times are not available, other airlines tend to chose alternative options. For the airport, this dependency on one major hub airline has advantages and disadvantages: as long as the airline is stable and successful in the market the airport can be sure of a consistent operation and therewith a steady income stream. As soon as the airline however struggles, this will have negative repercussions on the airport and might severely jeopardize (profitable) operations at the airport.

Pure hub and spoke vs. Hybrid hub and spoke

Pure hub and spoke (Figure 4-1) can be found in parcel or shipping industries where there is only one, centrally located hub. All routes originally travel to the hubs, receive localized goods that have already been separated, and return to their origins. And of course, the hub location must be located strategically. Cost, traffic and efficiency factors should decide which system is best for any organization.

Hybrid hub and spoke (Figure 4-1) is typically found in the Airline industry where most all flights that originate at some spoke location connect through one of a few hub locations and on to their intended desti-

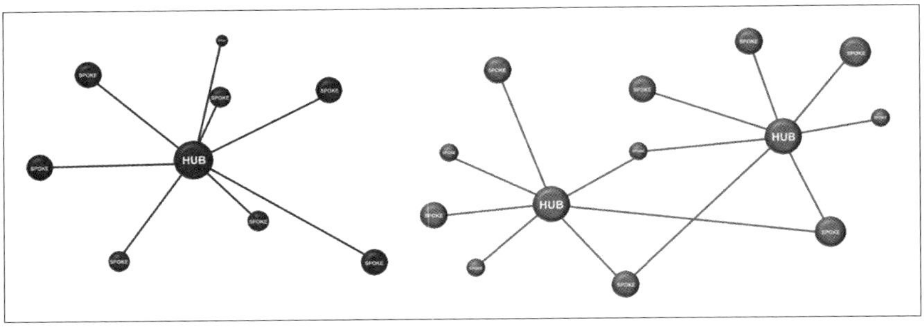

Figure 4-1 pure hub and spoke vs. hybrid hub and spoke

nation. Various airlines generally operate several hubs. At times, you can also find direct flights that do not connect through a hub. Direct flights are based upon demand and cost factors.

Point to point

Point to point system offers a direct movement from one point to another. There is no hub going through before reaching a destination (Figure 4-2) and this model is usually used by Low-Cost Carriers (LCCs).

Sine point to point model provides direct routes this positively reduces

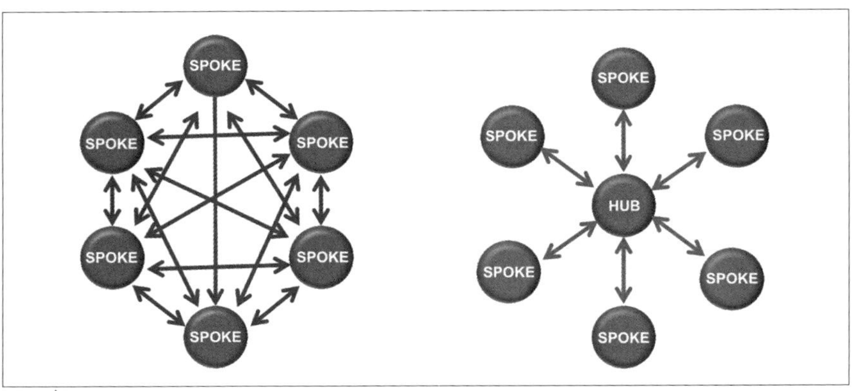

Figure 4-2 point to point vs. hub and spoke

travel time. Besides, it also offers less dependency since there is no need for connecting flights. Drawbacks of this model appear when aircraft still have to fly even if there are few passengers. The frequency of flights is usually reduced in comparison with Hub and Spoke models. Last but not least, passengers are forced to make connections or to travel by another airline if the particular one doesn't provide a specific destination.

CASE STUDY

DHL airfreight service

DHL, belonging to Deutsche Post DHL group, is known as one of the global leaders in the logistics industry. The company is responsible for 12% of the worldwide air freight marketing. They operate in over 220 countries and consist of three major business areas;

1. DHL Express
2. DHL Global Forwarding
3. Freight and DHL Supply Chain

In order to offer services their customers require, DHL's air freight offers various different services. These services include;

1. Fast, urgent but cost intensive deliveries via air (DHL AIR FIRST)
2. Cheaper deliveries that take longer time (DHL AIR VALUE)
3. Combined means of transportation to save costs for particular routes (DHL SEAIR)
4. Transportation of bulky deliveries (DHL AIRFREIGHT PLUS)
5. Newly launched service for transporting pharmaceutical or other life science industry related products that have to be transported within a certain period of time or at a certain temperature (DHL AIRFREIGHT PLUS PHARMA)

DHL works with commercial airlines as well as charter capacity. They mainly use the Airbus 300 and Boeing 757, but also own their own carriers. They are able to offer and ensure fast door-to-door priority air freight without limitations with their integrated carriers. As most of the major airfreight companies (UPS, TNT and FEDEX) DHL works with a hub-and-spoke system. In Europe DHL's main and largest (2million m^2 of land) air hub is located in Leipzig. When a cargo aircraft arrives in Leipzig, it normally requires seven staff members to unload up to 1,500 tons of parcels and mail approximately around 15 minutes.

Example of DHL's Airfreight System

A retailer in Germany orders a selection of clothes manufactured in Shenzen, China. When the manufacturer receives the order, he arranges the transport via DHL air freight. The same day, DHL sends a courier to the factory to pick up the load. The freight is sealed with a barcode containing the information of destination and time. The barcode is scanned by the courier so that sender and receiver can track down the sending. The courier brings the freight to a DHL distribution center where it is bundled with all the other parcels and then is transported to Shenzen airport. There, an automated sorting system scans and sorts the freight together with other goods according to their destinations. A DHL truck leaves Shenzen airport to bring the airfreight bundles to the nearest air hub, which in this case is in Hong Kong, the largest air hub in Asia, Australia and the Pacific region.

In the same night, all parcels are scanned and sorted by international destinations, planes are unloaded, refueled and then reloaded with the according freight. By 6am the next morning, the manufacturer's freight is already on its way to Germany, more specifically to Leipzig, the largest air hub in Europe and the central hub for Europe and Africa. At around 4pm the plane lands in Leipzig airport, where it is unloaded, the freight is rescanned and sorted, this time depending on their inner-state destinations to load them on the appropriate vehicles. The retailer's order is loaded onto another plane to Frankfurt International Airport.

The next morning, the cargo from Leipzig to Frankfurt takes off and arrives an hour later in Frankfurt where the freight again goes though scanning and sorting processes on a conveyer belt to figure out the fastest route to the local retailer. It is then transported to the nearest DHL distribution center, where a couple of hours later a DHL courier accepts the shipment, scans the freight to calculate the best route and starts off his journey. Arriving at the retailer in Frankfurt city, the courier scans the freight again and lets the owner sign the electronic hand scanner to confirm that the goods have been delivered.

Quiz

- When would you use air transportation for a package delivery? Why would you use this transportation mode?
- What is the biggest advantage of using air transportation?
- Can you think of any examples of point to point and hub and spoke?
- Can you think of any problems or benefits of hub and spoke model?
- Think about your journey to a foreign country sometime in the past and think about the followings;
  - _ Where was your destination country?
  - _ What airline did you fly with?
  - _ Was it a direct flight? If not, did you stop by elsewhere before reaching your destination country?

Notes

- Liu, J. and Yuanyuan, W. (2012), "Study of Competitiveness – A Case Study of DHL", Gävle: University of Gävle, Department of Business and Economics.
- Pak, M. (2011), Understanding International Logistics, Bobmumsa:Seoul.
- Upham, P., Maughan, J., Raper, D. and Thomas, C. (2003), "Towards Sustainable Aviation", Sterling: Earthscan Publications.
- Rodrigue, J., "Hubs of Major Air Freight Integrators", available at http://people.hofstra.edu/geotrans/eng/ch5en/appl5en/upshubs.html
- http://www.dhl.de/content/dam/dhlde/logistik/pdf/freight/dhl-logistik-air-freight-a4-6pg-web-en.pdf
- http://www.dhl.ch/en/logistics/freight_transportation/air_freight.html
- http://www.dpdhl.com/en/logistics_around_us/trends/parcel_on_tour.html
- http://www.dpdhl.com/en/logistics_around_us/from_our_divisions/leipzig_hub.html

ARTICLE

IFEZ emerges as international business hub: Commissioner Lee pledges deregulation to make Songdo more foreign-friendly

The Incheon Free Economic Zone (IFEZ) is being transformed into a "golden place," gathering investors as an international business hub.

IFEZ is attracting international organizations and firms thanks to its geographical benefits and eco- and business-friendly environment. The area was named a special district for a government project to boost the country's economy in 2003.

The IFEZ in Songdo, west of Seoul, aims to become the main business hub for northeast Asia by the end of 2020.

"We are forming this place as the center of global business by introducing many service sectors," Lee Jong-cheol, commissioner of the IFEZ, said during an interview.

"With its brilliant location in the center of the economic bloc in northeast Asia, the place is gaining attention from international investors."

Lee explained the differentiating feature of IFEZ from other business districts is its location, which is home to Incheon International Airport. The airport, which has been named as the top player in services for none consecutive times, has flights to 61 countries.

Lee emphasized that Songdo is also a self-sufficient city where residents can access everything they need to make a living within a 5 kilometer radius.

"The IFEZ is a compact, smart and green city where people can use internet anywhere," Lee added.

It has set a goal to become an eco-friendly zone with low carbon emissions and succeeded in making the land a greener area.

The case of development of Songdo International Business District as a designated free economic zone has been acknowledged at the 2014 Energy Efficiency Global Forum held in Walter E. Convention Center in Washington. It won Energy Efficiency Visionary Award (EEVA) at the forum.

With all those benefits, it already started functioning as an international hub for international organizations and multinational companies.

So far, there are up to 13 multinational organizations in the district. They include the Green Climate Fund (GCF), the World Bank Group's Korea Office, United Nations Economic and Social Commission for Asia and the Pacific (UN ESCAP) and the Association of World Election Bodies (A-Web).

The GCF is the entity of global funds supporting developing countries with the aim of diminishing greenhouse gas and countering climate change in the world.

The commissioner says he is placing a greater focus on easing rules in order to make the district more vitalized and a world-class hub. He said deregulation is the key to making the area more appealing to foreign companies.

The commissioner said red tape, if not addressed, could remain the biggest hurdle to the IFEZ's efforts to attract more investors.

"We need drastic, bold deregulation. Most importantly, the mindset of government officials must be changed in line with fast-changing global standards."

With the philosophy, Lee plans to educate government officials.

"We will make best effort to make the IFEZ a leading business-friendly zone in the world," he added.

Source : The Korea Times, June 4, 2014

Review

Songdo deregulated in an attempt to be more foreign-friendly

The Incheon Free Economic Zone (IFEZ) is attempting to become a major international business hub. It's an attractive area due to its geographical and business-friendly features. The South Korean government designated the area special status to boost the country's economy. This area in Songdo aims to become the top business hub for northeast Asia by 2020. It will include many different service sectors, and is vying to attract multiple international investors.

The IFEZ is differentiated from other economic zones due to its distinct and advantageous features. First, it has an unparalleled access to a world-class airport. Incheon airport has been rated the top airport in the world multiple times and is capable of handling flights to 61 different countries. Second, the IFEZ is a small and compact city that is designed to be eco-friendly and technologically connected with complete wifi-coverage. Finally, it has already attracted multiple international organizations and companies. Many of such have set up branches and offices in this district. Some of the organizations included are the Green Climate Fund, World Bank Group's Korea Office, United Nations Economic and Social Commission for Asian and the Pacific, and the Association of World Election Bodies.

Now, there is a great focus on creating an easier environment for businesses to setup shop. One specific goal is deregulation, which would serve to make the area more appealing to foreign investment and companies. This is the biggest challenge for the IFEZ. The first step and key to the success and growth of this area is bold deregulation. The mindset of the government officials must be changed to meet newly evolving global standards if success is to be ensured.

Question

1) Do you agree that deregulation of the IFEZ is the biggest hurdle for guaranteeing the success of such area?
2) Do you think that the IFEZ can reach its goal to become the biggest business NorthEast Asia by 2020? Why? Or why not? Support your answer with concrete details.

CHAPTER 5

Road

Road transportation has been a popular means of transportation for centuries. This means of transportation uses roads for transporting passengers or goods. In many countries, licensing requirements and safety regulations are in place in order to ensure a separation of the two industries. The vehicles mostly used on roads are cars and trucks, usually owned privately and therefore the cost for road transportation is split up into state costs for the roads and private costs for the vehicles.

Road transportation is the dominating mode for short-distance trips. For short distances and small shipments a van or pickup truck may be used. For large shipments, a truck will be more appropriate. Road transportation however brings pollution and road congestion problems. Congestion will be worse especially in urban areas.

This transportation mode is heavily used within countries and continents and usually also included in some parts of overseas transportation processes such as delivering the goods from a factory to an air hub.

More advantages and disadvantages can be listed as follows.

Advantages

- Relatively cheaper than other transportation modes
- Delivery is flexible
- Relatively cheaper than other transportation modes
- Cheaper for small quantities

Disadvantages

- Relatively less safer than other transportation modes
- Road traffics/ congestions may cause delivery delays
- Not suitable for large quantities
- Fares may be high for long distances

Quiz

- Is road transportation likely to be affected by the weather conditions?
- Think about the parcel delivery systems in Korea. How are the majority parcels transported within the country?
- Think about the road conditions and size of the country in Korea. What advantages and disadvantages of road transportation can you think of under such conditions?
- How has the use of Bus lane system in Korea improved the road condition and what changes have been made since? How would this help logistics conditions?

Notes

- Rodrigue, J., Comtois, C. and Slack, B. (2009), The Geography of Transport Systems, New York: Routledge.
- Pak, M. (2011), Understanding International Logistics, Bobmumsa: Seoul.

CHAPTER 6

Rail

Rail transport means the transportation of goods in freight trains. Freight trains consist of freight wagons and two or three locomotives. There are freight wagons for universal use but also for containers carrying cars, coal or wood. Besides that, liquid goods can be transported in tank wagons. Given the great variety of wagons, it is only logical that a freight train sometimes includes more than one type. Generally, trains run after a certain schedule. Nevertheless, unfulfilled capacity can be made use of with so-called ad-hoc trains running according to demand. There are several advantages and disadvantages of rail.

The main advantage is that bulky and large goods can be transported. Moreover, while hazardous goods can also be transported on a train it is a very safe method of transportation that is also very environmental-friendly even on longer distances. Unfortunately, it causes noise nuisance and is less flexible than road. Overall, different national regulations increase the difficulty of international rail transport.

More advantages and disadvantages can be listed as follows.

Advantages

- Considered to be environmentally friendly than other transportation modes
- No congestions (little delays)
- Offers affordable delivery costs
- Considered to be suitable for large quantities

- Suitable for medium to long distances (costs are relatively cheaper)
- Fewer accidents (safer than other transportation modes)
- Less likely to be affected by weather conditions

Disadvantages

- Routes are inflexible
- Limited number of locomotives and trains
- Expensive for short distances
- Not suitable to be used for emergency

Quiz

- Can you think of any other disadvantages of rail transportation?
- Why may rail transportation be safer than other transportation modes?
- How have your lives changed after the creation of KTX in Korea?
- The movements of goods have changed after KTX started to offer delivery services. What changes have been made? How has this enhanced the use of quick service?

Notes

- Corbat, P. (2009), Logistik in Vertriebsunternehmen (Books on Demand GmbH, Niederstedt)
- Pak, M. (2011), Understanding International Logistics, Bobmumsa: Seoul.
- http://www.kundenforum-bus-bahn.de/verkehr/mehr-gueter-auf-die-schiene-strassen-von-verkehr-entlasten.html
- http://www.logistiktrend.de/index.php/transport/schiene?showall=1&limitstart,
- http://www.transportberater.portal-c.info/vorteile_schiene.html

ARTICLE

Korea, Russia discuss railway, logistics projects

Deputy foreign ministers of South Korea and Russia met on Tuesday for bilateral consultations on topics including railway and logistics projects that involve North Korea, according to an official at the Russian Embassy in Seoul on Wednesday.

1st Vice Minister of Foreign Affairs Cho Tai-young and Deputy Minister for Political Affairs Lee Kyung-soo sat down with Igor V. Morgulov, Russian deputy minister of foreign affairs, for talks along with Russian Ambassador to South Korea Konstantin Vnukov.

Lee and Morgulov pledged to lift two-way trade to $30 billion annually by 2015. They also discussed the security environment on the Korean Peninsula and in Northeast Asia, and North Korean denuclearization.

During the Tuesday meeting, the two deputy ministers also talked about ways to increase South Korea's contributions to a proposed logistics and transport project.

Russian Railways and a consortium of major South Korean companies inked an MOU in a signing ceremony attended by Russian President Vladimir Putin and President Park Geun-hye in Seoul last November.

The deal would see South Korea investing in a Russian-led rail and port development project connecting North Korea's northern city of Rason with Russia's Trans-Siberian Railway.

The 54-kilometer, double-track railroad between Rajin Station in the North Korean city of Rason and Khasan Station in the nearby Russian town of Khasan reopened last year in September.

Source : Korea Herald, March 23, 2014

Review

Korea in talks with Russia to create a railway and logistics project

South Korea and Russian officials had a sit down meeting to discuss how to boost cross country trade to $30 billion annually by 2015. Furthermore, they discussed a variety of other topics including national security and North Korean denuclearization. They even proposed different ways to increase South Korea's contributions to a specific logistics and transport project.

Ultimately, Russian Railways and a collection of South Korean companies signed an MOU, which allows South Korea to invest in the Russian-led rail and port development project that connects North Korea's Rason city with Russian's own Trans-Siberian Railway. Also to note, the 54km railway between Rajin Station in North Korea and Russia's Khasan city reopened last September.

Question

1) Discuss what South Korea has to gain by contributing to this transport project.
2) Discuss what Russia has to gain.

ARTICLE

Will railway project lift ban on NK?

With Korean companies possibly set to join in a Russia-North Korean railway project, questions have arisen as to whether Seoul will lift a two-year-old ban — called the May 24 measure — on any fresh investments in the Stalinist nation.

On the sidelines of a summit between President Park Geun-hye and her Russian counterpart Vladimir Putin, Wednesday, Seoul and Moscow signed an agreement on potential cooperation in the railway venture.

Under the pact, POSCO and Hyundai Merchant Marine will go through due diligence next year to decide on its participation in the ongoing business of linking North Korea's Najin and Russia's Khasan.

"If POSCO and Hyundai take part, it is tantamount to investment in the North that is prohibited under the May 24 measure," said Chang Yong-seok, a researcher at the Institute of Peace and Unification Studies affiliated with Seoul National University.

"As the Park administration supports the business, it appears to give a green light to the project despite the May 24 measure. It can be a major breakthrough to improve stalled inter-Korean relations in economic areas."

In the aftermath of the sinking of South Korean frigate Cheonan on March 26, 2010, Seoul implemented the sanctions on May 24 after that North Korea was found responsible for the incident, which claimed the lives of 46 sailors.

The ship was destroyed in an unprovoked torpedo attack in the West Sea although Pyongyang has denied its involvement, refusing to accept the conclusions of an international investigation team.

The consensus is that Pyongyang has been deprived of some half a billion dollars in income thus far due to the punitive steps, which Seoul refuses to scrap without an official apology for the Cheonan incident.

However, the inter-Korean joint industrial complex in the North's border town of Gaeseong was exempted from the May 24 measure.

"Should Seoul agree to corporate investment in the Najin-Khasan project, there would be more operations by our companies around the Najin port," Chang said.

"They are also against the May 24 measure. It remains to be seen how South Korea will respond to them. It has a choice between just a one-off exception of the measure or substantially easing it."

In 2008, Russia and North Korea embarked on the $340 million project to connect the ice-free northeastern port of Najin, called Rajin in North Korea, to the nearby Russian town of Khasan.

POSCO and Hyundai are looking at being a part of the plan of refurbishing a 54-kilometer cross-border railway by purchasing a share from the Russian side, which holds a 70% stake.

Source : The Korea Times, November 14, 2013

Review

Possible Railway ban lifted in NK

As Russian and North Korea are working towards creating a joint-venture with a railway project, South Korea is questioning whether or not to join forces with these communist nations. Currently, under law, South Korea has a standing ban on any financial investments with Russia, its called the "May 24 measure". In 2008, Russian and North Korea made a deal to create a $340 million railway to connect Najin, North Korea or Khasan, Russia.

The current President of South Korea, Park Geun-hye signed an agreement on a possible joint venture with Russian President Vladimir Putin. They hope to collaborate on a railway venture together. The specific companies working the deal are POSCO and Hyundai Merchant Marine. They will have about a year to decide whether or not to participate in the business of connecting North Korea's Najin and Russia's Khasan together. POSCO and Hyundai want to invest in refurbishing a 54km stretch of railway on the Russian side. However, if Hyundai and POSCO decide to get in on the deal, it can be problematic since it is specifically prohibited under the May 24 measure. Despite this, the Park administration is supporting this joint venture and is seemingly ignoring the original May 24 measure. They argue that this deal can help rekindle the inter-Korean relationships in key economic regions.

Historically, the two Koreas have had tumultuous relationships. In 2010, the South Korean frigate named the Cheonan was attacked and sunk by North Korean forces, ultimately resulting in the death of 46 South Korean sailors. North Korea denied its involvement. Consequently, South Korea responded by depriving the North of over $500 billion dollars in economic revenue. Without an official apology for the incident from the North, the South refuses to lift such sanctions.

Question

1) Define and describe the advantages and disadvantages of POSCO and Hyundai cooperating with North Korean and Russia in collaborating in this international railway project.
2) Should the May 24 measure be revoked for this project? Why or why not?

CHAPTER 7

Sea

Definition of sea transportation is the commercial act of transporting people or goods by ship for pay. Due to its difference in mode of transportation, sea transportation is differentiated with lake or river transportation. Maritime transportation plays a significant role in intermodal transportation and integrated logistics system compared to other transportation modes and insures seamless global flow of goods. There are different types of sea transportation. Sea transportation involves the transporting of passengers or cargo across the oceans. It involves transporting them at extreme distances to different locations for a specified length of time.

Sea transportation consists of passenger vessels, bulk carriers, general cargo ships and roll-on/roll-off vessels. It can include the transportation of containers and large goods as well as the transportation of cars, trucks or trains via roll-on/roll-off vessels, or simply of passengers wanting to get from A to B or wanting to spend their vacation on a cruise ship.

Today's global economy is represented by widely spread, but interconnected supply of resources, division of labor, manufacturing, production, distribution, and logistics process. From the first stage of product production to the last stage of delivery to consumers, product elements are transported numerous times around the world. Sea transportation is an integral, but sometimes not always visible to the public eye, part of global economy and plays a key role in distribution, production, and flow of goods, thus promoting international trade.

Advantages and disadvantages can be listed as follows.

7.1 Advantages and Disadvantages

Advantages

- Attractive transportation costs (probably the cheapest transportation mode)
- Suitable for large quantities
- No traffic

Disadvantages

- More complicated packaging requirements may apply
- Difficulties with door-to-door delivery as inland transportation has to be organized separately
- Slowest transition time amongst the four transportation modes
- Relatively lower safety compared to other transportation modes (eg. due to piracy risks)

7.2 Functions of Sea Port

1) Economic aspect

Sea port is an important asset to city and local economy. Ports are closely related to activities of shipping, cargo and international trade. They at the same time play a vital role in contributing to the local economies since they tend to influence working areas of shipping such as ship repairing service, cargo custom, cargo security and many others.

Ports hence provide various types of jobs in its own field influencing the economic growth. However, the recent trends of port reflect the reality that containerization of cargo has changed the environment of port. Containerization has reduced the need for labor while reducing the port call. Historical characteristics of ports tend to disappear while new trends are taking its place.

2) Ecological aspect

Since the announcement of the redevelopment of the waterfront in the 1980s, it has become important to realize the existence of a healthy ecosystem. Environmental issues may not have been dealt with as one of the priorities before. But, since ports are closely related and can therefore have direct effects to the ecosystem, it is important to pay close attention to the environment.

3) Spatial aspect

In general, ports have established themselves along with cities forming port cities. There are changes that occurred in ports such as containerization in the face with spatial difficulties. This is because ports located within cities lack space and therefore it becomes difficult for ports to play its functions to the changes made. As a result of this, ports are now being separated from the main cities to secure more space.

Table 7-1 shows the modern policies of each transport agency which are used to improve the quality of transportation services as well as to propel efficiency and labor saving.

Table 7-1 Trends of modernization in transport agency

	Dedicated carriage	Intermodal carriage	Etc
Rail transportation	Material transport -Reinforcement of private transportations (grains, cement, cars, steel, fish food) -Maintenance of suitable base for certain material (petrol, chemical liquid, cement, steel, cars, paper, grains, fertilizer) -Reinforcement of lanes	Container transport -Reinforcement of containers -Maintenance of private container transportations -Maintenance of container base -Maintenance of marine container rail transport system Pallet transport (paper, plate glass, industrial products, vinyl chloride, chemical products) Maintenance of private wagons Maintenance of beltline railways	Express transport -Integration of cargo strategic stations -Express and one-way transport -Regional express transport -Development of high-speed cars (100km/h) Larger wagons Maintenance of cargo information system
Road transportation	Increase number of cars for special purpose (tank car, dump truck, concrete mixer, refrigerated vehicle)	Maintenance of marine container car transport system Maintenance of general terminal Maintenance of distribution center	Larger and trailerized vehicles
Sea transportation (Ocean-going shipping) (Inner-harbor shipping)	Dedicated transport service (petrol, coal, grains, steel iron) Maintenance of private terminals Maintenance of petrol transport base Private transport service Barge transport (petrol, LPG, coal, cement, steel, cars, chemicals)	Maritime container transport -Increased container ships -Maintenance of private ocean-going container terminal -Inner harbor container transport -Car ferry	Faster, larger, and automatized ships
Air transportation		Containerized air freight -Maintenance of airport cargo handling base	Larger aircrafts Cargo-only aircrafts

Source: Daily Economics of the East, Knowledge of logistics, 1994, p.113

ARTICLE

Making the sea our economic ground of the future

May 31 was the Ocean Day. As the maritime development competition intensified between countries after the United Nations Convention on the Law of the Sea took effect in November 1994, Korea designated the Ocean Day in 1996 to publicize the importance of the sea and inspire maritime pioneering spirit. However, in the aftermath of the Sewol ferry tragedy, this year's celebration events have been either reduced or canceled. The marine industry insiders are discouraged and feel guilty after the accident.

However, as we mourn for the tragic incident, we also need to think about the value of the ocean. Making up 71 percent of the surface of the earth, the oceans are the last remaining unexplored field. The value of the sea is especially significant for Korea, where three sides of the peninsula are surrounded by the seas and marine territory is more than four times the size of the land. The sea provides inexpensive and safe trade route, abundant seabed resources and marine products, creating great wealth for the nation.

The sailors who navigate the five oceans to transport Korean export goods, fishermen operating in the deep sea far away from Korea, the workers at the dockyard working day and night to build world-class ships and meet order deadlines, the researchers engaged in studies at the King Sejong Antarctic Research station, the Naval officers guarding the marine territories and standing face to face with North Korea, and the coast guards cracking down illegal fishing operations are the key players in the sea.

As Korea became one of the top 10 exporters from the poorest country in the world, Korea did not fear the ocean. Rather we challenged and controlled it. The shipbuilding industry, the marine transport industry, fisheries industry and the marine resources industry have made great contributions to the Korean economy. Moreover, marine life engineering is celebrated as a future industry, and marine leisure industry is emerging as a next-generation growth engine.

Instead of fearing the sea, we need to overcome and manage to make it our economic ground of the future. If we had managed the sea better, we could have prevented the Sewol ferry disaster. Let's remember what the seas mean to us.

Source : Korea JoongAng Daily, June 9, 2014

Review

Oceanic Economic Growth

In recent news, the Sewol ferry tragedy has brought a downpour of gloom to what would otherwise be a celebration of 'Ocean Day' on May 31st. This year's festivities were canceled out of respect for the tragic accident.

Despite these trying times, it is important to still view the ocean not as treacherous, but as a source of safe trade routes, resources, and economic potential. The ocean is especially important to South Korea due to the natural landscape being a peninsula. Many people depend on the ocean for their livelihood. The people range from fishermen, dock workers, researchers, navy officers, and coast guards. They all play key roles in the economy and safeguard of Korea.

Part of Korea's miraculous economic turnaround was due to its embracement of the ocean. South Korea utilized the ocean to create a world-class shipbuilding industry, marine transport industry, fisheries, and other marine resource industries. The ocean is also the birth place of future industries like marine leisure and marine life engineering. These emerging industries could fuel explosive economic growth for Korea's future.

In correlation with recent maritime accidents, fear has permeated into our sub consciousness. However, fear will only disrupt and delay our future economic growth in nurturing the oceanic economy. Through better management, disasters could be prevented. It is important to embrace the ocean, which has protected and served us so well in the past.

Question

1) Name the main Korean industries supported by the ocean and explain how each played a role in Korea's economic turnaround.
2) What do you foresee to be the biggest hurdle for Korea in developing their economy based upon the ocean?

ARTICLE

Hyundai Merchant to sell Pusan Newport

Hyundai Merchant Marine (HMM) is expected to sell its core assets, including Pusan Newport, to avoid a liquidity crisis following in the footsteps of Dongbu Group's self-rescue measures.

"We will reduce our outstanding debt by selling core assets and issuing perpetual bonds with the approval of creditor banks," an official at HMM, the flagship of the Hyundai Group, told The Korea Times by telephone.

HMM, the country's second-largest shipping company by sales after Hanjin Shipping, has raised 525 billion won ($500 million) since December through a rights offering and the sale of cranes. The state-run Korea Development Bank (KDB) recently bought corporate debt worth 280 billion from the shipping firm in October.

"We do not see any immediate liquidity problems through early next year but we will make a continued effort to sell our assets to cut debt," the official said asking not to be named.

However, such efforts are seemingly falling short of casting off investor worries as HMM is still struggling with a heavy debt-to-equity ratio of nearly 1,000 percent as of the end of September. Its debt currently stands at more than 6 trillion won.

Korea Investors Service (KIS) and Korea Ratings recently downgraded the corporate rating of Hyundai Merchant to BBB+ from A-.

"It is uncertain when the shipping industry will begin to recover amid oversupply and squeezed margins. Delayed recovery will continue to put downward pressure on shipping firms," Moon Chang-ho, head of KIS Fundamental Rating Group 2, said.

"The recent downgrade will have a negative impact on HMM when it applies for loans from banks as well as on the overall businesses of its parent Hyundai Group," Kang Dong-jin, an analyst at HMC Investment Securities, said.

HMM's additional restructuring moves include the sale of a 50 percent stake in Pusan Newport and asset-backed loans with three years of liquefied natural gas

(LNG) shipping charges as collateral, the official explained.

"Getting a loan based on LNG-carrying charges is only possible if the Korea Gas Corp. (KOGAS) approves the idea," Kang said. The company has a 20-year contract to deliver LNG for KOGAS.

On Sunday, Dongbu Group announced its plans to raise 3 trillion won by selling assets and streamlining four businesses - agriculture, electronics, finance and steel to avoid a companywide liquidity crisis.

Dongbu even put its core semiconductor business up for sale in order to cut its debt to 2.9 trillion won by 2015 from an estimated 6.3 trillion currently.

Financial regulators and creditor banks have been pressuring debt-ridden companies to take bolder steps to avoid having a grave impact on the economy.

"Instead of stopgap measures such as rights issue and stock collateral loans between affiliates, we asked financially-weak firms to sell their key assets for tangible results," a KDB official said.

The KDB is the main creditor bank of conglomerates such as Dongbu, Hyundai and Hanjin groups.

In late October, Hanjin Shipping said it would borrow 150 billion won in financial support from Korean Air, due to a lack of operating capital. The airline took a 15.4 percent stake in Hanjin Shipping held by Hanjin Shipping Holdings as security in return for the "emergency loan."

Hanjin Shipping and Korean Air are two major affiliates of Hanjin Group, the country's 10th-largest conglomerate by assets. Hyundai Group is a shipping to brokerage conglomerate.

Source : The Korea Times, November 18, 2013

Review

Hyundai Merchant sells Busan Newport

Due to outstanding debts, Hyundai Merchant Marine expects to sell some of its core assets to prevent a liquidity crisis similar to Dongbu Group's own emergency measures. One core asset of HMM includes Pusan Newport.

HMM is South Korea's second largest shipping company by sales, right after Hanjin Shipping. In order to raise money, HMM sold some rights offerings and the sale of its cranes for approximately $500 million. Furthermore, Korea Development Bank bought its corporate debt with approximately $250 million in October. These efforts to control debt have bought them some time to survive till early next year. However, it's current debt to equity ratio is still a staggering 1000%. It's debt is now at more than $6billion. This news has caused a ripple effect so that now Hyundai Merchant has been downgraded from a corporate rating of A- to BBB+. Experts are uncertain at the prospect of recovery. This downgrade in rating will negatively impact HMM when it applies for credit.

Part of this restructuring process includes selling off 50% of its stake in the Pusan Newport and loans with three years of liquefied natural gas shipping charges as collateral for those loans. The liquefied gas as collateral was an idea only possible if the Korea Gas Corporation approves of the idea. Currently, the HMM has a 20 year contract to deliver gas to the Korea Gas Corporation.

Dongbu Group is also restructuring and demands that they raise $3 billion by selling assets and restructuring 4 key businesses such as agriculture, electronics, finance, and steel. If done correctly, they can avoid a companywide crisis. They even put their semiconductor business up for sale in hopes to reduce debt by half. To prevent general economic aggravation, creditors are putting more pressure on companies to pay back their debts. Instead of making small fixes to their skyrocketing debts, creditors are asking firms to sell their assets for real tangible results. In related news, Korean Air loaned Hanjin Shipping 150 billion won for a 15.4% stock in Hanjin Shipping as security.

Question

1) What was the cause of Dongbu and HMM's economic troubles? Could it have been prevented?
2) Is selling off major assets a smart decision for these companies? Why or why not?

CASE STUDY

Rotterdam

The most famous seaport of the Netherlands is Rotterdam. It is not only important for the Netherlands, but actually has a region function for whole northwest Europe and is also used as an intermediate port to transfer goods to other ports around Europe.

The History of Rotterdam

The city of Rotterdam itself is not located at a sea. It is surrounded by several rivers that come together to flood into the sea. Over time this has proven an ideal point to connect sea trade and trade going further by rivers towards the connecting lands. The first time mentions of the port of Rotterdam are around the 15th century. Also around the time the Netherlands became a well-known seafaring nation that ruled the seas and had many trade connections all around the world.

What kind of port is Rotterdam?

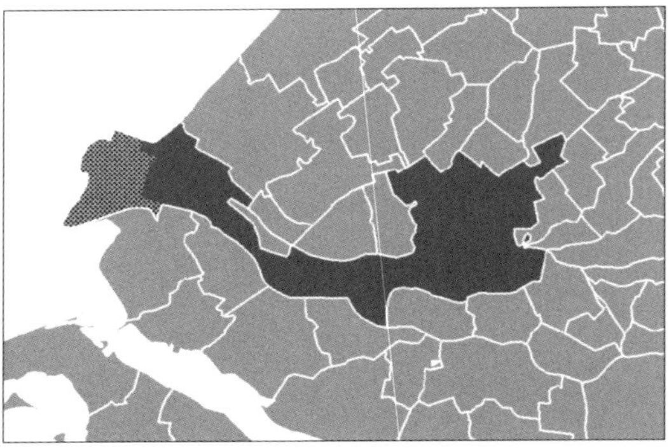

Source: Wikipedia

The dark colored area is known as Rotterdam, the dot-filled area represents the newly created Maasvlakte.

Early on Rotterdam started off as an inland port since it lay not directly at sea. The city had a good connection with both the sea, and the rivers connecting the countries surrounding it. But over the centuries Rotterdam developed itself and kept growing, which allowed the creation of the much needed " Maasvlaktes". The

Maasvlakte is an artificial created piece of land that directly lies in front of the rivers connecting Rotterdam and the Sea. At this moment the third Maasvlakte is being created after the first and second could not fulfill the extra need for capacity. Nowadays Rotterdam is both a normal seaport as well as an inland port.

What do they trade?

To further distinguish the port of Rotterdam we have to take a look at what type of goods and cargo are being transported to and from the port. We can conclude from numbers provided by the port of Rotterdam itself that it is a multipurpose port. Although it can handle both cruise ships and cargo the main area of interest for the port of Rotterdam lies in the cargo area. More than a total of 430 million metric tons of cargo were shipped to and from Rotterdam. The graphs below show the types of cargo handled and its amount in 2011 and 2012.

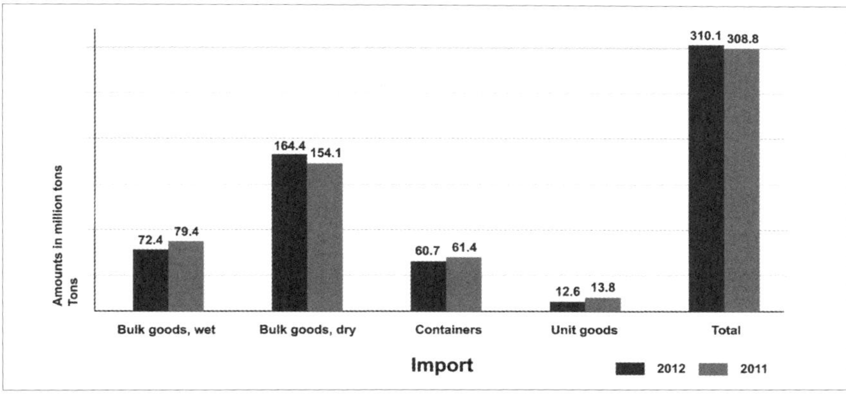

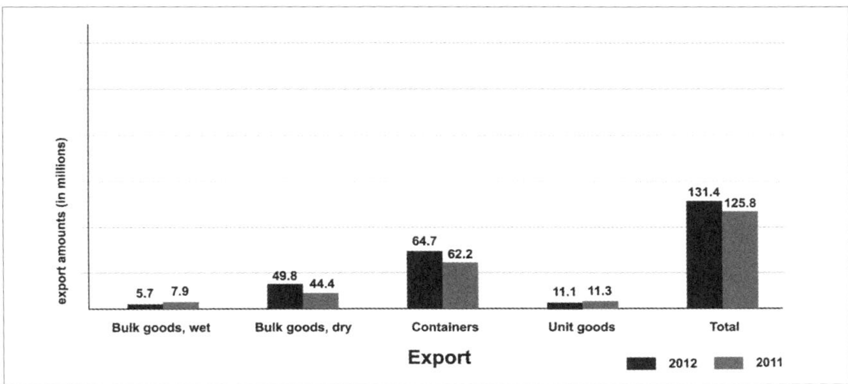

Source: Port of Rotterdam Official website

From this table it may be concluded that the port of Rotterdam is particularly specialized in dry bulk goods. Products that are classified as dry bulk are agricultural products, coal and ores (e.g. Iron). It is also clear that Rotterdam mainly imports good which will be distributed further over land.

Comparison to other ports

Rotterdam was the largest port in the world from 1968 till 2004 straight. Nowadays they remain in the top 5 and the total number of 441,5 makes Rotterdam rank fourth in size compared to ports all over the world. The busiest ports are Shanghai, Singapore and Ningbo. The largest port in the world, Ningbo China, is almost nearly double the size of Rotterdam with a total amount shipped of 744. Korea's Busan port ranks tenth on this list with almost 300 million ton of goods. Rotterdam is also the only European port in the top ten. When we take a closer look at the other European ports we can conclude that Rotterdam is almost as busy as the other European largest ports together that complement the top five.

Location

There are several factors that contribute to a ports success. The first factor is the location of the port of Rotterdam. The sea closest to Rotterdam is the North Sea. This sea is a warm water sea and does not freeze over in the winter. The rivers that connect Rotterdam with the North Sea are the Rhine and the Maas. The Rhine is one of the longest rivers of Europe with 1250 km and connects Rotterdam with Germany, France, and Austria and all the way to Switzerland. Especially the connection between the Ruhr-area (Germany's main economic part) and Rotterdam is an important one. Furthermore the Maas connects Rotterdam with Belgium and France, this river of 950 km allows for more possibilities to transfer goods into mainland Europe. Within a radius of 500 km the Port of Rotterdam can serve 150 million customers. Other infrastructure around Rotterdam is of a high standard as well. Close by is the 'The Hague/Rotterdam' international airport, the third largest airport in the Netherlands. Several pipelines connect Rotterdam with all of Europe. Some of the railroads around Rotterdam serve only a single purpose and that is cargo transport. The best known railroad is the "Betuwelijn" connecting Rotterdam in a straight line to the previous mentioned Ruhr-area. The Betuwelijn is nicknamed the Iron Rhine for its importance in transporting goods. Several other railroads connect Rotterdam with Amsterdam, Paris, London (through the

Channel tunnel) and other areas of economic interest. Where trains cannot come trucks can, the roads from Rotterdam lead straight into Belgium and the "Randstad", the Netherlands' economic heart. These possibilities allow for Rotterdam to have a smooth transition from port to other forms of Transport.

Additional support factors

Location is one factor; people and legislation is a second. Harbors need skilled employees and also an environment that sustains the activities of the port.

Rotterdam was bombed in the second world several times, first by the Nazi's and later by the allies to destroy the economic value for their enemies, thus leaving a destroyed city and port behind after the war. The Dutch government decided to appoint Rotterdam as area of main economic interest and invested heavily to create a top of the line new port. This mindset still plays a key role and plenty of investments (e.g. Betuwelijn, Maasvlakte) are made over past decade to ensure the economic importance of the port of Rotterdam. Legislation is often swiftly changed in favor of the port to allow its growth and to venture new possibilities.

Next to the government Rotterdam has one of the most renowned business universities in the Netherlands. Which provides a steady stream of highly educated personnel each year, together with the specialized "Zeevaartschool" for officers on ships and other educational infrastructure that is specialized in port and sea necessities. Of the population of Rotterdam, 600.000, nearly 70.000 work directly in the port, and another 220.000 in support industries related to the port.

Notes

- http://www.cbs.nl/nl-NL/menu/home/default.htm
- http://www.rijkswaterstaat.nl/water/feiten_en_cijfers/vaarwegenoverzicht/rijn/
- http://www.portofrotterdam.com/nl/Over-de-haven/havenstatistieken/Pages/default.aspx
- http://www.marineinsight.com/marine/top-10-biggest-ports-in-the-world-in-2011/
- http://en.wikipedia.org/wiki/Maasvlakte#

CASE STUDY

Changes in Block Exemption Applied to Maritime Transport and its Implication[1]

Liner shipping market has long been protected from capitalistic economy and its competition by block exemption. The market is well known to be highly inelastic, and in the case of liner shipping sector, it is often considered impossible to make profit while calling at ports on fixed schedule, unless there are enough cargos to load with enough ships to run the routes to provide frequent services to shippers. Also, with its unique characteristics of operating punctually regardless of fully loaded or not, competition between shipping companies could only lead to deficit operation. In order to prevent excessive competition which would lead to bankruptcy, companies have formed cartels, and this has been the rule over the last centuries. Since the very first cartel, UK/Calcutta Conference in 1875, being protected to price-fix under the law over a long period of time, now the market is facing a new era. In the US, deregulation in transportation sector began from 80's, and continuing through OSRA 1998, conferences were dissolving. In EU, Regulation 4056/86 contained block exemption for liner conferences with no review clause included, but in October 2008, EU has announced removal or the Regulation 4056/86 leaving conferences no longer permitted to fix the price. With this removal, now the US and EU are on the same approach to liner regulation by permitting to share general information and market conditions, but prohibiting collective rate setting capability.

Sea borne trade is run by different types of vessels according to various types of cargos its carrying, for example, dry bulk, tanker, and container. Also, it is operated differently according to its contract, such as tramp shipping and liner shipping industry. Liner shipping service can be defined as "a fixed itinerary, inclusion in a regular service, and the obligation to accept cargo from all comers and to sail, whether filled or not, on the date fixed by a published schedule is what distinguishes the liner from the tramp." Liner service has developed since the second half of the 19th century, after steam engines became common, which allowed vessels to sail itself without being affected by wind, thereby able to be scheduled. However, unlike tramp industry, which can react relatively fast to its imbalanced

1. Yoon, Pak and Hong (2010), Journal published at Korean Research Institute of International Commerce and Law, Vol. 48, pp. 57~76.

supply and demand by putting into lay ups, liner industry cannot respond by reducing number of vessels or changing the size of vessel according to cargo volume and maintain its characteristics as a liner service provider at the same time. Whether cargo fully onboard or not, it has to make its journey to next destination as scheduled, and this condition led to high fixed cost. The failure to co-ordinate such services often led to bunching of arrivals in ports, and competition for cargo among rival firms proved destructive; to increase profit, companies needed to collect more cargo, but unable to charge shippers higher freight to maintain the customers. Also as technology develops, there were more vessels coming into the market, causing not enough cargo to load, and eventually leading to provide service at lower price as possible resulting in deficit. Hence, liner shipping companies were facing bankruptcy, but only large companies that are financially well established were able to stand against the financial burden and manage the imbalances in traffic flow. Due to such imbalances in traffic flow, the market struggles at its unstable equilibrium. This is also related to inelastic market; freight rate variation (in short term). Shipping market could be divided into 4 segments - new building market, freight market, sales and purchase market, and demolition market. The tariff is affected by those 4 segments' movement, which even more complicates the freight fluctuation. A solution to such problems as these possibly called handicapped features, and most importantly to continue their service making profit, companies formed a group working together, a self regulation. The agreement is among scheduled carriers on a particular trade route to restrict competition among themselves by setting mutually agreed freight rates and conditions of service. Thus conferences could regulate of sailings and improve quality of ships, and thereby the UK/Calcutta Conference was formed in 1875, known as the first conference. The government also interferes in this market as the industry has great impact to national economy and security. With the various functions, countries have been more on supportive side of its forming of cartels, so that its shipping market accelerates for bigger share of international market.

Changes in block exemption

Council Regulation (ECC) 4056/86

Originally, European regulation began as Treaty of Rome, in 1957, which Art.855) and Art.866) contained the rules on competition. These rules were renumbered by the Treaty of Amsterdam, in 1999, to Art.81 and 82. It is perhaps natural to contain such legal restrictions to prevent any type of price fixing that would affect fair competition and economy structure. However, this was not to come into practice for maritime transport sector. The competition rules took into force to the Treaty in 1962, Regulation 121/62, but transport field was still excluded by Regulation 1017/62; it still was not noticeable sector by then. In 1974, European Court of Justice (ECJ) held that Art.81 and 82 applied to sea and air transport, but it took another period of time to put into practices, until European Commission (EC) published a Memorandum on Maritime Transport, and later on "1986 maritime package" adopted by the

Council of Ministers, which could be the basis of the European maritime common policy; the four regulations are 4055/86- Freedom to provide services, 4056/86- Competition regime, 4057/86- Unfair pricing practices, and 4058/86- Coordinated action. From the package, Council Regulation 4056/86 deals with Art.81 and 82 of the Treaty; the Art.37) of the regulation contains block exemption for liner conferences. The Art.3 specifies its objectives for example, coordination of time-tables and the allocation of cargo or revenue. "This block exemption is often called the most generous exemption ever given as it covers traditional hard-core restrictions and furthermore does not contain a review clause and remains in force for an unlimited period of time." Considering these assumptions that the shipping markets could be led to destructive competition and that without cooperation the market won't be able to provide service as it is supposedly but become bankrupt, carriers were able to form the conferences to provide reliable scheduled services.

Changes to traditional conference market

However, since the enforcement of the Regulation, shipping market conditions and other surroundings have been changed over decades, with high technology support. With the ever increasing overseas trade there are more customers with more cargos, and mostly shipping market is now heading for competition. Thereby conferences have been attempting for openness, to provide competitive services. Even so, EU has been standing on its traditional conference market, and the regulation has not been changed or reviewed as there was absence of its revision clause, but kept strictly applied. Below mentioned cases show strict application of the Regulation 4056/86, and this eventually led to some conflicts later on. Well known cases would be Trans Atlantic Agreement (TAA), Far Eastern Freight

Conference (FEFC), in 1994, and Trans Atlantic Conference Agreement (TACA), which replaced TAA in 1998, dealing with exemption for rate-fixing. Its decisions by the Court of First Instance (CFI) were; 1) TAA case prohibited two-tier pricing which applying different rates to former conference members and others, including discussion agreements, that all members of a conference should be offered the same rate, 2) FEFC case held that 4056/86 doesn't cover inland tariff, only limited to port to port sea transport, 3) and TACA case decided that joint service contracts are not covered by 4056/8610). The latest could be The Revised TACA which was declared in Nov.2003, that cargo-handling services in ports would fall within FEFC decision. However, these strict applications of the regulation could cause conflicts, especially after the United States reforming the Act in late 90's to adopt the trends, and considering the fact that shipping market is originally an international market; EU shipping market could not stand alone with its traditional conferences and its supporting regulations. In this context, EU perhaps had no other choices then to accept the changes brought into the market and OSRA 1998 and its impacts cannot be ignored.

US Shipping Act of 1984 to OSRA 1998

US Shipping Act of 1984

"The US Shipping Act of 1984, which repealed the 1916 Act, was enacted by the Congress and signed into law by the President on 20 March 1984." The United States has been working on deregulation in transport sector from 1970's, and the 1984 Act was logical extension of the process. "The three key goals of the Act were to encourage the development of an economically viable US flag liner fleet, provide for an efficient and economic transportation system in the US, and to establish a non-discriminatory regulatory process that would minimize the amount of governmental interference in the marketplace." The occurred changes were, accordingly, on antitrust immunity, service contracts, and independent action. The agreements under antitrust immunity were allowed to go into effect 45 days after filing13) , which used to be approved by Federal Maritime Commission (FMC) before going into effect.14) Until the 1984 Act was enforced, antitrust immunity was allowed only to ones that had been filed with FMC, but after the Act, it was extended to practices that have a reasonable basis under Sec.7 (a). Furthermore, it was no longer provided to sue for antitrust damages as it is prohibited by the Act15). Secondly, under Sec.8, it was permitted to provide service contracts, offering special tariff to certain shipper, and this could be joint agreements, agreeing not to undercut the price. However, with anti-competitive action allowed, it was also provided pro-competitive duties. Carriers had to file them with FMC, and terms were to be available to public. Hence all shippers with similar conditions were able to request the terms on their contract as well. This is known as the "me-too" provision. Lastly, through Sec.4, independent action became mandatory, and carriers were allowed to charge different prices. This was mainly to counter-balance the antitrust immunity. In addition, other provisions such as Sec.4 (a) (1) and Sec.10 (c) (4) states of intermodal rates, that conference authority to set intermodal rates but not able to negotiate with inland carriers within the US territory. This was to prevent small - in terms of cargo volume carried at once - inland carriers being overruled by sea carrier conferences, which can carry big number of containers at once. Moreover, it states to prohibit the dual rate16), and to be open conference to any carriers. Above all these provisions, under Sec.18, FMC was placed on duty to collect and analyze the data of five-year period within the industry, and report, known to be Sec.18 report.

OSRA 1998

In 1994, National Industrial Transportation League, known as NIT League, proposed a reform to the Act 1984. The bill requesting reform the Act was passed to the House of Representatives, but opposed to Senate in 1996, disagreeing on abolition of the FMC, which was one of the proposals given. Later on, this came into force on 1 May 1999; the US Ocean Shipping Reform Act of 1998 (OSRA), amending the Act 1984. One of the major changes was that individual service contract and its confidentiality was permitted18). Related to this, 10 days to give notice of independent action was reduced to 5 days, under Sec.5 (b) (8). The reform was to protect U.S. firms from foreign companies taking advantages by accessing to important contract terms, such as cost. Therefore previous "me-too" provision was deleted. This has affected the decline of conferences. Shipping conferences were set up mainly to stabilize rate among the members, but as the industry became globalized and needed intermodality to deliver cargos, firms required something more than just rate stability. Trade routes based conferences became an old obstacles, since the industry environment has been changed its base to global and thereby shipping companies were tending to be more preferable to alliances than conferences. Other changes were the replacement of filing tariff system to posting on internet, and freight forwarders and non-vessel operating common carrier (NVOCC) were placed under ocean intermediaries.

Conflicts among different regulations

One of the major differences between US regulations and EU regulations was that discussion agreements were available in US but not allowed in EU. Hence in the transatlantic lane, where carriers had to comply with both regulations of the US and the EU, the conferences, namely TACA (formerly TAA), became necessary in order to share information and setup the rate. In 1999, TACA submitted an application to amend provisions to comply with OSRA, and consequently the members were allowed to enter into non-conference service contracts. Moreover, while the US allowed to discuss information with outsiders of conference, EU did not allow this, hence conferences were prohibited to share information on the contents of the contract regarding non-conference service contracts. However they were able to form a model conference service and discuss of individual contract negotiations. This gave dramatically decrease in both market share and the number of conference membership. The market share dropped from roughly 80% to 50%, and the number of membership was 7 carriers, which used to be around 17 carriers in 1992. It was almost 600 conference service contracts in 1998, but the next year 80% of the cargos were moved under individual service contracts. Out of 1,000 service contracts of TACA, only 30 contracts were by the conference, and the rest were by individual. It was even reduced to 3 conference service contracts in 200021). Although existence of the conference rate, as shown above, massive increase of individual contract affected freight rate as well. Due to imbalances of the trade, higher growth cargos heading to the US and steady or fallen growth heading to the EU, accordingly freight rates has increased towards to the US and steady or fallen towards to the EU. This could be seen as the beginning of the changes, as well as the decline of liner conferences, although the EU was maintaining the regulation on liner conference strictly.

Removal of ECC 4056/86

While both the US and the EU provide ocean carriers with some form of immunity or exemption from respective antitrust/competition laws, each entity's approach leads to different and significant economic consequences. The United States have been moving towards more open and competitive while EU have been standing on strictly traditional conference based market. The establishment of OSRA 1998 brought different regulations to the market, especially in Trans Atlantic lane which could cause conflict. After all these changes made to the shipping markets, EU has been also began to review the market, and on Oct. 2008, Regulation 4056/86 has been removed from maritime transport sector, and forming cartels or any sort of price fixing is no longer permitted to ships that are operating in and out of Europe. And with this removal, now the scope of the regulatory regimes can be seen unilateral with the regime of the US. Although unexampled changes are made to the market, carriers and related parties are not in panic as one could have concerned, as this removal has been discussed since 2003. After reviewing the market status through various organizations, the White Paper was issued in Oct. 2004 and the removal was passed on Sept. 2006; Regulation 1419/2006 was entered into force which repealed the Regulation 4056/86 and the shipping industry became subjected to Art.81 and Art.82.23) Furthermore, in order to prevent confusion or disordered state, guideline has been issued so that relevant parties have enough time to settle. In the beginning of this process, the European Liner Affairs Association (ELAA) and carriers were against the removal, but later on they claim for alternative plans, insisting that the block exemption should be replaced with an information exchange system. As ELAA advises alternative measure, the removal of the regulation became clearer, and the issue was whether information exchange system would be selected as an alternative or not. Carriers also admit price fixing through conferences is no longer necessary to maintain the market. They suggested that the replacement of conference to information exchange system will eventually lead to more competitive market by providing more information to shippers and sharing core data among carriers.26) On the other hand shippers were supporting the removal and they opposed on information exchange system as well. They were seeking more competition in the market which could possibly provide cheaper and clear tariff than the tariff under the conference system by eliminating the block exemption. Although the two parties showed little differences in their views, both were advising that entering into more competition would lead to providing benefits to both parties. If the Regulation was to be replaced with information exchange system, then the market would show much similar structure to the US shipping market under OSRA 1998. It would not have too much of effects to but falling under similar structure reducing conflicts in transatlantic lane. However, it has been decided to remove it without any other system to assist, and therefore it would be an opening to a new era of shipping market, although the scope of the regimes being more unilateral than before, as it had not been under such a condition before. Liner industry is now facing diverse and various strategic options and would be difficult to predict the market, but this removal will have certain affect to other relevant Regulations to be revised, as well as ones in other countries.

Existing conferences are no longer permitted from October 2008; typically vessels operating in and out EU cannot fix the price. Thus there are some concerns regarding mega-sized shipping companies. For example Maersk Line, CMA CGM, MSC are well known large companies that take large portion of the European market, and they will be positioned advantageous than other non-Europe based companies in many ways such as obtaining information. Therefore small European shipping companies as well as non-Europe based shipping companies are expected some difficulties in European market.

However as the removal of 4056/86 does not interfere forming of consortia and alliances28), there are chances of carriers to form alliances to compete with mega-sized European companies.

The impact of the removal

Although the scope of the regime for both continents is now more unilateral than before the removal, they still not have met the agreement. The reform of the system in the US was done within the range of admitting the existence of conference, on the other hand the EU now has announced to abolish conference system. Hence both continents were seeking for more competition but one side allowing conference while the other doesn't. This does affect the US regime in some ways as it did to the EU regime causing the removal. The US created Antitrust Modernization Commission to review antitrust laws, and according to their report with the EU's recent elimination of its antitrust exemption for ocean carriers left "the United States as the only major country that still immunizes fixing shipping rates". They also have pointed out the efficient operation of ocean transport with competition, emphasizing on its quality of the service it matters not the price fixing to survive in the market; which has certain possibilities to abolish the conference system in the US as well.

The changes in the EU regime not only affect the US regime, but also shipping companies too. MOL has resigned from its conference as of Nov.2008. MOL did not prefer operating two different sets of rules - one for Europe lane and another for non-Europe lane. Carriers are still facing to operate under different sets of rules, and it is considered as only a matter of time for other carriers to follow MOL. Shipping companies will face more difficulties running in two different regimes with the intense competition, hence to select unified one. Perhaps it would be wise move to resign from the conference and seek for alliances to maintain the market share they had in and out of Europe, considering the fact that OSRA 1998 already rendered conferences virtually obsolete, although admitting its existence.

Moreover, the impacts would not leave out the Asian market, considering its borne characteristics of international market. Many Asian countries also are reviewing their antitrust law and under this tendency, dismissal of conference system would be only a matter of time. In the case of Korea, it would be required to be prepared for the possible changes in regime; Korean regulatory has not yet considered of antitrust law in ocean shipping industry, but it needs to review and clearly state regarding the exemption. Once conference system is removed, it does contain risks of market becoming quite unstable, especially due to freight rate changes. Hence, Korean regulatory should seek ways to minimize the risks but to encourage competition on the other hand – policies that could support reduction of operation cost would be more appropriate than to set freight rate at certain level.

Notes

- Alderton, P. and Rowlinson, M. (2002), "The economics of shipping freight markets." In: Grammenos, C. TH. (ed), The Handbook of Maritime Economics and Business. Great Britain: MPG Books Ltd., Bodmin, Cornwall. pp. 157-185
- Antitrust Modernization Commission (2009). Antitrust Modernization Commission Report and Recommendation. Imperial Graphics, Connecticut. 2007. Bourne, C. "European Liner Affairs Association", Journal of Commerce. 1/12/2009, p.118
- European Commission (2008). "Guidelines on the application of Article 81(3) of the EC Treaty to maritime transport services)", Official Journal of the European Union.
- European Commission (2008). "Preliminary Draft Commission Regulation (EC) No [XXX] of [XXX] on the application of Article 81(3) of the Treaty to certain categories of agreements, decisions and concerted practices between liner shipping companies("consortia")", Official Journal of the European Union.

- Federal Maritime Commission (2001). The Impact of the Ocean Shipping Reform Act of 1998.
- Frankel, E. G. (2986), "Economics and Commercial Implications of the U.S. Shipping Act of 1984". Logistics and Transportation Review. Vol.22, Iss.2, pp.99-114
- Fusillo, M. (2006), "Some notes on structure and stability in liner shipping", Maritime Policy & Management. vol.33, iss.5, pp.463-475
- Garnder, B., Marlow, P. and Nair, R. (2002), "The economic regulation of liner shipping: the impact of US and EU regulation in US trades". In: Grammenos, C. TH. (ed), The Handbook of Maritime Economics and Business. Great Britain: MPG Books Ltd., Bodmin, Cornwall. pp. 327-345
- Gardiner, P. (1995), The Liner Market 1995/96: An Analysis of the Major European Operators. London: Lloyd's of London.
- Gardiner, P. (1997), The Liner Market 1997/98: New Alliances and the New Era. London: LLP.
- Johnson, E. (2009), "Chain reaction?", American Shipper. January, pp.32-35
- Kil. KS and Ko, BW. (2010), "An evaluation of EU's abolition of liners' block exemption to competition rule and its implication for Korea liner market - using the difference-difference estimation concept", Journal of Shipping and Logistics. vol.65. pp.233-252
- Leach, P. (2006), "EU Sinks Conferences". Traffic World. vol.270, iss.41, p.31
- Lewis, I. and Vellenga, D.B. (2000), "The Ocean Shipping Reform Act of 1998". Transportation Journal. vol. 39, iss. 4, pp.27-34
- Marco, B., Claudio, F and Enrico, M. (2007), "The liner shipping industry and EU competition rules". Transport Policy. vol.14, pp.1-10
- Marlow, P. and Nair, R. (2005), "Liner Shipping and Information Exchange – A European Persipective". Marine Policy. vol. 30, iss. 6, pp.681-688
- Nitsche and Hinten-Reed. (2004), Competitive Impacts of Information Exchange. Brussels: Chales River Associates.
- Schaffer, R., Earle, B. and Agusti, F. (2005), International Business Law and its Environment, 6th edition. US: Thomson South Western.
- Stamatiou, C. and Neocleous, P. (2009), "The new era of EC Competition law in the shipping industry", International Company and Commercial Law Review. vol.20, iss.1,. pp.1-9
- Stopford, M. Maritime Economics. London: Routledge. 1997.

- U.S. Department of Justice (1990), The Department of Justice Analysis of the Impact of the Shipping Act of 1984.
- Van der Jagt, N. (2009), "European Shippers' Council", Journal of Commerce. 1/12/2009. pp.118-120
- US Department of Transport Maritime Administration, http://www.marad.dot.gov
- Federal Maritime Commission, http://www.fmc.gov
- European Commission, Competition, Maritime Transport,
- http://ec.europa.eu/competition/antitrust/legislation/maritime/index.html

—Guidelines on the application of Article 81 of the EC Treaty to maritime transport services

—European Liner Affairs Association Review of Regulation 4056/86: Comment on EC Commission Draft Guidelines on the Application of Article 81 of the EC Treaty to Maritime Transport

—European Community Shipowners' Associations: Consultation paper on the review of council regulation 4056/86 ECSA reaction to the questionnaire

—ELAA Proposal of 06 August 2004

—Response to the ELAA Proposal for a new regulatory framework for the liner shipping industry - Article 81 EC Assessment, 10th Mar. 2005

—IP/06/1283 Brussels, Sep 2006, Competition: Commission calls for comments on effects on competition of information exchange in liner shipping markets

—IP/06/1249 Brussels, Sep 2006, Competition: Commission welcomes Council agreements to end exemption for liner shipping conferences

—IP/08/1063 Brussels, July 2008, Antitrust: Commission adopts Guidelines on application of competition rules to maritime transport services

—MEMO/06/344 Brussels, Sep 2006, Competition: repeal of block exemption for liner shipping conferences - frequently asked questions

—MEMO/07/355 Brussels, Sep 2007, Antitrust: Draft Guidelines for maritime transport

Quiz

- What is the main problem of using sea transportation? What risks may arise?
- Have you used sea transportation for a package delivery before? Why did you decide to use this transportation mode? What was the main reason?

Notes

- Daily Economics of the East (1994), Knowledge of logistics
- Pak, M. (2011), Understanding International Logistics, Bobmumsa: Seoul.

ARTICLE

Arctic route to Europe for ships is being explored

The Korean government is organizing Arctic Ocean shipping routes to its shipping lines and to test them this summer.

According to Ministry of Ocean and Fisheries and local media reports, the government is talking with Russian authorities to open a commercial route across the Arctic Ocean. The ministry said details will be announced next month.

To reach Amsterdam, ships now cross the Indian Ocean, traverse the Suez Canal and ply the Mediterranean, a journey of about 20,000 kilometers (12,427 miles) from Busan. The Arctic Ocean route would reduce the distance to 13,000 kilometers and the time from 40 to 30 days.

Arctic routes were formerly limited to ice breakers, but global warming has allowed normal commercial vessels to ply them for about four months during the summer.

The plan follows Korea obtaining permanent observer status on the Arctic Council last month, allowing it to actively participate in Arctic-related issues including developing sea routes, environmental protection and scientific research.

From 2011, the Korean government formed a task force that includes officials from the Korea Shipowners' Association, shipping companies and researchers to explore Arctic Ocean routes. It has been talking with the Russian government to get sailing permission and escorts from ice-breaking vessels.

The ministry said it is also considering offering a discount on port usage for companies signing up for the Arctic routes. Shipping companies have said they are reviewing the logistics of the new route.

"Although we don't know how much we will gain or lose by operating Arctic Ocean routes, it's worth trying," an official from the nation's top shipping company said. "If there is enough cargo with good rates, who will not try the new route?"

Industry insiders expect bulk carriers transporting energy resources will be the first to use the routes. They speculate container ships would take longer to try them.

Last month, the Samsung Economic Research Institute said that Arctic Ocean route will provide new opportunities for Korea to try to become a center of Northeast Asia's maritime logistics and it said Busan would be the best port to benefit.

Shipping companies said the most important issue at the moment is to set up a "Shipping Guarantee Fund," as many firms are struggling with their businesses. The Chairman of the Korea Shipowners' Association, Lee Yun-jae, who also heads Heung-A Shipping, said a fund must be created within this year to solve liquidity problem of shippers. The situation recently became worse as STX PanOcean, the nation's largest bulk carrier, has entered court receivership.

"If the government establishes a 2 trillion won [$1.7 billion] fund, shippers will also support it with about 200 billion won," Lee said at an association meeting Friday.

Source : Korea JoongAng Daily, June 18, 2013

Review

Attempt to map an Arctic Route for ships

The Korean government has begun mapping out Arctic Ocean shipping routes to its shipping lines to be tested this upcoming summer after obtaining permanent observer status on the Arctic Council last month. The Ministry of Ocean and Fisheries states that South Korea is in communication with Russian authorities in hopes of opening a commercial throughway in the Artic Ocean. Currently, in order for ships to travel 20,000km from Busan, Korea to Amsterdam, ships have to pass the Indian Ocean, go through the Suez Canal and Mediterranean. If an Artic Ocean throughway is created, the distance could reduce to only 13,000km and reduce the time from 40 days to 30 days, a 25% decrease.

In the past, the Arctic routes were reserved only for ships capable of 'icebreaking', but due to global warming, normal commercial vessels can transverse the Arctic for about 4 months in the summer. South Korea has formed a task force which includes officials from the Korea Ship-owners Association, shipping companies, and researchers with the mission to explore and map out Arctic Routes viable for shipping. In order to do so, it is in cooperation with the Russian government in order to get sailing permissions as well as ice-breaking escorts. Incentives to use these new routes would include discounts on port usage.

With news of possible Arctic Shipping routes being developed, companies are willing to take the gamble to see if it will pay off. Experts believe that the first to benefit from these new routes would be bulk carriers transporting energy resources. Container shipping may follow suit afterwards. If the routes are successful, Busan port would gain recognition and rank as one of the most important hubs in this region. However, one of the main obstacles will be to first create a "Shipping Guarantee Fund," to help the struggling shippers with their liquidity problems.

Question

1) Why would the bulk shippers of energy resources be the first to take advantage of the new Artic shipping routes as compared to other shippers? Explain.
2) The article states that Busan would be a major port to benefit from new Artic routes. What other ports would benefit from new Artic routes and why?

CHAPTER 8

Selection of Transportation Mode

8.1 Transportation Mode

It is critical to realize the features of freights when deciding (allocating) appropriate modes of transportation. Such features are as follows;

Direct features

- Durability of products, trivialization and speed of decomposition
- Density or the reciprocal density
- Price of products

Indirect features

- Volume of daily sales
- Seasonableness
- Size and location of customer
- Market shares and competition

These features can be further explained.

Product life cycle, trivialization and speed of decomposition

It is obvious that those products with fast decomposition time and short life cycle are in need for fast transition. There is a fast growing demand in products which require special care and temperature control.

Density or the reciprocal of density

Weight to volume ratio is a critical element and this ratio is used when deciding a certain type of transportation mode. For marine transportation, the volume ratio (reciprocal density) is widely used as the optimization factor. For instance, coal, sand, and manufactured goods have completely different characteristics when seen from economic perspectives on transport.

Price of products

Price has an effect on two different factors. The higher the price of a good the lower the motivation to preserve stock. This as a result requires fast product rotation and transportation mode with fast speed and trust. High valued products require special care to transporters. High-tech products like computers therefore require extra care in handling. The types of transportation mode generally show the ratio of value to weight. This in other words means that the higher the price to weight ratio the higher the value of the good.

Volume of daily sales

Products with greater turnover require frequent delivery systems and mass transits. However, strict service conditions must be met when a certain type of transportation mode is being considered. Failure in delivery is led to a loss in sales.

Seasonality

Frozen foods or canned products are sold and consumed all year round, but the harvest is done during only a certain time of the year. On the other hand, chocolate is best consumed in the early spring when Valentine's Day is near. In this circumstance, the request of transport is straightforward. Fast and frequent services are required during the harvest times in order to minimize any delay that may occur. This is because intensive processing transactions and handling happen during the harvest periods.

Chocolates require a refrigerated transport from the factory to the warehouse which then further needs to be connected to a fast delivery to the customers' depot and retailers. Air transport is used for flowers and fish to be delivered to the market directly from the place of production in order to maintain the freshness and high prices.

Size and location of customers

It is possible to deliver products by large transport agencies when consumers are located nearby each other but it creates a problem when they are not, as total sale volumes drop. It is generally better to deliver products to other provinces and this is why brand companies choose to increase the minimum orders from customers and seek to select appropriate transport systems. They are as follows:

1) Use of logistics subsidiary - as a facility to handle mixed cargo this option offers relatively cheaper transportation costs
2) Joint enterprise with wholesalers – this offers appropriate prices since wholesalers do not need to compete with manufacturers

Market share and competition

The products under monopoly markets offer relatively lower level of service than those under intense competition markets. This suggests that market competition is closely related to the matters taken into account for transport.

Accuracy as a cost benefit analysis becomes important when deciding which transport mode to be selected. In other words, impacts that can be brought to other elements of logistics mix should be considered when analyzing the effects of certain transportation modes. Decisions made by transportation authorities have a huge impact on the level of inventory within the system since the speed secures inventory levels. In addition, when strong trust is built by the transportation authority the inventory level is likely to decrease. Finally, decisions made by the transportation authority cause impacts on requirements of delivery centers and warehouses as well as on the possibilities of unitization. Understanding of transportation modes with the least cost under the cost-benefit analysis becomes possible when all the above elements are considered.

8.2 Freight Forwarders

Trends of forwarding industry

While the forwarding industry continues to be a growth market its growth is expected to grow by 6.8% between 2012 and 2016, according to the new report by Transport Intelligence. The report added that the Asia-Pacific region is the largest for freight forwarding, with a 32% global market share that is set to grow to 37% by 2016. Although the region is heavily dependent on exports, domestic demand is growing, which is boosting intra-Asia services.

At the same time in Korea, with the current government continues to emphasize exports specialised shipping intermediaries are becoming more important than ever to global logistics operations. According to IMF, ABN AMRO estimates, the global outsourced logistics market enjoys growth rates two to three times that of global gross domestic product. The majority of companies in Korea export and import goods through freight forwarders. Korea International Trade Association reported that 96.1% of the domestic exporting and importing companies handle their export and import logistics through freight forwarding industries. In addition, 46.6% of consignors believe that having a forwarder for transportation reduces the overall logistics costs. Freight forwarding industry is and continues to be a growth industry.

Role of forwarders

A freight forwarder is one of the important links in the global supply chain. One of the main roles of freight forwarders is to act responsibly in his own name on behalf of the client and takes the role to facilitate the smooth transit of import or export goods through sea or air ports.

> "The freight forwarder traditionally acts as an agent who arranges for the shipment of goods belonging to his client or to the shipper. The freight forwarder as agent typically arranges for transportation, pays freight charges, insurances, packing, custom duties and then charges a fee, usually a percentage of the total expenses (Tetly, 2008)."

Although conditions vary from country to country, forwarders are expected to:

- Take reasonable care of goods entrusted to him;
- Comply with instructions of his customer in matters relating to their transportation;
- Avoid committing himself to any firm date of delivery at destination and has usually right to lien and detention over the goods in the event of customer's failure to pay for his duties related to the job (particularly freight) pertaining to those particular goods as per contract.

The main advantage of using forwarding service may be emphasized as such service handles ancillary services that are a part of the international shipping business. Forwarders are not just simply responsible for transit of goods but they also undertake responsibilities such as;

- offering supply chain management solutions
- advising on packaging and labeling of goods
- consolidating shipments
- assisting in claims processing

- cargo handling and distribution management
- preparing contracts such as Letters of Credit
- advising clients about the arrangements that have been made (consultancy/advisory services on international trade

Quiz

- Why do transportation costs matter a lot in logistics?
- Think of one type of product and decide what type of transportation mode you would like to use for the chosen product. Think about the followings; why you have chosen the product; why do you think the transportation mode is suitable for your product.
- Why the roles of intermediaries such as forwards are becoming important in the modern logistics?
- What other advantages of forwarders can you think of?
- Do you think the roles of forwarders will become even more important in Korea? If so, what are the reasons?

Notes

- Pak, M. (2011), Understanding International Logistics, Bobmumsa: Seoul.
- Tetly, W. (2008), "Marine cargo claims", 4th edition, Editions Yvon Blais: Canada.
- Korea International Trade Association (2013)
- Transport intelligence (2013), New report.

CASE STUDY

Multimodal Transport and Land Bridges in the Global Supply Chain: The Case of the ALB[2]

Transport in the Supply Chain

Logistics is more finely focused on the management of materials and their movement to the right place in the right amount at the right time. And, transport refers to the company or entity that physically moves the materials from one point to another. Containerization has had a huge impact in the market, in that it allowed for multimodal transport. A land bridge is a concept used to describe a route that crosses land in order to bridge two oceans. The American Land Bridge is one of the largest, in terms of size, and one of the most traditional, in terms of modes used.

The Role of Transport within the Chain

Logistics has been recognized as one of the more common but important concepts in business, as the global market has a great need for materials to be positioned in accordance with global supply and demand. A number of definitions of logistics exist, but these definitions share in common a rooting in physical distribution and a primary focus placed on transport itself. According to Coyle, Bardi and Langley, "logistics is the process of anticipating customer needs and wants and acquiring the capital, materials, people, technologies, and information necessary to meet those needs and wants; optimizing the goods- or service-producing network to fulfill customer requests; and utilizing the network to fulfill customer requests in timely way". The four subdivisions under this definition are business logistics, military logistics, event logistics, and service logistics. Among them, business logistics is defined as the "part of the supply chain process that plans, implements, and controls the efficient, effective flow and storage of goods, services, and related information from the point of origin to the point of use or consumption in order to meet customer requirements." The supply chain has emerged as a novel concept which may be considered a logical extension of logistics. The broader view of the entire procedure encompasses its very beginnings in raw materials to the ultimate end user, where the goods are finally consumed; consisting of "suppliers, manu-

2. Yoon, Pak and Kwon (2009), Journal published at Journal of Korea Trade, Vol. 12, No.2

facturing centres, warehouses, distribution centres and retail outlets, as well as raw materials, work-in-process inventory and finished products that flow between the facilities." "It is a collection of institutions, agencies and companies that support the ultimate goal of delivering products to the customer." In other words, by controlling the entire manufacturing process in order to deliver the right amount of the right product at the right time and place, value is added to the product.

Transportation, which basically involves the delivery of cargo from one point to another, is an important component of the chain. As Christopher mentions in one of his books, trade is gaining more power over the chain than the manufacturer, and thus transport is becoming ever more important by moving actual goods to different places in accordance with global supply and demand. Its fundamental objective is to close the gap between supply and demand. No matter what transport modality is employed, the basic rule in selecting the appropriate mode or modes involves the selection of the most cost- and time-effective route and transport modality. Transport, in and of itself, essentially creates value by virtue of creating space and time and may exert an influence within the logistics supply chain, and possibly on nations from a macro perspective. Transport accounts for the most salient resource commitment in logistics activity; thus, its relative cost/benefit profile must be established within the context of the level of customer satisfaction that is established as an objective. Owing to the connectedness of the aspects of the chain, a decision made in one area will exert some effect on other parts of the chain and possibly even to non-directly related logistics aspects. Saving costs on one side could induce higher costs on the other side or a newly introduced system could substantially alter the labor market. Thus, when making decisions within the chain, the whole process must be considered and this basically entails looking at cost trade-offs.

In today's markets, inventory and distribution must satisfy the key customer needs of time and place utilities, including item availability and delivery response time. It is important to manufacture and produce goods, but it is more crucial to sell those products to customers. However, as each customer places varying and different values on products, the arrangement and management of inventory and distribution is clearly an irreducibly complex proposition. For example, one could reduce transport cost, as well as the final cost to end users to a minimum by making sure that vehicles or containers were full to capacity and then dispatching them at a lower frequency. This would provide benefit through economies of scale, but might also result in a lower level of customer service and keep the goods from being delivered accurately and promptly. This might ultimately lead to a small market share. Therefore, it is crucial to find a reasonable compromise that both sides find acceptable. Different segments of business deal with various customers and the basic dilemma to be faced is: would a given extra amount of cost be reasonable or worth it in order to eliminate one or more days of transit time?

In considering the JIT concept in relation to logistics, perhaps transport has become one of the major factors to be considered as it is the factor that physically connects the entirety of the supply chain. By placing goods where they are needed at the right time, in the right amount, and all within a reasonable cost structure, transport functions as a value-addition to goods. Additionally, with finished goods travelling all around the world, it is almost impossible to employ unimodal transport, particularly when crossing borders. When products arrive at the final stage and before they fall into the hands of the customer, it is crucial that a competitive price is maintained in order that the products actually be sold. Once the product leaves its factory, it is no more than an extra cost or inventory cost within the supply chain until it is sold. However, regardless of the quality of the product, it will not be sold if it is not where it is needed and when it is needed. In an effort to keep costs down while delivering goods to the customers' satisfaction and in order to make profit for the company, the selection of transport is as crucial as any of the other manufacturing processes in the chain, and perhaps even more important, given choices of transport modes. Therefore, transport itself, whatever the mode selection, should be competitive. When selecting the modes or combining more than two modes, not only the cost, but also the frequency, speed, distance, and possible damage that may occur should be considered. Generally speaking, the longer the distance to be traversed and the more divertible the choices, the less chance there is that the product will ultimately be delivered. Additionally, there exists a risk that the product will be delayed over a long period of time, once it slips out of the given transport chain, unless the entire system is sufficiently flexible to make the journey whenever it is necessary. As all modes have different characteristics, each product will require its own suitable transport in order to reach its final destination.

Multimodal Transport and Containerisation

"International multimodal transport is one means of facilitating the orderly expansion of world trade." According to UNESCAP, "multimodal transport, which provides the opportunity to manage the transport chain more effectively through the integration of all modes of transport under a single transport document, is helping countries respond to this growing demand for just-in-time, door-to-door service." UNCTAD provides a similar definition; "The concept of international multimodal transport covers the door-to-door movement of goods under the responsibility of a single transport operator." Using different modes of transport, but with one person holding the responsibility, although there are several ongoing disputes about it, was perhaps an epochal change in the market when it initially appeared as shippers can now deal with only one person or a so-called multimodal transport operator and thus ship goods more efficiently.

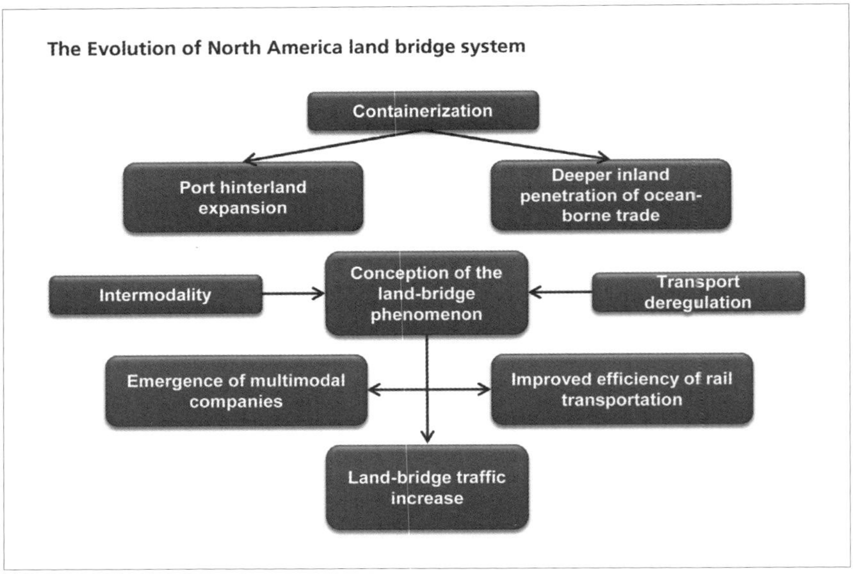

Source:Hayuth, 1992

Containerization is "a shipment method in which commodities are placed in a container and, after the initial loading, the commodities per se are not re-handled in shipment until they are unloaded at the destination", as defined by the Council of Supply Chain Management Professionals (CSCMP). Prior to containerization, break bulk cargos and significant human physical activities were required. The container, which was developed in the 1970's, was a huge sensation as it permitted cargo to be unitized in terms of size, which then increasingly enhanced the ease of transhipment. This changed the port market from a labor-intensive to a capital-intensive operation. Additionally, this reduced overall cost, transit time, and the risk of theft and damages, as the carrier had simply to deal with heavy, hard, regularly-shaped rectangular metal boxes, rather than a variety of different commodities in a variety of different packages. The most important advantage of containerization, though, is probably in that it allows for quick connection to other transport modes, regardless of weather conditions. Containerization is one of the most salient aspects in the development of multimodal transport and is also crucial to the exploitation of land bridges. The figure above shows the relationship between containerization, multimodal transport, and land bridges. However, in the United States, this method did not make significant progress during the 70's, owing to a shortage of cargo and the substantial investment required for the refitting of transport infrastructure to handle those containers. Also, US transport legislation didn't allow for any intermodal activities and a great deal of documentation was involved. Later, a series of deregulations were instituted, most notably the Staggers' Rail Act, allowed for faster market development.

"Perhaps one of the most significant manifestations of the intermodal concept -and competitive relations among transport modes- was the development of so-called 'land-bridges'." Land bridge transport refers to a combination of two or more transport organs, as opposed to the exclusive use of ships. "A land bridge, in biogeography, is an isthmus or other land connection between what, at other times, are separate areas which allows animals and plants to cross and colonise new lands". The Bering land bridge , which connects Alaska and eastern Siberia, is probably the best-known example. However, within the logistics industry, this term refers to "rail connecting ports on either side of a land mass." There remains some controversy regarding the beginning of the land bridge concept; some would argue that the concept has been extant since the Silk Road, and some assert that it began in the 60's with the American Land Bridge. However, it is clear that the land bridge reduces travel time and distance, and results in greater cost savings. Approximately 25~40% of the cost was reduced by the appearance of the double-stack train.

Major Existing Land Bridges

Currently existing major land bridges are known as the ALB, CLB and SLB. The

American Land Bridge (ALB) is a route from the Far East to the United States, which crosses the American continent from west to east, or vice versa, to its final destination in Europe or the Far East. The primary ports in the ALB are Los Angeles and Long Beach on the West coast, and New York on the East coast. The Canadian Land Bridge (CLB), which also links the Pacific and Atlantic Ocean, crosses Canada instead of America, under the very same rationale as the ALB. As cargo traffic grows world-wide, Canada also faces continuous growth, and as the West coast ports of the USA become congested, there may be an increase in the traffic flow via Canada, as the result of attempts to avoid congestion.

The Siberia Land Bridge (SLB) crosses Russia. It is probably the shortest route linking the Far East and Europe and is also probably the longest land bridge currently in existence. The TSR, or Trans-Siberian Railway, is 9,288km long, running from Vladivostok to Moscow, and takes roughly 7 days to traverse. Owing to cold weather and the prodigious distances required for transport within the country, rail has been the most appropriate means of transportation for Russia; 85% of inland cargo is moved by rail. This route is usually used by Korea and Japan; due to its location, China and other Asian countries achieve no real benefit by selecting this route rather than shipping or using other means of transport. If the railway reconnecting the two Koreas materializes, it will permit full rail service from Korea to Europe. As a part of the SLB, the Trans China Rail (TCR) crosses China to deliver freight from the Far East to China and Europe. When cargo arrives in China by ship, it makes transhipments to trucks and rails to different Chinese landlocked cities or is transferred to Europe via the TSR. The rail connection between Rotterdam and Liangyungang is 13,050km long. Using the TCR from Shanghai to Rotterdam would result in a reduction of 7,200km as compared to the usual all-ocean route. As China is currently undergoing rapid growth and produces millions of goods that are exported to many different countries, the TCR appears to carry more cargo originating in China than goods of other origins passing through, as does the TSR.

Although all of the mentioned routes are referred to as land bridges, some of them are arguably not technically land bridges. A land bridge is defined as "an intermodal connection between two ocean carriers separated by a land mass, linked together in a seamless transaction by a land carrier." Some 'land bridges' meet this definition literally and some do not exactly connect two ocean carriers, but rather make transhipments in order to deliver goods to their final destinations, which happen to be located in landlocked cities. For this reason, the TSR and TCR may fit the definition less closely, as neither terminate on both sides with an ocean carrier. In fact, the TCR is really just an inland rail route. As no definition makes it perfectly clear as to whether these can truly be considered land bridges, and because other routes branch out from both, there is some room for ambiguity in this regard. However, as time passes and newly developed countries expand their share in the market, this concept may have to be reconsidered.

American Land Bridge

As all continents are divided by oceans, most international trade has been conducted via shipping. Although it is possible to deliver cargo to different places by air and sometimes via railways, major trade is still conducted principally by vessel as it is frequently necessary to cross oceans. With the wide variety of available transport modes, shipments often travel via more than one mode of transport; for example, via ocean carrier followed by transhipment to rail over a land bridge. According to the definition of the Keihin Port Development Authority, "A Land Bridge is an intermodal connection between two ocean-carriers separated by a land mass, linked together in a seamless transaction by a land carrier." As per this definition, any ocean mile substituted by a land mile can be referred to as a land bridge, and thus, the ALB is just one type of land bridge. However, the ALB can be differentiated from others by its cargo volume flow and its size (probably the second longest after the SLB) as well as its frequency. Although the SLB may be the longest existing land bridge, considering the cargo flow and its usage frequency, the ALB is probably the most important. The CSCMP definition of a land bridge is "the movement of containers by ship-rail-ship from Japan to Europe; ships move containers to the U.S. Pacific Coast, rails move containers to an East Coast port, and ships deliver containers to Europe". This definition clearly includes the ALB.

The American Land Bridge services began in the summer of 1972, when a company called Seatrain Lines opened a container route for the Far East/West Coast of North America. Their container ships were used on the Pacific and Atlantic Oceans, and railroads were used on the American continent for container transport between the Far East and Europe. By shortening the journey, both in terms of distance and total transit time, it brought a new impact to the market. However, it has also resulted in some conflicts. Since the passing of the U.S. Shipping Act, shipping lines formed conferences and basically provided the same services at the same prices under the law. However, as inland transport became a component of the supply chain or the transport service, which at the beginning didn't exist as a part of the conference system, there was a great deal of controversy as to whether or not to include inland transport within the conference, until this matter was settled under a 1984 law, the reformed U.S. Shipping Act. It might be readily concluded that a route from Asia to Europe via America is unreasonable. However, it actually depends on from where in Asia and to where in Europe it will travel and, in some cases, it is certainly appropriate to use the ALB.

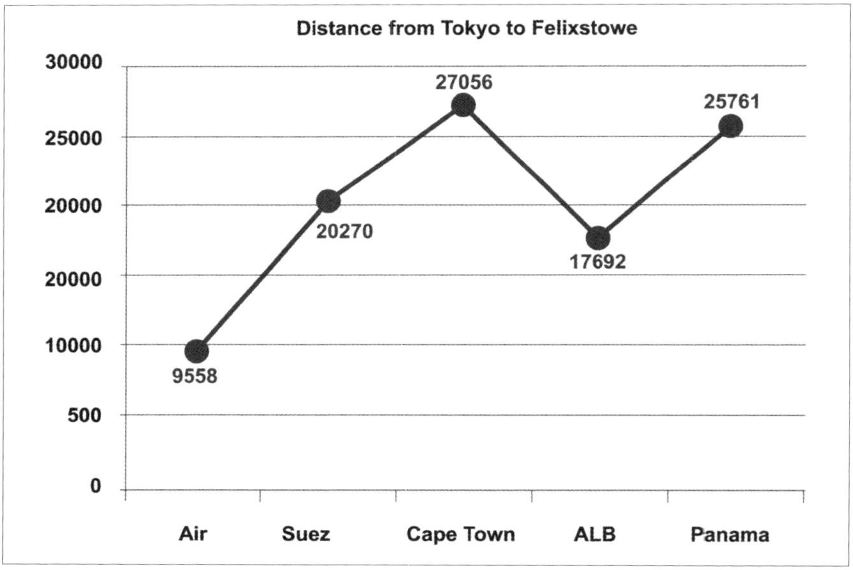

Source: Planes website

The distance from Far East Asian countries to Western European countries will roughly fall within a 10,000km direct line. For example, the distance from Tokyo, Japan to Felixstowe, UK would be 9,558km via air, which would be as close as possible to a straight line. Considering the distance a vessel travels, which will then be the distance to traverse the Suez Canal or go around Africa, passing Cape Town, the distance is realistically much longer, roughly 10,945 nautical miles and 14,609 nautical miles, respectively. This distance can be reduced by utilizing the American Land Bridge which brings the distance down to 8,168 nautical miles by vessels at each end connected by 2,454 miles by rail, and 13,910 nautical miles using a vessel going through the Panama Canal. According to this calculation, the ALB represents the most direct route between Tokyo and Felixstowe.

Analysis: Comparison between Different Routes

It is not surprising how many containers travel around the world today. As Asian countries undergo rapid development, more and more cargo travels from Asia to the U.S. and European countries. This section discusses routes specifically from Busan, South Korea to Felixstowe, UK. There are several methods by which the two points can be linked, as follows;

1) ship to Vostochny, Russia, and make a transhipment to the TSR, to cross Russia, and then use another shipping or rail service, or even travel by air, to Felixstowe,
2) ship westbound via the Suez Canal,
3) ship via Cape Town, around Africa,
4) ship eastbound via the Panama Canal,
5) ship to the West coast of the US, then make a transhipment to rail to the East coast, then again ship to Felixstowe, and
6) using air, any combination of more than two air transportation segments.

According to shipping companies currently operating those lines, it takes approximately 26 days to ship eastbound via the Suez Canal, 35 days via the Panama Canal, and 15 days using the land bridge, although different companies may provide different transit days according to their number of calls to ports within the route. As a matter of cost, the Suez route would be the cheapest among three, and the ALB would be the most expensive due to high inland transport costs, as has been mentioned in Beresford's research and his cost model.

Alternative Ways

Some newly developed or discussed routes may pose threats to the existing land bridges. As increased amounts of cargo go through ports with limited handling capacity, some serious congestion can be expected during peak seasons. In order to circumvent this possible crisis, shipping lines are currently searching for alternative ways to reach their destinations. In order to satisfy both customers and companies, there are no other choices but to develop cost- and time-effective new ways to destinations.

1) Panama Canal:

In 1914, a new 80km route was developed that significantly shortened the maritime distance between the Pacific and Atlantic Coasts of the United States, and is known as the Panama Canal. Originally, the shipping route around South America was 21,000km, but the Panama Canal reduced that distance to 8,000km. This was a great opportunity for shipping lines, but as container ships got larger and larger, the Panama Canal could no longer accommodate all ships. As the intermodal system developed with smooth connections to railways and shorter transit times, more and more cargo began to traverse the American Land Bridge rather than the Panama Canal. In 2007, 312 million PC/UMS passed through with 13,234 transits, and with the growing traffic volume, it is expected to meet its maximum capacity between 2009 and 2012. In July 2006, a project to widen the 92-year old canal was implemented, with the blessing of Panama's President Martin Torrijos, as well as a landmark vote in October in which the project gained 78% of the vote. The plan was initiated in early 2007 and is expected to be completed by 2014. It will cost approximately US$5.25 billion. According to the Panama Canal Authority (ACP), the expanded canal will garner $6.2 billion in revenue per year until 2025, which is approximately six times its current annual revenue. This will also bring more than $4 billion in annual contributions to its government, which had total revenue of $489 million in 2005. The current size of the Canal is 32.31m in width and 294.13m in length, with a draft of 12.04m, and the average transit time necessary to traverse the Canal is approximately 9 hours. The newly widened canal will be 54.86m wide and 427m long, with a draft of 16.5m. As it is expanded and its size limitations are ameliorated, the term 'panamax' may have to be redefined. The typical panamax vessel is now able to carry 65,000 tons, but after the expansion project this number will probably be more like 12,000TEU for containers and 170,000dwt for tankers, and bulk vessels will be the maximum size that can enter the canal.

The expansion has been nominated for the Samoter 2008 "Best Construction Project in the World" award. As the canal expands, the transit fee is expected to increase as well with an average toll increase of 10% per year over three years. However, even with the increased fees, shipping lines will be able to save some extra cost by using bigger vessels and moving more cargo at one time. These cost savings are expected to be around 16% as has been reported in ACP studies, in cases in which shipping lines are operating 8,000 TEU vessels rather than 4,200 TEU vessels. According to the ACP, the canal handles approximately 4% of world trade. Additionally, during the seven-year expansion project, the canal is to operate normally, and traffic should not be affected by the work.

2) Suez Canal:

At the end of the 18th century, Napoleon Bonaparte began construction of the Suez Canal. After passing through many other regimes, it was finally completed by the British government and opened in November 1869. The Suez Canal brought Asia and Europe much closer, eliminating approximately 6,000 km of distance. For example, from London to Bombay, the distance is shortened by 41%, and the distance between London and Shanghai is shortened by 32%. Presently, up to 16m or 53ft draft vessels are permitted to pass, and there may also, as with the Panama Canal, be the possibility of expanding the Canal. Currently, for example, in the case of a 22m super-tanker, some cargo is unloaded to a canal-owned boat and is reloaded after passing through the Canal. According to Egypt's Suez Canal Authority (SCA), 17,224 ships passed through the Canal in 2003. In regard to total world shipping cargo, approximately 8% passes through the Canal. This passage takes between 11 and 16 hours at a speed of around 8 knots. The passing ships must move relatively slowly in order to prevent any erosion of the Canal banks.

According to an article in the American Shipper, China Shipping Container Lines began a service to the US and Canadian Atlantic coast from Asia through the Suez Canal and the Mediterranean, which seems a most unlikely route from Asia to America at first glance. Ports of call are in Halifax, New York, Norfolk, and Savannah, as well as other ports if the shipper so chooses. It appears that the Suez route was used as a solution to infrastructure constraints occurring at the major ports on the US Pacific coast in 2004 during the peak seasons. The MLB and the Suez route are not too different in terms of distance and transit time, but there is a gap in terms of cost. As was assumed earlier in the paper, the cost will not exceed that of the Panama route, as the travelling distance is shorter. The Panama Canal expansion plan may also affect this calculus. However, considering the possible transit time with MLB service, even with the expansion plan, the Suez route would still be the most preferable route among the three.

The above data may indicate that Asian countries located east of Singapore may perhaps find more advantage in using the MLB. However, if one wished to cross in a way other than the usual method via the Malacca Strait route, the Suez route is a viable option. Another route might involve the Kra Isthmus in Thailand. The Malacca Strait is well known for being crowded, risky and prone to both accidents and piracy. If the Kra Isthmus could be developed and utilized as a new shipping route, it would clearly be a shorter route with shorter transit times and would also be less risky. However, as a huge amount of investment would be required to adapt this passage to large vessels, an alternative land bridge scheme across Southern Thailand has already emerged. Either way, once the new route opens, it will definitely affect current shipping routes, as well as the freight market. China, Korea, and Japan are particularly interested in this scheme.

3) Northern Sea:

The Northern Sea route is "a shipping lane from the Atlantic Ocean to the Pacific Ocean along the Russian coasts of the Far East and Siberia." According to a Russian ministry official, the shipments will provide a service from Yokohama to Rotterdam, making only one call, at Arkhangelsk (Archangel). If the Arctic sea area can be travelled under conditions similar to other ocean routes, it might prove to be the most productive and efficient way to deliver cargo in terms of distance and transit time. The Arctic sea route is 7,000 km shorter than the usual route from Japan to Europe via the Suez Canal. Considering that the usual route is approximately 20,694 km, the Northern Sea route is roughly two-thirds of the current operating distance. Using this route, the Russians claim, will result in a savings in costs of up to 40%.

However, with all the possible advantages such a route would bring, there exist some major problems. Ice is the most obvious problem. For only 2 months is this lane free of ice. Ice-breakers could probably solve this problem, though, and as matter of fact, as the average temperature of the Earth is increasing every year, there has been a reduction in the ice, and the Northern Sea route may already be much more passable. However, there aren't any sufficient ports of call along the route at this point. Inadequate infrastructure for navigation, fuelling, repairs and cargo handling also pose large issues. The main reason for Russia to invest in a new route to the Arctic sea would be to expand oil fields in the Arctic. Additionally, this route may be controversial, due to environmental concerns about development. Global warming is currently an issue being discussed all over the world and every year, as temperatures increase, ocean levels are increasing as well. If more ships travel the routes, there is a possibility of an accelerated meltdown.

The Northern Sea route was officially opened for commercial exploitation in 1935. However, after the breakdown of the Soviet Union, the route fell into decline during the 1990's, as state funding decreased. The majority of shipping lanes were in operation on the east side and the west side, separately, but not in the middle between Dudinka and Pevek, and thus the two sides lacked an adequate connection. By 2005, approximately 9 million tons of cargo was transported via the Arctic route and it is hoped that the volume will increase. Although it is run nominally at the moment, the Russian government is looking forward to increasing its traffic and making an investment in its development, hoping that it will eventually become a route connecting Asia to Europe.

4) Sea & Air

Based on the land bridge concept, ocean and rail combinations have been the main subjects under discussion here. Although Sea & Air combinations are clearly less relevant to the land bridge concept, this combination is also used fairly frequently. From China to Korea via ocean, then to the US via air would be a good example of this. Hanjin and Korean Air together provide joint service from Korea to the East coast of the US via ocean and to inland destination points via air. This might help to avoid traffic congestion at the port, from vessel to rail. For seasonal shipments, such as Beaujolais Nouveau from France to Japan, which must be released to the customers within a small time window from production, the cargo is not only flown directly to Japan, but is also flown to Korea and shipped to Japan.

Notes

- ACP (2006), Proposal for the Expansion of Panama Canal: Third Set of Locks Project. <http://www.pancanal.com/eng/plan/documentos/propuesta/acp-expansion-proposal.pdf>
- Aldworth (ed) (2003), Lloyd's Maritime Atlas [map] of World Ports and Shipping Places. Informa Publishing Group: Essex.

- Barret (ed) (2000), "Russia in Quest for 'Northern Sea Route'." Maritime Asia. Dec.
- Beresford (1999), Modelling Freight Transport Costs: A Case Study of the UK-Greece Corridor. International Journal of Logistics: Research and Application, vol.2, no.3, p.230-246.
- Bryman (1989), Research Methods and Organisation Studies. Unwin Hyman Ltd: London.
- Christopher (1979), Logistics: the Total Distribution Concept. In: Wentworth and Christopher (ed), Managing International Distribution. Gower Press: Hants p.3-13.
- Christopher (1986), Strategy of Distribution Management. Heinemann Ltd: Butterworth.
- Christopher (ed) (1992), Logistics: the Strategic Issues. Champman & Hall: London.
- Christopher (1998), Logistics and Supply Chain Management: Strategies for Reducing Cost and Improving Service. Financial Times/Pitman: London.
- Christopher (2005), Logistics and Supply Chain Management: Creating Value-Adding Networks. Prentice Hall: UK.
- Coyle, Bardi and Novack (1994), Transportation. West Publishing: Minneapolis.
- Coyle, Bardi and Langley (2003), The Management of Business Logistics: A Supply Chain Perspective. South-Western, Thomson Learning: Canada.
- Cooper (ed) (1990), Logistics and Distribution Planning: Strategies for Management. Kogan Page: London.
- Damas, (2005), "New Suez Routes, Gateways for Pacific." American Shipper. September, p.53-54.
- Drewry (1991), Strategy and Profitability in Global Container Shipping. Drewry Shipping Consultant Ltd: London.
- Fossey (ed) (2006), "Panama Canal Confidence." Containerisation International. July, p.12.
- Fossey, (2006), "End of an Era?" Containerisation International. July, p.38-41.
- Garnder, Marlow and Nair. (2002), The Economic Regulation of Liner Shipping: The Impact of US and EU Regulation in US Trades. In: Grammenos (ed), The Handbook of Maritime Economics and Business. Great Britain: MPG Books Ltd., Bodmin, Cornwall. pp. 327-345.
- Gummesson (2000), Qualitative Method in Management Research. Sage Publications: London.
- Harrison, Lee and Neale (ed) (2003), Practice of Supply Chain Management: Where

Theory and Application Converge. Kluwer Academic Publication: Boston.

- Hayuth (1987), Intermodality: Concept and Practice. Lloyd's of London: Colchester.
- Hayuth (1992), Multimodal Freight Transport. In: Hoyle and Knowles (ed), Modern Transport Geography. Belhaven Press: London.
- Hensher and Brewer (2001), Transport: An Economics and Management Perspective. Oxford University Press Inc.: New York.
- Jung (1996), China as an Intermodal Link between the Far East and Europe. Thesis-Department of Maritime Studies and International Transport University of Wales: Cardiff.
- KBS (2003), Iron Silk Road-Busan to London. Korean Broadcast Service (KBS) television programme, 6th March, 2003.
- Keihin Port Development Authority (1979), Land Bridge Transport. Keihin Port Authority: Tokyo
- Kim (1987), Innovation in Liner Shipping: The Round-the-World Service as a Global Strategy. Institute of Shipping Economics and Logistics: Bremen.
- Koh and Pak (2001), A Proposal for an International Logistics Network System in Northeast Asia. The Journal of Korea Trade, Vol.5, No.2. p.85-112.
- Mangan (2000), Logistics and Transport in a Fast Growing Economy: Managing the Supply Chain for High Performance. Blackhall: Dublin.
- Marlow and Boerne (1992), Case for Inter-Modalism in Freight Transport. Department of Maritime Studies and International Transport, University of Wales College of Wales: Cardiff.
- Murphy Jr and Wood (2008), Contemporary Logistics 9th ed. Prentice Hall: New Jersey.
- Nelson, "Panama faces landmark vote on expansion of canal" Lloyd's List 19th. July 2006 p.
- Nelson, "Voices of doubt overshadow Panama's $1bn port project" Lloyd's List 20th. July 2006 p.1.
- Pak (2003), International Logistics. Bobmunsa: Seoul.
- Pellew (1990), The Internalisation of Retailing: The Impact of Physical Distribution. In: Fernie (ed), Retail Distribution Management: a Strategic Guide to Developments and Trends. Kogan Page Limited: London. p.59-74.
- Rodrigue, Comtois and Slack (2006), The Geography of Transport System. Routledge: Oxon.

- Rushton, Oxley and Croucher (2000), The Handbook of Logistics and Distribution Management. Kogan Page Ltd: London.
- UNCTAD (2005), Trade and Development Report, 2005. United Nations Publication: New York.
- UNCTAD (2007), Review of Maritime Transport. United Nations Publication: New York.
- Waters (2002), Purchasing Transportation.In: Day (ed), Gower Handbook of Purchasing Management. Gower Publishing Ltd: Aldershot. p.343-358.
- Weeks (1990), Trade-offs, service and cost.In: Fernie (ed), Retail Distribution Management: A Strategic Guide to Developments and Trends. Kogan Page Limited: London. p.107-132
- Wilding (2002), Purchasing, Logistics and Supply Chain Management. In: Day (ed), Gower Handbook of Purchasing Management. Gower Publishing Ltd: Aldershot. p.117-140.
- Wong (1997), The Development of Multimodal Transport Systems in China. Thesis-Department of maritime Studies and International Transport University of Wales: Cardiff.

Also cited from:

AAR- http://www.aar.org
APL- http://www.apl.com
BNSF- http://www.bnsf.com
Busan Port Authority- http://www.pba.or.kr
CN- http://www.cn.ca
CSCMP- http://www.cscmp.org/Downloads/Resources/glossary03.pdf
DOT- http://www.dot.gov
Hanjin- http://www.hanjin.com
IANA- http://www.intermodal.org
OOCL- http://www.oocl.com
Panama Canal Authority- http://www.pancanal.com/eng/index.html
Port of Los Angeles- http://www.portoflosangeles.org
Port of New York and New Jersey- http://www.panynj.gov
UNESCAP- http://www.unescap.org/ttdw/index.asp?MenuName=MultimodalTxandLogistics
UNCTAD- http://r0.unctad.org/en/subsites/multimod/mt2brf0.htm
UP- http://www.up.com
http://www.planes.com/airports_distances.htm, sited on 29 Mar, 2008

CASE STUDY

A plan for co-operation in transport between South and North Korea

As the end of the Cold War era leads to the reshaping of the international order, northeast Asia is also seeking out a new inter-relationship. The trend of regionalization, transformation of the former Soviet Union, China's continued efforts towards openness and reform, and North Korea's attempt to expand its external economic relationship, are basic conditions for the realization of the great development potential. The northeast Asia region has become an area which has received a lot of attention, and is closely watched by the rest of the world community for various reasons. This area consists of South Korea, North Korea, Japan, Mongolia, China (specifically the provinces of Heilong-Jang, Jilin and Liaoning), Inner Mongolia and the Russian Far East with a total area of about 10 million square kilometers.

In the northeast Asia region, we have countries with different levels of development which could compliment and help each other. They range from an underdeveloped country like Mongolia to a highly industrialized country like Japan. This region is also endowed with the largest concentration of natural resources in the world. To develop and utilize these resources, Japan possesses large amounts of capital and advanced technology, South Korea has experience in successfully achieving economic development with quite a high standard of technology and capital. China has a vast labour force which also provides a huge consuming power. China is the most distinctive case in the region.

Some economists predict that China will surpass Japan in GNP after 2020 if she keeps her high growth rate in the future. With the establishment of a socialist market economy, the total amount of economic income will grow rapidly and the people's standard of living will get closer to that of affluent societies. Transport as the infrastructure of the national economy and social development will then face new situations and new patterns and assume an increasingly important role. On the other hand, Japan and South Korea, both densely populated countries, are poor in natural resources and depend largely on foreign trade. North Korea has ample mineral resources, and is attempting to liberalize its closed economic structure gradually; it looks likely that North Korea will adopt a Chinese style of market oriented economy step by step. For example, North Korea is also adopting a limited opening in the TREDA (Tumen River Economic Development Area) by allowing it to develop as a special export-oriented free economic trade zone along the Chinese model. TREDA is an area bordering China, Russia and North Korea.

The combination and complementariness of various forces, capacities and opportunities will undoubtedly help foster the development and growth of this region. For efficient economic co-operation here a transport network in the northeast Asia region appropriate must be established. Transport is a crucial link in the world economy, both as a servant and as a creator of trade. Cheap and efficient transport services are a prerequisite to an expanding world trade. As Stubbs et al. (1980) put it: Transport is a keystone of civilisation. The spread of production, trade and ideas and the economic ascendancy of mankind all depend upon movement. Personal mobility is one of democracy's most valued freedoms, and a surprisingly high proportion of our income is devoted to our movement and to the movement of the goods that we buy. The transport network development strategy for the Korean peninsula is the development of contiguous routes between South and North Korea. Transport routes that are the most rational for the entire economy of northeast Asia should be considered.

The Korean peninsula is situated between the Yellow sea where it faces China and the East sea (sea of Japan) where it faces Japan and Russia. Thus it is the centre of the northeast Asia region. The East sea maritime transport network should link the ports of Busan, Sokcho (South Korea), Najin (North Korea), Niigata (Japan) and Vladivostock (Russia). Express highway and express rail routes are to be constructed between Busan and Vladivostock. All of these express highway and rail routes are to be connected to Japan through an undersea tunnel constructed under the strait between Korea and Japan. The Yellow sea transport networks for both sea and air should link cities on the Korean peninsula with Kyusha (Japan), Dalian (China), Beijing and Shanghai. In the past, the intermodal transport network linking northeast Asia with Europe focused on the Trans-Siberian Railway (TSR), the alternative to the all-water service via the Suez canal. Today, however, the world's interest is in potential landbridges that link China (Trans-China Railway, TCR) with the Korean peninsula (Trans- Korean Railway; TKR) as well. Exploitation of a trans-continental railway is regarded as the most important development in the supra-regional transport system as it has remarkable impacts on transport cost and time savings.

PART. 2

Distribution

Learning objectives

- Understand the functions of distribution
- Learn how distribution process is carried out
- Learn the purpose of distribution

CHAPTER 9

Function and Composition of Distribution

9.1 Functions of Distribution

In the self-sufficient ancient society, customers and suppliers were considered one and the same. But there is a clear classification between customer and suppliers forming time and space differences between the two. Also, differences in quantity demanded and quantity supplied is inevitable. The role of distribution is to decrease the space, time, and quantity gap between supplier and customer.

There are three social functions of distribution;

1. Location adjustment function
2. Time adjustment function
3. Supply and demand adjustment function

"Location adjustment" function is utilized to bridge the gap in space and time between customer and supplier. Transportation of goods is one way of bridging the gap in location and warehousing (storing) goods from the moment of production to the moment of consumption. It is another method of creating time utility (time adjustment function). Thus, location and time adjustment function are physical characteristics of distribution.

Economic characteristics of distribution include a balance and adjustment between quantity demanded and quantity supplied. For instance, seasonal products or agriculture products (products which are produced or supplied in mass only at a certain period) are processes and stored in warehouses and supplied to customers in a continuous manner throughout the year. Providing products as demanded without fluctuation has the intention of price manipulation. When quantity demanded and quantity supplied is not met or balanced over time, excess demand or excess supply occurs eventually leading to price fluctuation. Thus, distribution plays a key role in the circular flow of the economy.

Moving away from the social aspects, distribution can be easily found near us in everyday life. Essential commodities of life are groceries and we can easily purchase them in local grocery stores or supermarkets. Even small convenience stores carry groceries making purchases available 24/7.

The convenience due to products being located close to customers not only applies to groceries, but to daily necessities as well. Distribution makes this social structure (ease of purchasing products due to short distance travel) possible. Well-established distribution systems are prerequisites for a stable and affluent society.

9.2 Composition of Distribution

Distribution process is the act of moving manufactured products to customers. A real life example is described below.

Typically when goods are produced, it is stored in the manufacturer's warehouse. Goods are then moved to a wholesaler's warehouse when a wholesaler buys the goods from the manufacturer. The goods in a wholesaler's warehouse are once again moved to a retailer's warehouse after it is sold to the retailer. Finally, goods are moved to retail stores or other small stores for final purchase by the end-user. In most cases, distribution is divided and carried out by 3 parties (manufacturer, wholesaler, and retailer). But in some cases, mostly seen in the United States of America, the distribution process is divided and carried out by only two parties (manufacturer, retailer) excluding the wholesaler.

Whether or not three or two parties carry out the distribution process, the distribution process can be classified into two categories.

1. Process related to trade and sales (marketing distribution): selling, marketing, purchasing, promoting sales, confirming orders
2. Process related to the physical transport and management of commodity (physical distribution): storing, transporting, delivery, packaging, loading and unloading process, inventory process.

In the past, the two distribution processes were considered separate as sales activity (marketing distribution) was completed first, and then followed by physical distribution. Physical distribution initiation was signaled after the completion of the marketing distribution process.

But in recent days, this concept of sequential order has been challenged due to the holistic view of marketing distribution and physical distribution. Marketing distribution and physical distribution is seen as one complete process with close relations with one another. Thus, giving rise to the holistic term, logistics. Computer information systems allowed the overall management of the marketing distribution and physical distribution, thus integrating the two to form a new and holistic distribution system.

Quiz

- Explain about the function of distribution in your own words.
- Why distribution is important?
- How will product flow from supply points to multiple distribution centers?

Notes

- Pak, M. (2011), Understanding International Logistics, Bobmumsa: Seoul.

CHAPTER 10

Distribution Process

Today, the distribution facility is fully linked into the supply chain. Its roles and responsibilities are changing at a rapid pace. It is not only a warehouse in which to store inventory. Distribution process may refer to activities of re-packaging, adjustments made for orders and assembly. For example, assembling home products such as furniture and placing price tags on items in stores. Such activities are managed in order to satisfy customers' needs. As a consequence of such activities, the value of products increases while customers' convenience increases as well at the same time.

There are often conflicts of opinions on whether such distribution processes should be excluded from the logistics activities for its primary function or whether it lies in production. However, as this process plays a significant role in designing the total logistics system it should be included as an element of logistics components. The purposes and types of distribution process can be summarized as shown in table 10-1.

Table 10-1 Purposes, types and places of distribution process

Purpose	Promoting sales (suitable for customers' needs) Supporting production efficiency (plans, mass production supports) Rationalized logistics (control timing)
Types	Sub-division, placing price tags, placing labels, marking, assembly, heating, cooling, surface finishing and etc
Places of performance	Distribution center, during delivery, stores, during sales and etc

CASE STUDY

Woolworth in Australia

Woolworths Limited was founded in 1924 and has besides its name no affiliation to the U.S. Woolworths Group. It owns and operates a magnitude of retail stores throughout Australia and New Zealand. It is headquartered in Bella Vista, New South Wales, Australia, and employs more than 190,000 people. The company is Australia's largest retail and recorded revenues of A$55.2 billion during the financial year (FY) 2012, an increase of 4.8% over FY2011. Although operating profit increased during FY2012 (3% to A$3.3 billion) Woolworth's net profit decreased by a staggering 14.5% to A$1.8 billion in FY2012. While Woolworth operates retail stores which in addition to food and groceries also sell alcohol, gasoline, general merchandise and consumer electronics, this analysis limits itself to a brief introduction of the company's food retail business in Australia.

Best Practice Distribution

Woolworth has to overcome 7.6 million km^2 of landmass to reach its customers and has, for this reason, installed 26 distribution centers thought the country. Most of these facilities are not owned by the company though rather than leased on usual 10 to 15 year terms. The company itself claims that its sophisticated supply chain creates a comparative advantage and continuously delivers financial benefits. Woolworth transformed its supermarket supply chain through the implementation of various systems including a specially designed distribution centre forecast based warehouse management system called StockSmart and forecast based replenishment system called AutoStockR and other integrated warehouse and transport management systems.

The new systems gradually reduced day's inventory as well as save costs in stores, distribution centres and transportation. Replenishments are requested fully automatically and AutoStockR will determine from which DC the store will be supplied best. 'Best' is a balance between several criteria such as urgency, costs, already planned shipments etc. This is possible as stores are can be supplied by more than one DC. In remote areas transhipments between DC's can be arranged to finalize an order. Woolworth also upgraded its National Distribution Centre (NDC) located in Mulgrave(✶) near Melbourne, Victoria.

Mulgrave is the company's main DC and is currently distributing over one million cases per week to 800+ stores nationwide and will increase its throughput volume capacity by up to 80% to service over 1000 stores a week by 2020. This integrated network DC's increase the company's overall order processing capacity and ultimately reduce costs. DCs are designed according the above mentioned PQRST key with a focus on processing speed. To further optimize handling capacities, different warehouse facilities are used for different kind of storage requirements. Facilities for frozen and chilled food are physically detached from the warehouses for extended shelf life (ESL) goods.

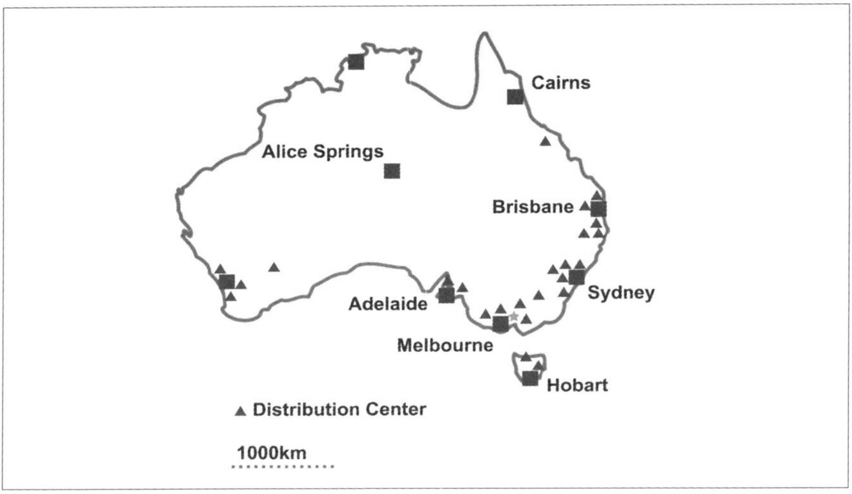

Source: Dematic (2012)

Woolworth DCs are also a critical control point in checking the quality of fresh food. DCs are strategically located within a 250km proximity of the countries three most populated urban areas (Sydney, Melbourne and Brisbane) and one near Perth to supply Western Australia. Far north Queensland as well the Northern Territory however lack an extensive DC network with only one and nil centres respectively. The countries centre and the Northern Territory are both supplied from the Adelaide facilities; letting some deliveries exceed distances of 2000km. These outstations however offer a limited assortment and although delivery costs are substantially higher than those to other urban areas, DCs simply do not pay off in these regions.

The actual deliveries take place with traditional trucks in urban areas while for deliveries in remote areas and long routes so called road trains – trucks with two or three trailers – are deployed to keep delivery costs at an optimum. As this suggests, Woolworth freight is divided into categories. Three to be precise: NDC

Linehaul, Primary Freight and Secondary Freight. The NDC Linehaul operation is in charge of all deliveries to and from the NDC in Mulgrave and the respected manufacture or point of entry if goods are imported (Harbour or Airport). Primary Freight handles all shipments between the NDC and regional DCs and may include at times transhipments between DCs. Lastly Secondary Freight overtakes the task of the end delivery of goods from regional DCs to and from the retail stores. In practical terms, this involves thousands of trucks transporting goods from ports and moving goods from over a thousand suppliers into distributions centers before being delivered to all Woolworth's retail outlets.

Woolworth uses a mix of company owned trailers and outsourced freight operators as part of its transport operations and is currently exploring the usage of an inter-modular rail/truck primary freight alternative between Sydney and Melbourne. Woolworth's AutoStockR for example maps and manages freight movements to ensure efficiency. It calculates for every truck route, distance and travel time based on safe speeds and expected traffic. Ordering and delivery processes are then precisely coordinated against these travel times so it can manage trucks arriving and leaving at DCs to minimize congestions and increase efficiency of its limited resources.

CASE STUDY

Wal-Mart's Distribution and Inventory System

Wal-Mart's distribution system and inventory management is one of its kind and have pioneered effective cost and time cutting measures that affected the entire business sector. According to Wal-Mart "logistics and distribution: the heart of its operation, one that keeps millions of products moving to customers every day of the year".

Wal-Mart is famous for efficient high-volume distribution and its distribution system is built around many distribution centers around the world. Wal-Mart has a total of 158 distribution centers and each distribution center is more than 1 million square feet large, has up to 12 mile conveyor belts to handle products and serves 90 to 100 stores in a 200-mile radius. Highly automated 24-hour operating distribution centers combined with private logistics fleet-6,500 tractors, 55,000 trailers, more than 7,000 drivers-constitutes Wal-Mart's powerful distribution system. Wal-Mart employs 'hub-and-spoke' distribution network where hub is distribution center and spoke is individual Wal-Mart stores. Goods are centrally ordered and directly sourced from the manufacturer and transported by Wal-Mart's private logistics fleet. Products are assembled at the distribution center and shipped to individual Wal-Mart stores daily.

Wal-Mart's expansion strategy was to first build a distribution center and individual stores were gradually built around the distribution center so distribution center could support about 100 stores within a 200-250 mile radius. Once the area is saturated with Wal-Mart stores and distribution center, the distribution network undergoes a process called 'reoptimization'. The distribution network is reconfigured so trucks do not have to travel a long distance from and to stores. Shorter distance between distribution centers and stores leads to transportation cost and lead time reduction which in turn leads to fewer inventories to hold. Every time a new store is added to the area, the distribution network undergoes a new reoptimization process to ensure maximum efficiency in delivery. The average distance between a distribution center and an individual store is approximately 130 miles Since trucks are privately owned, they create 'back-haul revenue' by bringing back unsold merchandise to distribution centers.

As mention in the previous section describing evolution of supply chain management, Wal-Mart developed cross-docking that changed inventory operations once and for all. Cross docking eliminates unnecessary inventory by sorting and packaging products upon arrival and directly transships products according to their destination. This process is carried out to its full potential when the final destination is already known upon product arrival. When inbound products from manufactures arrive at the Wal-Mart distribution center, they are break bulked, sorted, labeled, tracked, and consolidated according to final destination and directly transshipped to outbound trucks. Cross docking also ensures fully loaded trucks since Different bulk products from different manufacturers are sorted and combined into full shipments.

Products bypass the storing process which increases inventory speed and efficiency while reducing inventory costs. Products are not stored in distribution center since 85% of Wal-Mart's products go through the cross docking process within 24-48 hours and distributed to local stores. In order to increase product handling efficiency, Wal-Mart cooperated with manufacturers to standardize labeling and case sizes. Also similar products are packed together in outbound trucks to ease the unloading and inventory management of individual stores. Cross docking requires efficient and continuous communication between suppliers and distribution centers. To achieve seamless product flow and information exchange, Wal-Mart operates their own satellite.

Quiz

- What is the purpose of distribution process?
- How does Woolworth operate their distribution process? Why do you think they may have one of the best distribution practices in the world?
- How does Wal-Mart operate their distribution process? Why do you think they may have one of the best distribution practices in the world?
- Based on your findings from the above two questions, compare Wal-Mart and Woolworth.
- What are the main benefits of cross-docking?

Notes

- Woolworths Limited. (2013, Mar 15). Submission responding to theDraftNSW Freight and Ports Strategy. Della Vista, NSW, Australia. Retrieved from http://www.woolworths-limited.com.au/icms_docs/136724_Draft_NSW_Freight_and_Ports_Strategy.pdf
- Woolworths National Transport. (2010, Jan.). Woolworths National Transport. Road Runner Newsletter. Bella Vista, NSW, Australia.
- Woolworths Limited. (2012). Australia's Fresh Food Farmers. Bella Vista: Woolworths Limited.
- Dematic. (2012). Dematic upgrade refreshes Woolworths Mulgrave. Belrose: Dematic Pty Ltd.
- Coriolis Research. (2005). An Overview of Woolworths Australia. Auckland: Coriolis Research.
- Supply Chain Management, 2012 http://cmuscm.blogspot.kr/2012/09/week-2-post-crossdocking.html (accessed on January 29th 2014)
- Trends & Challenges of Warehousing 2009 http://trendschallenges-warehousing.blogspot.kr/(accessed on January 29th 2014)
- Jim West Photography http://www.jimwestphoto.com/gallery/displayimage.php?album=3&pid=14218(accessed on January 29th 2014)
- P. Fraser Johnson(2006) "Supply Chain Management at Wal-mart", Richard Ivey School of Business
- Pak, M. (2011), Understanding International Logistics, Bobmumsa: Seoul.

UNIT. 3

ELEMENTS OF SUPPLY CHAIN MANAGEMENT AND ITS OPERATION II

CHAPTER 11

Storage & Warehouse

Learning objectives

- Understand the evolution and definition of storage
- Understand the functions and importance of warehouses
- How inventory management is managed

11.1 Evolution and Definition of Storage

There is a time interval between production and consumption (sales) and this is where storage becomes important. In other words, the main function of storage is to increase the time efficiency. Storage not only controls the time intervals, but also has a direct impact on prices. As a result, it is often argued that it has two main functions; 'time adjustment' and 'price adjustment'.

Storage activities are usually carried out in warehouses, but can be done in other places such as business facilities. Warehouses are not only for storage since they do other functions like packing and unpacking. For this reason, warehouse activities and storage activities shall not be seen as the same. Functions of storage are rapidly changing due to today's mass production and consumption that are managed under forecasted demand levels. Therefore, production is done based on a scheduled timeline and shipping and delivery are arranged as soon as orders from customers are received.

Storage warehouse refers to the original type of warehouse while distribution warehouse refers to the ones created with modernized logistics. The latter warehouse offers shorter storage time and frequent flow of products. This is a good example that shows one side of modernized logistics. Another change that occurred due to the modernized logistics is that privatized warehouses have been established as a result of economic growth. Depending on the quantity of logistics, different types (in terms of size, temperature and weight) of warehouses are needed. In order to function as a distribution warehouse and logistics base it is important to offer computerized and most updated data such as information on delivery and products. Especially, information processing technology through computers has led to the increased numbers of automated warehouses.

The functions and roles of warehouses were not considered as significant as compared to current days. Warehousing now plays a vital role in the logistics system and therefore its role should be realized in delivering new opportunities for overall improvement of businesses.

Evolution of warehouse service

Historically, factories were located near to raw material procurement points and this was to store products close to manufacturing facilities. However, development and extension of railway systems have allowed these warehouses to be placed closer to the cities where consumption continues to increase. Moreover, as transportation efficiency of truck vehicles improves, warehouses have started to be positioned close to the main highways. However, this has not always been the case. For example, some local companies (wholesaler and retailer) positioned their warehouses in the center of sales market in main cities. The warehouse networks have even become more complicated if companies grew in size as a result of a merger.

The key successes of business have become the sales function and the marketing function due to increased use of truck transportation. Before this happened, the spot used to be the place for handling warehouse service and loading and unloading service while strategic decision makings for warehouse facilities belonged to the logistics managers. Nonetheless, the field of logistics has become an independent research area and logistics costs have become a vital cost element that affects the price of products. Besides, logistics costs are considered to be eligible for control and management which made the field to be even more important. Positioning warehouses and delivery centers where minimum transportation costs and inventory maintenance are guaranteed has become an important consideration for businesses today.

Functions of warehouses

Warehouse costs are an important and inevitable cost. Companies therefore need to realize the importance of managing warehouses effectively in terms of their locations and operations. Table 11-1 shows how warehouse costs can be reduced. It is also important to realize the functions of warehouses depending on their purposes since they tend to differ from one another. The main functions of warehouses are as follows.

1. Storage
2. Consolidation
3. Production logistics
4. Delivery
5. Response plans for unexpected events

Warehouse activities can be considered as a physical system. Such physical system ① allows the physical flows ② secures nothing is lost during the flows ③ records all activities carried out within the warehouses. These warehouse activities are summarized in table 11-2.

Table 11-1 How warehouses affect overall costs of production

Example 1		Example 2	
When factory warehouses and transportation centers used	Cost unit	Direct delivery to customers	Cost unit
	(Unit: Won)		(Unit: Won)
Raw material marker		Raw material marker	
Arrival transportation of Raw material	2,000	Arrival transportation of Raw material	2,000
Factory warehouse raw material	1,000	Factory warehouse raw material	1,000
Manufacturing process		Manufacturing process	
Factory warehouse Finished goods	1,000	Factory warehouse Finished goods	1,000
Transportation Between facilities	3,000		
Delivery center	3,000		
Consignment transportation	1,000	Consignment transportation	3,000
Total costs of warehouse and transportation	11,000	Total costs of warehouse and transportation	7,000

Types of warehouses

Warehouses are where storage activities take place and there are a variety of kinds. The term 'Sales warehouse' is used when products are received

Table 11-2 Summary of warehouse activities

Input →	Process →				Output
Arrival	Movement of arrivals	Storage	Order pickings	Packaging, marking and ready for shipping	Shipping
Unload cargo from transportation vehicles Check for any damages	Identify storage place for products Update inventory records	Store products physically	Remove products from storage Update inventory records	Packaging of products Or Add labels	Load to transportation vehicles Fill in consignment note

from the third-party and stored in warehouses. Warehouses are used as storage to keep goods, but vehicles can also be used as a storage place if they are put in a certain place for keeping goods in them. Warehouses can be divided in terms of purpose, structure, stored products, and locations.

Division by purpose

Self warehouse, sales warehouse, public warehouse, bonded warehouse

Division by stored products

Raw material warehouse, product warehouse, refrigerated warehouse, dangerous-product warehouse, agricultural warehouse, open yard warehouse

Division by structure

Multi-story building warehouse, automated warehouse, silo

Division by location

Harbor warehouse, inland warehouse, station warehouse, terminal warehouse, city warehouse, factory warehouse

Quiz

- What are the functions of warehouses? How would warehousing help firms? In what ways?
- What are the advantages and disadvantages of using warehouses?
- What are the advantages and disadvantages of not using warehouses?
- How would you summarize warehouse activities?

Notes

- Pak, M. (2011), Understanding International Logistics, Bobmumsa: Seoul.

CHAPTER 12

Inventory Management

12.1 Definition of Inventory Management

Inventory management involves controlling the production processes such as ordering and storage as well as forecasting the sales of the finished products' quantities. In other words, it helps to forecast the demand so that firms can defend themselves against the chance of running out of important materials or goods for their sales. Inventory management is a major asset to a business since it directly affects the costs. Mismanaged inventory may result in excess or shortage of products and this in turn may create significant financial problems for a business.

Good inventory management brings benefits to businesses. First of all, the inventory management improves the accuracy of inventory orders. When inventory is properly handled and managed this helps firms to forecast the exact amount of inventory to have on-hand. Keeping materials or finished goods in inventory cost money but managing it properly can reduce or eliminate to have unnecessary amounts. Firms also have no concerns over shortages.

Inventory management can also lead to a more organized warehouse. Organizing warehouse is as important as having good inventory management. Warehouses should be organized well in order to benefit from inventory management. Many organizations try to optimize their number of warehouses by having highest selling goods together and having warehouses in easily accessible place. This will speed up the process of order fulfillments and companies may expect high levels of satisfaction from their customers.

Inventory management is controlled with devices such as barcode scanners, EDI and RFID. These devices greatly increases firms' productivity and efficient. Computerized systems minimize errors and as manual processes decrease the human resources can be used elsewhere – more important areas of the business.

12.2 Loading and Unloading Activities

Activities of loading and unloading occur on arrival and departure of products. Any activities involved during this process shall be considered as loading and unloading activities.

Depending on the place where the activities occur it can be divided into 'warehouse loading and unloading' 'port loading and unloading' and so on. Transportation mode can also be divided into 'cargo loading and unloading', 'shipping loading and unloading' etc while cargo types can also distinguish them into 'bulk cargo loading and unloading', 'container loading and unloading' 'pallet loading and unloading' and so on.

There is an increasing importance of 'classification' and 'picking' among loading and unloading activities as the logistics centers become modernized. 'Picking' refers to the activities of cargo arrangement from warehouses when an order or other tasks are given. All the loading and unloading activities were managed by labor in the past, but in modern times the majority of these activities are managed by machines and efforts to increase the productivity in this area continues to rise. Effective management of loading and unloading activities can be managed through unit load, containerization, and palletization.

The purposes of unitization are as follows.

- To increase work efficiency by expanding the handling unit
- To increase convenience of transport
- To promote standardization of work by equaling the handling unit
- To increase the protection levels by placing products safely

Quiz

- Why inventory management is important? What is it?
- What are the objectives of inventory management?
- Why is inventory management important to firms? What benefits may this bring to them?

Notes

- Pak, M. (2011), Understanding International Logistics, Bobmumsa: Seoul.

CHAPTER 13

Information & Technology Innovation

As briefly mentioned before, information and technology revolution starting from the end of the twentieth century has brought about immense changes in the business world as well as to mankind. Throughout this book, the importance of information and technology has been emphasized many times and there is no sense in re-emphasizing that technology allows information to disseminate much faster, reliable, wider, deeper, integrates different industries and eliminates silo effects. Information and technology has greatly impacted the logistics, international trade and supply chain management system. With physical and system infrastructure (sourcing, supplier selection, storage & inventory management, transportation) already in place, the flow of information is considered more important than flow of goods or services since information facilitates the fast and smooth flow of goods and services. Nowadays information and technology is used to track and manage goods, efficiently manage systems, ebbed security and transparency to supply chains, help supply chain's greening efforts, risk management and so on. Information and technology's application is limitless and so are examples of information and technology changing the works of supply chain management (we have seen several cases in previous sections) but in this section, we will focus on how information and technology revolutionized logistics in the very beginning.

13.1 Electronic Data Interchange

Before Electronic Data Interchange (EDI), international trade was accompanied by immense, tedious yet important paperwork documenting origin, destination, ownership, information of goods carried, terms of delivery (incoterms), partnership agreements, terms of production and purchasing, etc. Traditionally, documents between logistics providers, importers, exporters, customers, and everyone involved in international trade was sent and received by fax, mail, or telegram. Creating and filing documents were such a hassle, one study even stated that a crucial element of freight forwarders survival was its ability to manage information.

Electronic data interchange (EDI) is a communication system that exchanges structured data and documents electronically such as purchasing orders, invoices, funds transferees, packing list, shipping instructions, delivery status, proof of delivery and other key information from business's computer to another business's computer. Standards such as ANSI, EDIFACT, TRADACOMS and ebXML have been developed so business can agree upon which standards to use and easily send and receive data and documents through appropriate channels. Data can be transferred by branch transfer (sending accumulated data in specific intervals), event driven transfer (sending data on request) or interactive transfer (requesting data from host system on a real-time basis). Businesses enjoyed major benefits as they deviated away from paper-based documents.

For example, companies may enjoy reduced costs since EDI system replaces faxing and mailing of paper documents. While these replacements reduce costs they can also reduce the amount of time spent by workers. In other words, processing time becomes faster and this allows more time for employees.

Electronic commerce is growing and electronic network exchange plays a key role in business communication between firms, and their external environments for example, suppliers. Electronic commerce has developed from early EDI applications in the automotive industry in the beginning of 1970s and has since spread to almost all industries and business sections. Subsequently, it is a useful method to improve the flow of information between companies. Electronic commerce has become common among businesses in recent years and can be defined as the electronic exchange of information, goods and services. In order to take advantage of the e-commerce, it is necessity that information can be transferred between parties in the most effective manner.

Advantages

- EDI provides quick access to information and cost savings by reducing paper, increasing quality and quantity of information and eliminating paper processing.
- Time savings and eliminating repetition are other benefits from the reduction in paper processing (elimination of manual intervention, checking)
- Documents can be transferred more quickly and processing errors can be decreased allowing business to be done more efficiently.
- More efficient processing will likely lead to improved customer service, which will ultimately expand the customer base.
- Facilitate stable relationships with business partners since EDI hardware, software and operating expenses are expensive, thus less incentive to change partners.
- Improves visibility and transparency since different business partners have access to the same information and data which eliminates the possibility of concealing and fudging data from each other.
- In the case of manufacturer and retailer sharing data and information from EDI, they can reduce costs by minimizing inventory levels. Since forecast demand is generated using the same data without concealment, both parties can accurately request the quantity and eliminate unnecessary inventory (elimination of bullwhip effect).

- Security- Much less likely to lose information transmitted through EDI than information sent via mail. Only authorized users can access EDI, and then there are audit trails and archives of data. Unauthorized users cannot easily change EDI data. It is also not subject to viruses.

Quiz

- What are the key benefits of the automated system?
- How will the automation impact the operational flexibility?

Notes

- Gray, R., Kim, G., (2001), Logistics and International Shipping, Institute of International Maritime Affairs, Korea Maritime University, 230-240
- Ozsomer, A., Mitri, M and Cavusgil, S.T. (1993), Selecting International Freight Forwarders: and expert systems application, International *Journal of Physical Distribution and Logistics Management,* 23,3,11-21
- Pak, M. (2011), Understanding International Logistics, Bobmumsa: Seoul.

CHAPTER 14

Operations and Strategies

In this chapter, the strategies and operations which are adopted and used by businesses will be studied. Businesses' priority lies on increasing efficiency and thus reducing costs. This priority could be achieved through the use of the following strategies.

14.1 Just In Time

Just-In-Time (JIT) is one of the fastest and newest methods of logistics. Understanding the philosophy of JIT is not difficult at all. Everything happens just-in-time. Have a look around your life. You need to leave a house just-in-time to catch a bus, just-in-time to arrive at a university and just-in-time to meet your friends.

JIT was originated in Japan. This may be known as an inventory strategy firms use in order to improve their productivity and decrease waste. The idea of JIT is very simple but, it is essential in modern supply chain management. In a broad sense, its aim is to meet customers' demand in time in terms of both quality and quantity. In doing so, JIT tries to reduce the level of stock a business holds and thus cuts costs.

For a successful adoption of JIT, the following conditions should be met by firms. They must know what they need, how many and when. The production under JIT should be 'pulled through' rather than 'pushed through'. This is because production should be for specific customer orders. Stocks will be delivered when they are needed. This automatically increases the frequency of deliveries of stocks. Accurately forecasted demand is vital for this method since production cycle starts only when an order from a customer is received.

Advantages

- Operation costs will be reduced
- Higher quality is expected
- Lead time and respond time are reduced
- Saved working capital as stock is only obtained when it is needed
- Less time is spent on checking and re-working the product of others as the emphasis is on getting the work right first time

Disadvantages

- Only little room for mistakes as minimal stock is kept for re-working faulty product
- Production becomes heavily reliant on suppliers and can cause the whole production delays if stock is not delivered on time
- There is no spare finished product available to meet unexpected orders, because all product is made to meet actual orders – however, JIT is a very responsive method of production

CASE STUDY

The Tulip industry in the Netherlands

The Dutch society was introduced to the Tulip by Augier Ghislain de Busbecq in the 16th century. The Tulip owes its names to the Turkish word Turban, which is almost identically to the form of the flower. Busbecq exported the Tulip from Anatolia, Turkey to Vienna Austria first, where he became a successful horticulturist in the gardens of the Austrian Kingdom palaces. After almost twenty years, Busbecq moved to Leiden, The Netherlands, and introduced the flower. By 1636, the unregulated Dutch tulip industry became booming, while the demand for the flowers could not keep up with supply and the price of single bulbs soared.

The first half of the seventeenth century was marked by formidable economic growth and a period of prosperity for the Netherlands, which was called the Dutch Golden Age; merchants became rich from International trade. In the late 1630s, a speculative market of bulb trading developed quickly, where the history books speak of a "Tulip mania", which can be characterized by an extremely increasing and uncontrolled Tulip bulb market. At the top of this period of speculation, some bulbs reached extremely high prices, which discontinued for several years. The price of one Tulip bulb even reached the equivalent ten times the annual income of a skilled craftsman. However, after a couple of years, the market collapsed in 1637, which led to the day of the first economic crisis in history. Since Tulips had become so popular in the most of Europe and the Netherlands became the main exporter for the European continent.

Today, 93% of all bulbs in the world are exported from the Netherlands, planted in October and November, and blossoming in April until June. There are over 52,000 acres of bulbs produced by 2,700 suppliers, counting 20,000 employees. Over nine billion bulbs are produced annually of which are one-third Tulips. These three billion Tulips, if planted four inches apart, would circle the globe at the equator seven times. The Tulip industry is important in the Dutch economy, not only in terms of international trade, but also in tourism. For every tourist, who visits the Netherlands during the months April until June, a trip through the bulb fields of the Netherlands is a must. The highlight is a visit to the famous Keukenhof with its Bulb Gardens, the world's largest floral display. Today, Tulips are still one of the most popular export products from the Netherlands.

Tulip industry using JIT

Plants and flowers are living products; they are perishable and especially fragile, also changes in temperature are detrimental. For these reasons, specialists of cut flowers developed special distribution circuits, a logistical system, adjusted to these fragile products. Flowers are living, fresh and fragile products which do not like storage and transport, this is why the logistics used in the distribution of flower appears to be very complex and applies the concept of "Just in Time". Furthermore, it is very important for a market leader to use this method, keeping the leader spot in the market.

Distributions networks include distribution centers, which are platforms for cross docking to reduce inventory to minimum and speed up the flow. Cross docking is a logistics procedure where products from a supplier or manufacturing plant are distributed directly to a customer or retail chain with marginal to no handling or storage time. Cross docking takes place in a distribution docking terminal; usually consisting of trucks and dock doors on two (inbound and outbound) sides with minimal storage space. The name 'cross docking' explains the process of receiving products through an inbound dock and then transferring them across the dock to the outbound transportation dock.

Monceau Fleurs, who is the market leader in wholesale of flowers and vegetables, took a step there five years ago. The franchise network was created in 1998, and then settled in the Netherlands and now they use a platform and logistics, which enable them to remove the intermediaries and actually they dominate the Dutch market. The direct relationship, which then exists between the producer and the shopping centre, requires a perfect mastery of logistics.

The quality, price and logistics are critical elements in the game of global competition. Moreover, the requirements of sustainable development will impose more constraints. This is why a company must continue to invest, create and innovate in their logistics.

The Dutch horticulture is one of the major sectors, being 7% of the total agricultural sector. The largest flower productions of cut flowers are rose, chrysanthemum and tulips. This sector is highly fragmented and highly specialized. The Dutch Flower Council of Holland developed this sector with the creation of producer groups. All products are grouped and marketed in auction, for example in the famous markets of Aalsmeer and Westland Rijnsburg. The Dutch horticulture is mainly produced in very efficient greenhouses and highly optimized, then she is marketed through a logistics with a lot of powerful techniques. This explains the presence of a volume of 70% from the Dutch flowers in Rungis. Rungis is the biggest fresh products market in the world and is accommodates close to Paris, France.

Quiz

- Think of one JIT example in your real life. How does JIT strategy is used in your daily lives?
- Do you think the JIT strategy is used well in the tulip industry? Why do you think so? What benefits does JIT bring to the industry?
- Who else uses JIT strategy?

Notes

- rungisinternational.com
- aalhysterforklifts.com
- Shiller, 2005
- Floralia-Brussles
- Essortment.com
- Histotheek.nl

14.2 Packaging

People often consider packaging a part of the marketing process. But the truth is, packaging is essential to logistics. If companies combine the right packaging with the corresponding distribution process, they gain efficiency and can considerably reduce their costs. Packaging and distribution processes are a source of competitive advantage. The following paragraphs detail how and why.

"Packaging is a coordinated system of preparing goods for safe, secure, efficient and effective handling, transport, distribution, storage, retailing, consumption combined with maximizing consumer value, sales and hence profit". Packaging is essential and must be taken into account, especially in the last logistics stage, the distribution process.

The main functions of packaging in the logistic process are;

1) Protective function

Products may support mechanical and climatic stresses during transportation. Good packaging ensures the delivery of merchandise in satisfactory conditions.

2) Storage function

Packaging is designed to facilitate the storage of a product. It should be practical to move, to store (for instance, companies can optimise their space and costs if products are stackable in a warehouse). Packaging should therefore be adapted to individual company storage equipment.

3) Transportation function

Packaging must facilitate the product's transportation: its size, its form and its material should be as light and manageable as possible.

4) Handling function

Packaging is supposed to simplify the handling of a product. For example, individual yoghurts are annoying to handle, thus they are placed in bags or cartons.

5) Information function

Packaging provides information about products such as the expiration date, fragility. This information can be provided by automatic recognition such as barcodes or RFID, which are also imprinted on the packaging.

Furthermore, more and more companies are concerned about sustainable packaging, either because of obligation or with a view to give a good image of themselves. It can boost sales as well as product reputation. Once the packaging process is the last stage of production. Once it is finished the product enters into the distribution process.

CASE STUDY

Introduction to Sirops Monin in France

Monin is first and foremost a brand that sells "sirops". The best English equivalent for this word is "syrup", which will be used from now on. Syrups in France are the equivalent of Kool Aid in America, but in liquid form. A small dose of syrup to which you add water (or any other drinkable liquid) colors the water and gives it the taste of the flavor. These flavors can be classical (such as mint, or "grenadine") or very original (Monin has a cucumber flavored syrup, for example!). Syrups are common household goods in France, but the professional market is much more developed, as many bartenders or baristas use them in their compositions. Monin's relative anonymity hides a very strong presence in this market; the brand is in fact the world's foremost producer of high quality syrups intended for professional use.

The Frenchman George Monin created Monin in 1912, in the Belgian city of Bourges. The company was subsequently moved to France and started exporting internationally in 1930. In 1945 the company started concentrating on the production of syrups. The brand has manufacturing sites in Florida and Kuala Lumpur, and international transactions represent 75% of the group's 100 million euro yearly revenue. Monin cultivates its international presence, and its success is due to its quality products, but also to its distribution strategy and packaging.

Packaging to fit constraints

Monin's wide range of products, with more than 140 different flavors, attracts a great number of professionals and individual consumers. As the world's premium syrup brand, Monin markets its goods as luxury products. The packaging helps to maintain this image. Monin was able to position itself on the professional market, and it is the only brand to have successfully done so. But this market segment does not represent its only consumers, and Monin caters to many different customers. Its success is due in part to its adaptability to provide all its customers with efficient and adapted packaging.

Professionals use Monin syrups across the globe. All international cocktail and bartending competitions and championships use Monin syrups. In bars, bottles are displayed and affect the choice of cocktails for clients. Therefore, barmen need elegant glass bottles, but they also need high capacity containers. Thus the creation of two-liter glass bottles, that are manageable yet sufficiently large to suit barmen's needs. For baristas on the other hand, ergonomic and esthetic bottles are not very important, and they do not have to carry the containers. Thus Monin created specific plastic containers that contain up to 5 liters of syrup, that have a push valve at the top, to speed up the creation of smoothies, lattes etc. Finally, individual households also consume these products, and Monin has designed one-liter bottles and half-liter bottles to cater to this market. Despite these different containers, the brand maintains only one image, thanks to its understated and classical labels. They have created a very unique image for the group.

All Monin product bottles and packaging materials are recyclable. Bottles are for the majority in plastic or glass. Plastic bottles are lighter and easy to transport since they are not fragile, but Monin has also chosen to use glass bottles. Glass involves a higher logistics cost, but Monin has made this choice because glass is a more noble material than plastic, and it is a question of image, which is always important for companies selling luxury products. The company's manufacturing sites are on the cutting edge of technology, which allow them to guarantee a quality packaging while reducing labor costs. Their machines are highly automated, which is why the intervention of their employees is required only moderately. To illustrate how technologically advanced this company is, one only has to mention that it only has 320 employees.

Monin spends a fair amount on the transportation of its products, seeing as at least half are glass bottles, and thus, highly fragile. However the brand has earned the reputation of a quality supplier because their boxes are designed to secure the bottles and prevent any breaks or leakage. On arrival, products go to warehouses, which are at a specific temperature to keep products in optimal conditions and to avoid altering the flavors. Monin has chosen to have a considerable transportation and packaging budget, because they seek to maintain the quality and nobility of their products. The syrups have to reach their destination in perfect condition to respect their luxury image.

Quiz

- Do products require different types of protection during shipment?
- Why is packaging important?
- What would happen to products without packaging?
- How Monin manages their packing process?

Notes

- http://www.monin.com/en-gb/home
- http://www.ebs-paris.com/pdf/20122013/olivier-monin-octobre-2012.pdf
- http://www.lesechos.fr/14/09/2011/LesEchos/21016-95-ECH_les-sirops-monin-regnent-sur-le-monde-des-cocktails.htm
- http://www.leberry.fr/cher/actualite/2012/10/19/les-sirops-monin-centans-de-succes_1300904.html

14.3 Cross-docking

Cross-docking is a distribution system where goods from a supplier or manufacturing plant are distributed directly to a customer or retail chain. Simply speaking, under this system items received at the warehouse are not received into stock, but are prepared for shipment to another location or for retail stores. This process hence eliminates handling or storage time since the goods are not received into stock.

The main purpose of cross-docking system is to save time and costs. Because the products received do not spend any time in the warehouse the overall time is saved. Besides, the system reduces costs associated with excess inventory because it either reduces or removes the unnecessary handling of goods. When the level of inventory decreases it also reduces the handling and storing products. This eventually will lead to reduced product damages which will then directly reduce the costs.

Advantages

- Product handling time is reduced
- There is no need to store products in warehouses
- Labor cost is reduced since there is no need for handling/packaging/storing
- Products move more quickly
- More frequent deliveries become possible
- Just-in-time strategy for customer

Disadvantages

- In order to make the system work more efficiently, more dedicated management is required such as time management
- Cross-docking terminals are required but this takes time and money
- Risk of stock-out due to the zero inventory

CASE STUDY

FloraHolland in the Netherlands

The Netherland is known for over a century for its contribution to the floriculture sector. At the same time, the floriculture sector is expanding in Eastern Europe. Therefore FloraHolland focuses mainly on the relationship between all the parties involved in a unique combination to optimize their position in the international market. Specialized growers, collective trade platforms, salespersons specialized in trade and logistics, form the basis of strong positioning in the international floriculture sector. The annual turnover is around €4.4 billion with sales of 12.5 billion items a year. There are 20000 different varieties plants and flowers auctioned at the 38 auction clocks located in the auction houses in Aalsmeer, Bleiswijk, Eelde, Naaldwijk, Rijnsburg and Rhein-Maas, that are opened from Monday to Friday (except for holidays).

The auction process

The process of the flower auction at FloraHolland starts at the flower growers. Whenever the flowers matured they are cut and transported to the various auction houses. Via Internet the grower has select where he wants his flowers to be auctioned. Not all flowers auctioned at are from the Netherlands; every day flowers from 50 other countries are also auctioned. As shown in the appendix, FloraHolland's worldwide import top 5 exists of Kenya, Ethiopia, Israel, Belgium and Germany. The imported flowers usually arrive by airplane, as the flowers have to be as quick as possible in the Netherlands due to perishability.

After the flowers are collected, had a quality check and the flower's information is in the auction house's database – described in 'The logistics process'- the auction can begin. There are three ways of buying flowers at FloraHolland. The first is as the Dutch say: "going under the clock". Referring to moving trolleys with plants and flowers making their way under the clock (see second picture on the cover page). Bidders, located at a tribune facing the clock, will start to bid for their clients. With the products' information provided and the instructions of the clients, bidders will press the bid button when the clock reaches the desired price. Another way to bid on flowers is via Internet or in specially designed rooms in one of FloraHolland's locations. Flowers can also be bought without auction; FloraHolland can also intermediate between growers and buyers to provide price and quantity contracts. In this way, assurance can be provided for both parties. The buyer is sure to get the needed quantity and quality for a setup price. The growers' advantage is mostly the assurance that his flowers will be bought and can partly adapt his harvest to it. After the flowers are bought, the flowers have to be transported to the buyers as quick as possible.

The logistics process

Logistics is one of the most important factors in the process of the floriculture sector due to the perish ability of the flowers (and plants). The grower has to submit his product list via Internet to FloraHolland, in this way the information is stored and used for the internal logistics. The information is also used for the 'Tracking and Tracing' system. FloraHolland distributed their own logistics supplies to the growers. The fusts are used to protect the products during transport, it also set a standard to the amount of, for instance, flowers. These fusts are loaded on auction trolleys, and loaded into a truck. Unless special arrangements are made with FloraHolland, the growers have to arrange own transportation to the auction locations. Because the growers forwarded their product information, special Tracking & Tracing chips with customized barcodes are integrated and packing slips are provided.

With this system, the flowers are followed throughout the whole auction and logistics process. For the plants and flowers imported from other countries, the process is slightly different. The foreign growers have to send a conformation if the agreed quality and quantity is met before the products are loaded into truck to the airport. Airfreight is the quickest transportation option and therefore used for this perishable product. When the plants and flowers arrive at the Dutch airport, usually Schiphol, trucks are arranged to get the products to designated auction locations. Even though the auction process is the same in every auction location, the distribution process may vary slightly. The auction locations have different capacities and groupings. Therefore, we focus on the internal logistics process of the auction location 'Rijnsweerd'. As the trucks with the flowers arrive during the night, the barcode and the packing slip are checked and an overall quantity check is done. Before the auction starts and the flowers and plants will go through the whole auction process, they are kept in cooling cellars. Each cellar has a specific temperature according to the requirements for the plants and flowers. During the time the products are stored into the cellars, quality tests are done on random basis to assure the flower quality and the growers' information.

At six in the morning the auction starts and the plants and flowers will make their way to the "Meinzaal", the Dutch auction hall. As the products roll into the auction hall, the clocks are ticking and bidders start bidding. After a half trolley/trolley/multiple trolleys are sold, the trolleys will be fully automatically brought to the sorting floor for packaging and further distribution. Before the sold products leave the auction location in Rijnsweerd, the large buyers can have the plants and flowers packed and rapped. Several companies have contracts with FloraHolland to immediately use to flowers to make bouquets before entering the trucks. Wrapping the trolleys is done for every sold trolley for the protection and cooling during transport. Small companies will provide their own transportation for distribution but for large clients, FloraHolland also offers a distribution service. This service is also extended for export to other countries.

Quiz

- How would you define cross-docking?
- When is cross-docking appropriate?
- What are the prerequisites of cross-docking?
- Can you think of any other advantages or disadvantages?

Notes

- Alicke, K. (2003). *Planung und Betrieb von Logistiknetzwerken*. Springer Verlag.
- Heiserich, O.-E. (2002). *Logistik. Eine praxisorientierte Einführung*. Gabler Verlag.
- Mathar, H.-J. J. (2009). *Unternehmenslogistik. Grundlagen für die betriebliche Praxis*. Zürich: Compendio Bildungsmedien AG.
- Rallis, K. (1997). *Materialwirtschaft, Grundlagen, Methoden, Techniken, Politik*. Wien: Karl Hanser Verlag München.
- Stölzle, W. K. (2004). *Erfolgsfaktor Bestandsmanagement*. Zürich: Versus Verlag AG.
- Wannenwetsch, H. (2010). *Integrierte Materialwirtschaft und Logistik*. Springer Verlag.

14.4 RFID

RFID stands for Radio-Frequency Identification. The RFID device has the same functioning purpose as a bar code or a magnetic strip which can be found at the back of a credit card or ATM card. This device provides a unique identifier for a certain object and must be scanned in order to obtain information on that object.

Examples may include:

- ExxonMobil uses RFID technology for its "SpeedPass," which instantly collects payment on gas stations from a tag on a driver's keychain
- United Airlines uses RFID tags to track passenger bags, which reduces the number of lost bags essentially

There is a big difference between barcode and RFID. Differently from barcode system, RFID uses radio signals. This means that the device does not need to be scanned directly. More in specific, it uses a wireless non-contract radio system to transfer data between a tag and an object (Figure 14-1). Automatic identification and tracking become possible under this system. Barcode system sometimes faces difficulties in reading the code but this problem is not found on RFID system. Since RFID uses radio signals it works within a given range (this can be up to 20 feet for high-frequency devices). It has been more than half a century since RFID became available but, it has just not been until recently that the device has started to be used more commonly.

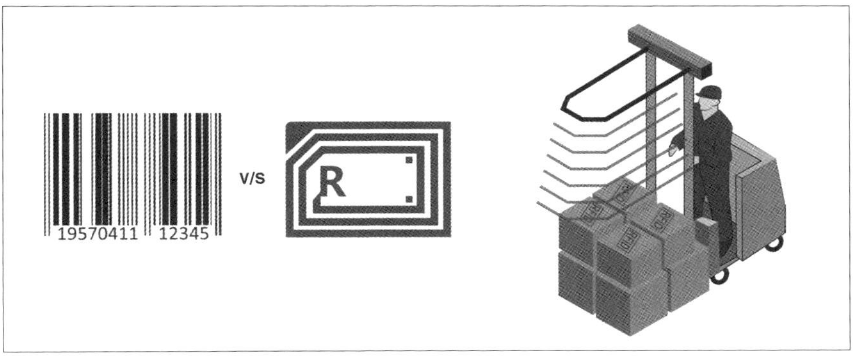

Source: http://msdn.microsoft.com/en-us/library/aa479362.aspx

Figure 14-1 reading RFID tags in a warehouse

CASE STUDY

Case study- Hi-pass system in Republic of Korea

South Korea has adopted a Hi-pass system to allow car drivers to pay highway tolls without having to stop for payments. This system is widely used on roads in Korea. In order to use this system, OnBoard Unit (OBU) and a Hi-pass card need to be presented. The OBU has to be installed inside a car (at the front of the vehicle) and the Hi-pass card has to be inserted into the OBU. The Hi-pass card can be purchased and is available to be charged from minimum of 10,000 won. As of August 2013, the payment became possible with credit cards. This reduces the hassle of having to charge the card every time it runs out of credit.

The system overall does a great job of getting cars through the gates quickly, especially when traffic is in place during rush hours.

How the system works

The way the Hi-pass system works is simple. Once a driver has OBU and the HI-pass card installed in his car he can benefit from the system on road. When drivers need to pay tolls he will see roads with indication and different colors. Those who wish to pay the tolls by Hi-pass card should take lanes with blue colors. When the car approaches near to the toll gate the driver should slow down the speed within a given range and let the RFID to be read from outside. The driver does not need to do anything else. Once the car passes through the given range the Hi-pass card will be read automatically and the driver will be able to check the amount of tolls being paid and the credit on card from the screen that is placed on the left side at the end of the given range.

Such payment becomes even handier when cards travel a long distance. When a car travels from one city to another, the driver has to collect a ticket from the departing city and once he has to pay the toll at the destination city by handing over the ticket to identify the distance that has been travelled. If the ticket is lost accidently the situation becomes complicated. However, with the Hi-pass card the driver just needs to remember to take the Hi-pass only lanes (with blue colors) when leaving the departing city and once he reaches the destination city he once needs to take the Hi-pass lane for the payment to be checked out. The card will automatically identify the distance the car has travelled and will take the payment out of the card.

Quiz

- Think of any examples of RFID system in your real life. How convenient are they? Are there any problems you face with them?
- Can you think of one area where the RFID system can/need be expanded?
- What do you think about the Hi-pass system in Korea?

Notes

- Krieger, Prof. Dr. Winfried. *Wirtschaftslexikon*. Edited by Springer Gabler Verlag. Gabler Wirtschaftslexikon. 2013. http://wirtschaftslexikon.gabler.de/Archiv/83828/rfid-v5.html (accessed 09 25, 2013)
- *United Airlines*. 2013. http://www.united.com (accessed 10 03, 2013).
- http://msdn.microsoft.com/en-us/library/aa479362.aspx

14.5 Economic Order Quantity

Order and storage costs occur when companies order goods and keep them in warehouses. Optimal orders can be made when these order and storage costs are minimized. The following pressures occur under this situation.

- Pressure to purchase larger lots to minimize order cost and order frequency
- Pressure to purchase smaller lots to minimize inventory holding cost

Hence, order quantity should be where the combination of these order cost and inventory holding cost are minimized. Such order quantity is called as EOQ (Economic Order Quantity) or ELS (Economic Lot Size).

In order to calculate this EOQ, 'inventory holding cost' and 'order cost' should be considered first.

Annual inventory holding cost can be calculated as follows;
Inventory holding cost = annual inventory x unit price x annual inventory holding ratio Here, annual average total stock = order quantity x unit price x annual inventory holding ratio/2 **(Equation 1)**

Order cost can be written as follows;
Order cost = per order cost x annual order frequency
In this case, per order cost = annual usage/order quantity
Hence, per order cost x annual usage/order quantity **(Equation 2)**

As previously stated, EOQ is where the combination of inventory holding cost and order cost is minimized. Hence, equation 1 and 2 should be seen as the same.[3]

3. Order cost and inventory holding cost, used to define optimal order lot size, can be used to find the balance point. Let's assume the annual average inventory level is half of annual total sales.

X: order quantity
A: order cost (fixed)
S: annual sales (usage)
P: annual average inventory level (X/2)
N: annual order frequency (S/X)
i: annual inventory holding cost per product (= annual inventory holding ratio x unit price)
TC: total inventory-related cost
TC= AN + Ip

$$= \frac{AS}{X} + \frac{iX}{2}$$

Here, differentiate the equation by X and assume it to be equal to 0 to get the order quantity that minimizes the total cost.

$$\frac{dAS}{dx} = \frac{AS}{X^2} + \frac{iX}{2} = 0$$

$\frac{AS}{X^2} + \frac{iX}{2}$ (do multiple x on both side then it becomes as $\frac{AS}{X} + \frac{iX}{2}$ Hence, order cost and inventory holding cost becomes the same)

Thus, $X = \sqrt{\frac{2AS}{i}}$

EOQ therefore can be calculated as follows;

$$\text{EOQ} = \sqrt{\frac{2 \text{ x annual usage x per order cost}}{\text{annual inventory holding ratio x unit pric}}}$$

The annual inventory holding ratio is usually 20~30% which includes 13~20% of profit, 5~8% of obsolescence and 1~3% of storage expense.

CHAPTER 15

Supply Chain Security & Transparency

Nowadays, lengthy geographically dispersed supply chains are servicing international markets across the world. If a single process goes wrong, the effect can be disastrous. A minor security issue along the supply chain can threaten the physical infrastructure underpinning globalization. It compromises nation's abilities to trade goods and services internationally, in turn affecting economic growth, employment, overall prosperity, and may lead to higher prices with fewer goods. Smooth and seamless operation of international trade and logistics infrastructure must be a fundamental element for global well-being. As seen in 9/11, security is a must and a crucial element of the supply chain but not always appreciated. In order to ensure security, security has to be designed into the international supply chain rather than seek to mitigate consequences after the fact. Many companies are concerned with the cost of re-engineering the supply chain in order to incorporate security, but short term costs of implementing security measures can be balanced against the long-term gains from improved customer relations. Especially, security is important for strong brands in order to protect their brand value and corporate reputation.

Urciuoli advocates seven recommendations to consider when improving supply chain security. First of all, comply with compulsory regulations issued by the government around the world since compliance will ensure free flow and reduce uncertainty delays. Secondly, establish and exploit the logistics multi layered framework -identify elements (horizontal protection), layers (vertical protection), and weak points-to protect distribution chain. Additional recommendations include increasing the hardness of supply chains by using hybrid security systems and developing real time monitoring capabilities in order to respond adequately. Lastly, identifying and promoting security measures that are efficient, integrating security and supply chain management, and ensuring the comprehension of security across the whole supply chain is also recommended. After the attack on the twin towers on September 11, United States Customs and Border Protection (CBP) has implemented several initiatives to ensure supply chain security. Section 1 will briefly cover other initiatives CBP implemented, CSI and 24 Hour Manifest Rule, before concentrating on C-TPAT. Section 2 will cover the main topic, C-TPAT. It will discuss the process, benefits, and cost of C-TPAT. In Section 3 global harmonization issues between security initiatives around the world will be discussed. The concept of Mutual Recognition is discussed, especially what is necessary and what actions to be taken for the establishment of Mutual Recognition between countries.

15.1 Supply Chain Security Initiatives

In the wake of the September 11, 2011 terrorist attacks on America, The Customs Service was in charge of expanding America's borders to facilitate the early detection and prevention of further terrorist attacks. To that end, Customs implemented the Container Security Initiative ("CSI"), the 24 Hour Rule, and Customs-Trade Partnership Against Terrorism ("C-TPAT"). This section will cover other initiatives than C-TPAT, the U. S. government implemented for supply chain security reasons.

Container Security Initiative(CSI)

About 108 million cargo containers are transported through seaports around the world each year, making containers the most critical component of global trade. Each year, some 16 million containers move through U. S. ports, representing some $475 billion worth of commerce. Statistically speaking, approximately 40% of all containers in the world pass through U. S. ports each year. Approximately 70% of all U. S. bound containers originate or pass through some 20 foreign container ports. Prior to September 11, Customs' prime concern in identifying suspect containers related to narcotics, foreign invasive species, and contraband. After September 11, the focus was shifted to weapon of mass destruction possibly being transported. Container Security Initiative (CSI) was launched in January 2002 as a part of the U. S. Customs and Border Protection's (CBP) layered cargo security strategy. CSI operates in 58 ports worldwide, in regions including North, Central, and South America; the Caribbean, Europe, Africa, the Middle East, and throughout Asia. CSI is a cooperative program between the U. S. government and foreign governments that identifies and pre-screens high risk cargos. Currently, over 80% of all maritime cargo imported into the United States is subject to pre-screening.

CSI consists of four core elements: (1) Using intelligence and automated advance targeting information to identify and target containers that pose a risk for terrorism; (2) pre-screening those containers identified as high risk before they arrive at US ports; and (3) using state-of-the-art detection technology to scan containers that pose a risk.

In fiscal year 2010, more than 10.1 million maritime shipments were reviewed in CSI Ports before arriving at United States seaports, an average of 27,600 a day. CSI also has the goal of taking these measures without slowing down trade. Because CSI is not mandatory it does not theoretically impose any specific new obligation on the commercial shipping community. But CSI needs information in order to identify, target and pre-screen possible high risk shipment. So Customs has enacted the 24 Hour Rule, which does impose increased obligations and potential liabilities and provides information for pre-screening.

"24 Hour" Manifest Rule

Prior to September 11, Customs regulations required the filling of cargo manifests 48 hours before vessel arrival. This meant, in the vast majority of cases, that the containers covered by the manifest were already onboard a vessel bound for a U. S. port, which limited any screening efforts prior to the port arrival. In an effort to enhance security, Customs enacted the "24 Hour Rule" on February 1, 2003.

In contrast to CSI and C-TPAT, the 24 Hour Rule is mandatory. Federal Regulations now require electronic transmission of vessel cargo manifest information directly to Customs 24 or more hours before the cargo is loaded to a vessel destined to U. S. at a foreign port. The rule allows U. S. Customs officers to analyze the container content information and identify potential terrorist threats before the U. S. bound container is loaded at the foreign seaport. Due to new rules enforced by the 24 Hour Rule, cargo descriptions such as "said to contain" or "freight all kinds" or other general descriptions of cargos are forbidden. Cargo descriptions must include precise descriptions, weight of cargo, and the complete name and addresses of the shippers and consignees. If cargo descriptions were not filed in a timely fashion, it would be left behind at various ports with "Do Not Load" orders.

15.2 Customs-Trade Partnership Against Terrorism

Nevertheless, the most elaborate and complex but most efficient security initiative implemented by the CBP is considered to be Customs-Trade Partnership Against Terrorism (C-TPAT) which was launched in November 2001 in response to the September 11 attack on the twin towers. C-TPAT sets standards, checks compliance and offers incentives for adopting secure practices such as speedier processing on arrival. It has four clear objectives: (a) To ensure that members improve their supply chain security; (b) To provide incentives and benefits to speed up the flow of goods within the system; (c) To introduce its security principles into the international community on the basis of cooperation and coordination; and (d) To support other initiatives of United States CBP.

C-TPAT is a voluntary government-business initiative to build cooperative relationships that strengthen and improve overall international supply chain and U. S. border security by tightening security and tracking cargo at points along the cargo transit and supply chain. CBP officials review company's security procedures, make recommendations with an audit as well as an annual assessment. Supply chain specialists within the CBP organization help recruit new companies into the C-TPAT program and assist them with their security programs and in establishing their security profiles (according to such factors as security related anomalies, geographic regions, other risk related information, or import volumes). Based on these reviews, companies are assigned scores which, if favorable, give them expedited processing through U. S. ports, and a reduced likelihood of physical inspection. C-TPAT ensures security practices' integrity and also verifies the validity of their business partner's security practices. C-TPAT recognizes that U. S. CBP can provide the highest level of cargo security only through close cooperation with the owners of the international supply chain. As of March 2010, C-TPAT has more than 8,200 certified members and account for over 50% (by value) of what is imported in the United States. These members include U.S importers, U. S./Canada highway carriers, U. S./Mexico highway carriers, rail and sea carriers, licensed U. S. Customs brokers, U. S. marine port authority/terminal operators, U. S. freight consolidators, ocean transportation intermediaries, non-operating common carriers, Mexican and Canadian manufacturers, and Mexican long haul carriers. There are several different minimum security criteria for different types of companies that must be met before certification. (e.g. minimum security criteria for third party logistics providers, marine port authority and terminal operators, long haul carriers, customs brokers, etc).

Certification and Validation Process

Collection of advanced information becomes a relevant operation in order to decide if container inspection is to be performed or not. Entering in to the program, companies sign an agreement to work with CBP to protect the supply chain, identify security gaps and implement specific security measures and best practices. C-TPAT requires companies to document and validate their supply chain security procedures in relation to existing CBP C-TPAT criteria or guidelines as applicable. Companies provide CBP with a company profile and security profile outlining the specific security measures the company has in place. Applicants must address a broad range of security topics and present security profiles that list action plans to align security throughout their supply chain. Once this is complete, CBP will assign the applicant a Supply Chain Security Specialist (SCSS) who will review the application. The review process by the SCSS consists of two components; (a) approval of the security profile and (b) the vetting process. This is when CBP conducts its investigation of the applicant's company. When the company becomes certified it is eligible to generate a Status Verification Interface ("SVI") number. A C-TPAT certified company supplies this SVI number to importers or service providers, who are C-TPAT members themselves and are interested in knowing the company's C-TPAT status.

The SAFE Port Act mandates that C-TPAT members undergo a validation process within one year of becoming C-TPAT certified. Validation process is to ensure the existence of security measures documented in one's supply chain security profile and in any supplemental information provided to CBP. The validation process is essential to verifying the company's commitment to C-TPAT. Also members must undergo a revalidation process within three years of the last validation or sooner based on cause or incident. The timing of validation is based on a company's past compliance history, security profile and other circumstances.

Benefit-Cost Analysis of C-TPAT

Benefits

C-TPAT program establishes clear supply chain security criteria for members to meat and in return provides incentives and benefits such as secure and expeditious supply chain for their employees, suppliers and customers.

Benefits of being a C-TPAT member include;

- Reduction in time and costs of cargo release by CBP
- Reduced number of CBP inspections (reduced border delay times)
- Priority processing for CBP inspection leading to reduced time in CBP inspection lines (front of the line processing for inspections when possible
- Increase predictability in moving goods (14.5% of members indicated increased ability to predict lead time)
- Eligibility to attend C-TPAT supply chain security training seminars
- Assignment of a C-TPAT Supply Chain Security Specialist (SCSS) to help validation process and enhance security throughout member's international supply chain
- Potential eligibility for self-policing and self monitoring of security activities through the Importer Self-Assessment Program (ISA)
- Increased supply chain visibility (29.5% of members), Increased ability to track orders (18.0% of importer members)
- Increased ability to asses and manage supply chain risk (59.9% of members)
- Intangible benefits such as "increased security awareness" and "demonstrating corporate citizenship"

Additional benefits are increased number of customers and revenue for 2 out of 10 members. Although the effect varies by business type (importer, non-importer), business size, and number of years participating in the C-TPAT program.

Normally, the listed benefits increase in degree as the number of years participating in the C-TPAT program increases.

Costs of Implementing the C-TPAT Program

Across all businesses, "improving or implementing physical security costs (doors, windows, electronic access, cameras, fences, gates, lighting, etc.) received the most mentions of all the potential C-TPAT implementation costs (71.1%). Next on the list of potential costs with most mentions include "Improving cargo security" costs which were mentioned by 59.0% of all businesses. The costs associated with "salaries and expenses of personnel hired/contracted specifically to implement and/or manage C-TPAT program" received the lowest mentions with 51.3% of all businesses. Also "cost of improving identification system" was mentioned by 58.1% of businesses. For Importers, more than half (59.3%) reported that they have incurred costs related to "updating existing foreign supplier, manufacturer, or vendor security evaluation survey process." Next on the list of implementation costs incurred by Importers were "educating foreign suppliers, manufacturers, or vendors about security requirements" and "developing a new supplier security evaluation survey process."

Maintenance costs are ongoing expenditures businesses experienced to maintain the C-TPAT program. Of all the maintenance cost items, "maintaining the physical security" and "maintaining cargo security" were the most frequently mentioned by all the businesses. Next on the list of maintenance costs was "maintaining in-house education, training, and awareness."

Table 15-1 Potential implementation costs for all businesses

	Cost incurred (%)
Improving physical security	71.1
Improving cargo security	59.0
Improving identification system	58.1
Improving personnel security	57.2
Improving in-house awareness	56.7
Improving personnel screening	55.3
Salaries and expenses of personnel	51.3

Source: C-TPAT Partner Survey, 2010

Benefits versus Costs

In addition to being asked to specify what costs and benefits were associated with their participation in C-TPAT, businesses were asked to make an overall cost-benefit assessment of their experience with C-TPAT. The question was: How would you describe your company's overall experience with CTPAT thus far? Overall, 42.1% of businesses reported that the benefits of participating outweighed the costs, approximately a 10 percentage point improvement over the 2007 survey. Exactly one quarter of businesses reported that the benefits and costs of participation were about the same, 14.9% reported that the costs of participation outweighed the benefits and 18% reported that it was too early to tell. Companies' overall cost-benefit rating varied significantly by business size, business type.

Encouragingly, but perhaps not surprisingly, businesses that had been certified longer were systematically more likely to report that the benefits of participation outweighed the costs. Perceptions of net benefits increased in a linear fashion with years in C-TPAT, ranging from 30.2% among companies certified less than one year to 47.7% among companies certified more than five years.

Also studies indicated that larger companies are systematically more likely to perceive greater net benefits from C-TPAT membership. The benefits outweigh the costs increased in a linear fashion with company size.

15.3 Global Harmonization

According to a survey conducted by CBP on companies compliant with C-TPAT, 8.6% considered a lack of mutual recognition or harmonization among security programs to be a "serious problem," while 33.8% considered it "somewhat of a problem". There are some efforts being made towards integrating security initiatives from different countries or recognizing the compatibility but more work has to be done for global harmonization and global security. In the midst of globalization, convergence of international regulatory standards will reduce compliance burden on companies and improve overall global security. This section will cover Mutual Recognition (MR) among countries and discuss in detail the necessity and steps towards MR between different security initiatives implemented by different nations.

An emerging focus: Mutual Recognition Arrangements

Mutual Recognition (MR) refers to the act of signing documents between foreign Customs Administrations that provides for the exchange of information. The essential concept of MR is that "foreign programs are compatible in both theory and practice so that one program may recognize the validation findings of the other program". Customs administrations work together to improve their capability to detect high-risk consignments and expedite the movement of legitimate cargo. Through

MR, international industry partnership programs are linked so that together they create a unified and sustainable security posture that can assist in securing and facilitating global cargo trade. It means end to end supply chain security based on program membership.

Benefits of MR include;

- Efficiency: Customs do not have to expend limited resources to send its staff overseas to validate a facility that has been certified by a foreign partnership program.
- Risk Assessment Tool: The status of the foreign partnership program participant is recognized by national program and it is used as a risk-assessment factor. national program validation visit will be conducted on a different segment of the national program importer's supply chain.
- Less Redundancy/Duplication of Efforts: Foreign companies do not have to go through two separate validation visits: the first one conducted by the local Customs administration as the company is initially certified by its business partnership program is followed by another validation process by the national program if no MR was in place. Moreover, companies only have to go through one revalidation visit in the future.
- Common Standard/Trade Facilitation: Companies only have to conform to one set of security requirements. Avoiding the burden of addressing different sets of requirements as a shipment moves through the supply chain in different countries.
- Transparency: With close collaboration among Customs administrations and between their partnership program, companies will benefit from increased supply chain transparency. Similar security platforms and the exchange of information between all of these partners expedite and facilitate the movement of commerce across nations.

There have been many MRs signed by various countries during the last

Table 15-2 Mutual Recognition status concluded MRs

Date	Country
June 2007	New Zealand-USA
May 2008	Japan-New Zealand
June 2008	Canada-USA
June 2008	Jordan-USA
June 2009	Japan-USA
July 2009	EU-Norway
July 2009	EU-Switzerland
June 2010	Canada-Japan
June 2010	Canada-Korea
June 2010	Canada-Singapore
June 2010	Korea-Singapore
June 2010	Korea-USA
May 2012	USA-EU
November 2012	Taiwan-EU
June 2014	Israel-AEO

Source: *Mutual Recognition Information, 2011*

decade. Table 15-2 shows the complete list of MRs concluded in the past.

Towards "Mutual Recognition"

In order for the signing of MR between countries, there are operational issues as well as political, legal and cultural issues to be considered. There are several steps needed to be taken in order to accomplish MRs.

<Operational/ Technical actions to be taken>

Information technology: Under joint effort the countries have to discuss which data elements will be exchanged for purposes of mutual recognition and additionally agree on guidelines of data transmission. Also an IT system has to be established for automated data exchange between countries.

Updates and training: Both countries have to communicate changes in a legal environment that might have an effect on the mutual recognition of the programs. In addition, conferences and training modules have to be exchanged and joint participation is anticipated. Also audits and validation visits are to be carried out together in order to understand one another's methods. Best Practice Seminars are being held, so that experts from both countries can exchange. Government representatives from both sides have to be informed about mutual recognition and its benefits.

Communication and cooperation with businesses: Businesses shall be informed about the progress of mutual recognition, especially regarding the benefits. Also feedback from the private sector has to be gathered in order to incorporate them in the roadmap.

AEO

Authorized Economic Operator (AEO) is a security initiative implemented by the EU which certifies economic operators in order to promote supply chain security. AEO is based on the SAFE framework in order to ensure mutual recognition globally. Like C-TPAT, AEO offers incentives to its members such as physical and document-based controls, priority treatment of consignments, choice of place for inspection, customs simplifications, simplified summary declarations, and prior notifications. AEO also has cost reduction measures as they direct their efforts towards checking non-certified companies to increase the security of international supply chain, while reducing the administrative burden for AEOs. To qualify for AEO status, economic operator performs self assessment according to the Community Customs Code and the AEO guidelines, identifying the risks its exposed to and security measures that must be implemented to mitigate the risks. Customs perform an audit to check whether the self-assessment is performed correctly, whether the company identified all the risks and has taken appropriate measures, and whether these measures are operational. When an economic operator is certified in one member state of the EU, certification is automatically recognized in other member states.

Both AEO and C-TPAT show "trust" to its members, and therefore grants benefits which are same or at least very similar. Benefits include fewer inspections of cargo and complete priority when mandatory examinations are necessary. The "soft benefits" appear to be the same: both programs canvass their benefits with the access to certain information, possibilities to promote the company's secure image through marketing activities and emphasize that membership means a better relation and cooperation between the customs authority and the business itself.

Notes

Alston, R., "Customs Enforcement Actions for C-TPAT Non-Compliance," *Journal Managing Imports & Exports*, Vol. 14, 2010

Anon, "C-TPAT Expands Benefits, Considrs Including Exporters", *Journal Managing Imports & Exports, Vol.* 10, 2008

Burgemeestre, B., Hulstijn, J., Tan, Y., "Rule-Based versus Principle-Based Regulatory Compliance", *Amsterdam Press*, 2009

Anon, "C-TPAT Soon to Be Compatible With EU's AEO System", *Journal Managing Imports & Exports, Vol.* 8, 2007

CBP, "Mutual Recognition-Frequently Asked Questions", *Customs and Border Protection*, 2011

CBP, "Customs-Trade Partnership Against Terrorism 2011 Costs & Savings Survey", *Customs and Border Protection*, 2011

CBP, "Fact Sheet", *Customs and Border Protection*, 2007.

Diop, A., Hartman, D., Rexrode, D., "Customs-Trade Partnership Against Terrorism Cost/Benefit Survey", *U.S. CUSTOMS AND BORDER PROTECTION*, 2007

EC, "Abridged External Partner Version of the U.S.-EU Joint Customs Cooperation Committee Roadmap Towards Mutual Recognition of Trade Partnership Programs", *European Commission*, 2009

EC, "Authorized Economic Operator (AEO)", *European Commission*, 2009

Edmonson, R.G., "C-TPAT Looks Within", *The Journal of Commerce*, Vol 12, 2011

Facilitation of Trade and Transport in Latin America and the Caribbean, "C-TPAT and AEO: New Channels for World Trade," *Bulletin FAL*, Vol 258, 2008

Furia, P., Lee, J., Rexrode, D., Ellis, J., "Customs-Trade Partnership Against Terrorism 2010 Partner Survey," *U.S. Customs and Border Protection*, 2010

Jaspan, R., "Avoiding Trouble in a C-TPAT Validation," *The Journal of Commerce*, Vol.12, 2011

Jordan, C, "Convincing Senior Management to Join the C-TPAT Program," *Journal Managing Imports & Exports*, Vol. 5, 2009

Murnane, D.P., Ross, J.L., Kahn, L.J., ""CSI", "C-TPAT", The "24 Hour Rule" and Vessel Security Plans: Do New U. S. Security Programs Result in New Liability Issues?", *Freehill Hogan & Mahar, LLP*, 2003

O'Connell, J., "C-TPAT: Major Challenges", *Springer Science + Business Media*, Vol. 2, 2009

Sarathy, R., "Secruity and the Global Supply Chain," *Transportation Journal*, Vol. 45, 2006.

Sheu, C., Lee, L., Niehoff, B., "Volunatry Logistics Security Program and International Supply Chain Partnership", *Supply Chain Management: An Interantional Journal*, Vol 11, 2006

Szelp, A., "Cargo Security Initiatives in the EU and the USA, their Impact on Business Operations and Mutual Recognition with Focus on AEO and C-TPAT", *WU Vienna University of Economics and Business*, 2010

Urciuoli, L., "Supply Chain Security-Mitigation Measures and a Logistics Multi-layered Framework," *Springer Science+Business Media*, Vol 3, 2009

WTO, "Trade Profiles", *World Trade Organization*, 2010

GREEN SCM

CHAPTER 16

Necessity and Growing Importance of Sustainability and Green SCM

16.1 Green SCM

Why Green SCM is Needed

The environment-related issues have always existed but the 21st century may be remarked for the most attention being paid. Being green and sustainable is no longer an option for everyone and businesses are not an exception. They especially need to lay down their priorities on environment and hence, it is rather a necessity for them. The environmental issues need to be taken into account for all participants in supply chain management.

Of course one of the main reasons for this argument is due to the climate change. But besides this matter, there are other key drivers of green supply chain management. These can be summarized as follows:

1) Changes in the preference of customers and hence changes in market demand

In the past, customers did not care much about the environment. But, it will be easily noticed that they are no longer ignoring what they used to before. There is an increasing level of interest in environment from customers. They care about the environment and started to look for environment friendly products. Some customers are even willing to pay higher costs for these types of products. Businesses can no longer ignore these changes and hence they need to take such matters into account for their productions. Moreover, people are getting more aware of the environmental issues going on in the world, companies are forced to engage in pro-environmental behaviour. This environmental behaviour was expressed by using the word 'green'. Companies should become greener in their activities.

2) Regulatory pressures

There are government policies that place pressures on companies to produce environment friendly products so that they produce less pollution and manage the natural resources in a sustainable manner. Companies need to comply with the regulations being posed to their home countries.

16.2 Concept of Green Logistics

Companies showed interest in the environmental issues by trying to transform their supply chain into a green supply chain. Since logistics is a part of the supply chain, companies are also focused on exploiting concepts of green logistics management. Traditional companies were just attentive on producing goods and services and store in warehouses without paying attention to efficiency and pollution. Environmentally aware companies applied concepts of green logistics management. One concept is focused on the environmental performance and the other on operational performance. Environmental performance is related to the reduction in emissions, pollution and waste incurred from the logistical process.

One way to improve the environmental performance that has been applied in several companies is reverse logistics. This concept was opening new logistical markets and reduces the costs of the production process. It is focused on getting back waste materials from customers to recycle it and re-use it in the production process. This concept fits in the thoughts of green logistics because its logistical system is totally focused on avoiding pollution by being environmentally aware and disposal of waste. To be effective the transportation industry should become green as well to improve the environmental performance. Many concepts in this industry have been developed to make this logistic system green as well. In the airfreight industries a new idea has developed.

It tries to look for alternative fuels and stop pollution by using oil. The industry is now using bio-fuel for the airplanes which is less harmful for the environment and reduces a waste product from other activities. By this way airlines and airfreight is getting less polluting. Land logistics is getting more environmentally friendly by using less polluting electric and hybrid engines in the trucks and train companies negotiate with electricity companies to use green energy as one of the power sources for the trains. Operational performance is related with the product development and delivery. Packaging is an example of operational performance. Environmentally aware companies have developed new ways of packaging their products such that production process became more environmentally friendly and the delivery of products could be more efficient.

Quiz

- Recall your daily activities. Are there any activities that concern environment issues? How do you help the environment? Any commitments you make towards to it?
- Where improvements could be made?
- Can you think of any companies that carry out green marketing for their brands?

16.3 Sustainability and Resource depletion

Sustainability

The words 'sustainable' and 'sustainability' are heard almost every day. What do they mean exactly? Sustainability is very important in green

SCM. There is no single universally agreed definition on what it means but it may refer to the ability or capacity of something to be maintained. The idea was originated from the sustainable development concept which became common language at the World's first Earth Summit in Rio in 1992.

The original definition of sustainable development is usually considered to be:

> "Development that meets the needs of the present without compromising the ability of future generations to meet their own needs."
>
> Bruntland Report for the World Commission on Environment and Development (1992)

Sustainability is easily found in Economics. It simply argues that since the natural resources are limited the current generations should not use up all the available resources and leave some behind for the next generations. This idea is also applied to the green SCM. Supply chain sustainability is a business issue affecting their supply chain in terms of environment and waste reduction for instance. Traditionally, the challenges businesses faced were included lowering costs, ensuring they deliver JIT to their customers, maximizing profits for their organizations. However, the increasing concerns on the environment have changed the patterns of challenges. Besides, the growing pressure from consumers for eco-friendly products has led many businesses to look for and adopt sustainable supply chains.

Sustainability of course includes caring for environment but there are other key issues in international supply chain sustainability. Working condition has ranked in the first place which is followed by environment and green issues.

In the past, 'caring about the environment' was simply a nice thing to do. But this no longer makes sense in that way. Companies who have failed to manage issues related to the environment and even in social exposed themselves to huge risks. There are few good examples which support this argument.

1) Nike

Nike was accused of hiring child labor in 1996. Children were employed to work in overseas factories and this was publicly criticized until 1998. They had to come up with significant plans to improve their working conditions at supplier factories. The damage Nike received in that year was so severe that it took them a good length of year until the brand image recovery took a place.

2) Apple

Apple's case was another famous story in this century. They were criticized for a lack of transparency in their supply chains. Their poor working conditions such as not paying a minimum wage to their workers and environmental standards were exposed in 2008 but this once again was faced in 2011. Their image has been damaged and it will take some time to recover from it.

Resource depletion

All the living beings largely depend on natural resources for survivals. This may include for food, generating energy and protections. Using natural resources have always been on a main issue as they are limited. The current consumption patterns tell us that they are being used at an unprecedented rate and thus, they are faced with risk of becoming irreversibly depleted.

Resource depletion hence refers to the reduction of natural resources such as trees and minerals. There are many reasons for such depletion. One of the main causes is due to the increasing use by people. Over the last century or perhaps even before that, humans have become very efficient in extracting the earth's resources. For example, mining for gold and cutting tress to build houses and buildings. Such activities produce pollution and also cause deforestation as they remove tress to increase the land usages for human activities. Of course these activities have to be carried out for survivals but, the problem is that people are acting beyond consideration for the environment. Natural disasters can of course be one of the causes as well but, technological development has largely contributed to the resource depletion. Resource depletion can also contribute to climate change and other damages to earth's atmosphere. That is why it is important to tackle problems related to the global warming. It is vital that people realize the importance living together.

More causes of resource depletion

Population growth

The population growth and natural resource usage tend to move in the same directions. As the number of population grows the depletion of natural resource will also increase. This is because of the necessary activities of human kinds. As long as humans alive he will continuously demand resources from the environment for his comforts. Natural resources will eventually face scarcity as the population grows.

Over consumption

In Economics, they distinguish need and want from one another. While need refers to the objects that are required for survivals such as food, clothes and houses want refers to those people consume for pleasure. This may include jewelries and cars which people can live without. As this type of consumption increases the natural resources disappear even at a faster speed. Moreover, the use of cars increases the use of petrol and gas. If consumption on these goods increases they will disappear from the world.

Quiz

- What is depletion of resources?
- Can you think of any other causes of resource depletion?
- Why may the effects of natural resource depletion be drastic?

16.4 Kyoto Protocol

As the environment-related issues become severe the world has realized the importance of having to take care of the matters more in depth. One of the efforts that have been made is the Kyoto Protocol. The Kyoto protocol was the first agreement established between industrialized nations to mandate reductions in greenhouse gas emissions. Kyoto emerged from the UN Framework Convention on Climate Change (UNFCCC). Having been finalized in Kyoto, Japan in 1997 it went into force in 2005. It was after years of negotiation being carried out. The purpose of this agreement was to stabilize greenhouse gas emissions at an acceptable level. In other words, to prevent nations from producing carbon emissions that would harm the earth. It was thought that some level of pressure had to be placed for the good of everyone living on the earth. The EU has been at the forefront of international efforts. They have long been a driving force in international negotiations on climate change and were instrumental in the development of the Kyoto Protocol.

The Kyoto Protocol Mechanisms

One of the characteristics of the Kyoto Protocol is that it has three mechanisms involved under the treaty. This mechanism allows countries and companies to buy, generate, or trade emission credits. This is known as International Emissions Trading Scheme. This scheme is the world's biggest scheme for trading greenhouse gas emissions allowances. The idea of this scheme is straightforward. Certain level of emissions is allowed for companies. They need to measure and report the carbon emissions in order to see whether they have exceeded the allowance usage or not. Those who have left with the allowance can sell the remaining while credits can be bought from other industrialized countries those who have exceeded their reduction targets.

Quiz

- What is Kyoto protocol? What do you understand by it?
- Do you know the key facts about Kyoto targets?
- What Kyoto targets does the EU have?
- What is a Kyoto target?
- How can a country achieve its target?
- Why do we need to achieve this target?

ARTICLE

Businesses object to carbon trading introduction

Companies are strongly protesting the government's plan to introduce a greenhouse gas emissions trading system. Analysts say the government should take into account diverse factors instead of just pushing the plan forward.

The Ministry of Environment announced that the country will start the emissions rights trading on the Korea Exchange from 2015. The ministry will set quotas for energy-intensive businesses, and those successfully cutting emissions can sell the remaining rights to those failing to meet their obligations. Gas emissions trading dates back to the Kyoto Protocol, which set the obligation for developed countries to cut them.

However, the Kyoto Protocol was essentially cancelled in 2011 after major gas emitters abandoned it. Instead, the issue was discussed under a new climate change regime, which included developing countries as well as developed countries. As a result, only 38 countries, including the 28 EU countries, New Zealand, Switzerland and Kazakhstan are implementing the greenhouse gas cut obligations.

Germany is the only country with a huge manufacturing industry that is adhering to the old scheme. Korea was given developing country status in the Kyoto Protocol, but it has been pushing for cuts especially after the inauguration of former President Lee Myung-bak who pushed "green growth" as the country's vision.

The ministry recently announced a plan to cap total gas emissions by large businesses at 1.64 billion tons by 2017. It aims at cutting emissions by 30% by 2020 compared with the BAU (business as usual), or the amount estimated without additional efforts to cut emissions. Business groups represented by the Federation of Korean Industries (FKI), however, announced in a joint statement that the government plan will eat into their corporate competitiveness, placing excessive burdens on them. They said that it will cost them 28.5 trillion won over the next three years to meet conditions under the plan; and nearly 6 trillion won to buy emissions rights.

If firms fail to cut emissions and there are too few rights trading in the market, they will have to pay fines. Then, the cost could snowball to nearly 30 trillion won. The FKI said this would lead to companies relocating factories overseas, raise electricity prices due to the costs to power companies, and layoffs.

"Countries that emit most of the gas, like China, the United States, and Japan, aren't implementing the scheme ... Korea, which is responsible for only 1.8percent of the gas emissions, has no reason to lead in emissions trading," the FKI said. China emits 28.6percent of the world's greenhouse gases, the United States 15.1percent and Japan 3.8percent .

"The trading system will be effective in greenhouse gas cuts only when it is implemented with major gas emitting countries like China and the United States," it added, demanding the government review its plan.

The ministry, however, said the FKI was overestimating the costs. It added that emissions rights transactions have been implemented in some provinces of China and the United States. "China plans to adopt it nationwide from 2016," said Park Ryun-min, a ministry official.

He explained that compared with other plans for gas cuts such as a carbon tax, rights transaction lessens the burden on businesses. "It will work as an incentive for them to develop new technologies, transforming the industrial structure to low-carbon. It will create jobs and contribute to economic growth."

He said that the EU succeeded in cutting more gas than their target thanks to the transaction scheme. "It is the best scheme based on the market ... Some adopted carbon tax, but the problem here is that it places a burden on the public."

Do Eun-jin, a researcher at the LG Economic Research Institute, said the government should understand why businesses are unhappy with the plan. "The industries that emit gas most are steel, petrochemicals and cement, and most of the companies have to compete globally. They fear that costs will rise," he said. Too strict regulation may tempt them to relocate their production facilities overseas.

He pointed out that while the transactions scheme is based on market mechanisms, it may fail sometimes. If the economy turns sluggish, for instance, companies that failed in management and thus slashed production can get a windfall profit by selling emissions rights.

"The government plans to set a quota (for each company) this year, but it is yet to be seen whether it will be done rationally. Setting the quota is most crucial," he said.

Source : The Korea Times, June 4, 2014

Review

Businesses resist carbon trading

The Ministry of Environment announced that South Korea will begin the trading of rights emissions on the Korea Exchange from next year. However, many companies are strongly protesting this plan. Experts criticize the government's hasty introduction of the plan, saying that more factors need to be accounted for before such a plan can be adopted. The way that the plan will work is that the ministry will set quotas for businesses that use lots of energy and businesses that successfully cut their emissions can sell their extra "credits" to those who are failing to meet their obligations under law.

The idea of gas trading comes from the Kyoto Protocol, which called for developed nations to cut their emissions. However, the Kyoto Protocol was abandoned in 2011 when key carbon emitting countries refused to sign it. Instead, the idea rolled over in the wake of climate change talks, which included all nations and not just developed ones. Consequently, only 38 countries are pursuing carbon-emission cutting.

South Korea was designated as a "developing country" in the Kyoto Protocol, but it has been pursuing "green growth" since President Lee Myungbak. South Korea intends to cap total gas emissions by 1.64 billion tons by 2017. Furthermore, it plans to reduce emissions by 30% by 2020 compared to if they weren't making any effort at all.

Companies criticize this plan by South Korean officials as they state that it would hurt their bottom line and hinder their competitiveness in the market. They even state that it would cost them 28.5 trillion won over the next 3 years to make the necessary changes to meet the minimum conditions of the plan. Additionally, nearly 6 trillion won would need to be used to buy emission rights from others to meet requirements.

If companies fail to meet the requirements or fail to buy enough credits, they will be susceptible to fines of up to 30 trillion won. The result could mean that factories would relocate overseas and the cost of power would rise.

One criticism of this new campaign is that South Korea only contributes to 1.8% of the world's gas emissions, while places like China, the USA, and Japan produce 28.6%, 15.1%, and 3.8% respectively. The trading system will only work and make an impact if the major emitters are on board. Without their participation, there is little incentive for other countries to follow through with their commitments to reducing green house emissions. However, some regions of the USA and China have started to adapt similar trading schemes for their emissions. Some experts say that it will lessen the burden on businesses and work as an incentive for them to develop new technologies which in turn will create new jobs and fuel economic growth in the green sector.

In Europe the trading scheme has been found to be successful. The scheme has been praised as the best on the market, yet the problem is that it places a burden on the public. Furthermore, the industries that are most unhappy with this scheme are steel, petrochemicals, and cement. As these companies must compete on a global scale, competition is fierce and any increase in cost can encourage them to relocate their facilities overseas. This scheme can also create a secondary market for the trading of emission credits during a slow economic year. The government is setting the quotas for each company this year, and the most important part is to see whether they are done fairly and rationally. The quota is the most crucial number in this game.

Question

- Clearly describe and illustrate an example of how carbon trading works using companies and situations. Use a chart or graph in your explanation.
- What are some possible pitfalls of carbon trading scheme?

16.5 ISO 9000 and ISO 14000

The International Organization of Standardization (ISO) is a worldwide federation whose aim is to develop international manufacturing, trade and communication standards. They enhance international trade by making industries more efficient and breaking down trade barriers. This becomes possible since their international standards help reassure consumers that products are safe and good for the environment.

International standards are important strategic tools and guidelines which can be used to help industries to tackle the challenges they face in modern business. Under these standards, the firms' productivity is likely to increase.

Other benefits may be obtained through such international standards and these include:

Cost may be saved

Having international standards may help optimize operations (eg. through increased productivity) and thus help reduce the costs

Customer satisfaction is likely to increase

The importance of ISO 9000 lies on the quality. Since the international standards help to improve the products' quality it will in turn increase the customer satisfaction which will lead to increased level of sales

Access to new markets

International standards allow open access to the global markets as they prevent trade barriers. Companies obtain better opportunities to extend their business fields.

Increased market share

One of the biggest advantages of the international standards is that it encourages the abilities of production. In other words, productivity increases as a result of operation optimization. When productivity increases it makes the products more competitive. Firms are likely to obtain competitive advantage in the global markets.

Environmental benefits

Environmental benefits are very important in this regard. International standards may help reduce or eliminate negative environmental effects. This may attract consumers who greatly care about the environment.

ISO 9000

ISO 9000 is a series of standards which was developed by the ISO. It deals with quality management systems and is one of the most recognized series in the world. The importance of ISO 9000 is the importance of quality. While companies offer their own products and services it is still their responsibilities to make those products and services as best and efficiently as possible.

There are numerous benefits businesses may obtain through the ISO 9000 quality management system. For example, profits and customer satisfaction may increase through reduced waste and rework, improved problem tracking and resolution and better supplier relations.

- This standard makes sure of products' quality. Hence, quality will be maintained.
- Companies will have better chances of extending its businesses to the global market. They will have opportunity to compete with larger businesses.
- Customer satisfaction is very important. Hence, companies will spend good amount of time for their customers.
- The international standards prove and confirm the products' quality. This will leave a strong remark to the customers. Sales will likely to increase.
- Good quality of products in turn will increase the customer satisfaction. This will be a great benefit to businesses.

It is now common for companies to implement the ISO 9000 standards for their products. Besides, it is not only the businesses who have realized the importance of these international standards. The customers today have recognized the importance of quality as much as the businesses have. As customers' one of their priorities start to lie on the quality businesses cannot ignore these changes because they are the most important source to the businesses. ISO 9000 enhances businesses to focus on the quality as a result.

ISO 14000

ISO 14000 is published in order to reduce environmental damages and industrial wastes. The standards are practical tools for businesses who realize the importance of implementing these standards as a way to care about the environment and bring benefits to themselves at the same time. Thus, the ultimate goal of these guidelines is to promote useful tools to organizations to reduce negative environmental effects and manage the environment in a sustainable manner.

The main difference between ISO 9000 and ISO 14000 is that ISO 9000 cares for the quality by achieving control of processes and encouraging continuous improvements in the area while ISO 14000 cares for the environments. There are of course some overlaps and similarities between these two types of standards. Both use the same fundamental systems such as document controls and management policies as well as trainings. Besides, both of them also require organizations to provide on-going management reviews of the management systems and their objectives.

However, differences also exist between the two. The ISO 9000 international standards have been designed in order to fulfill the customer requirements. This means they need to satisfy the customers' expectations on their products' quality. Therefore, the businesses processes for those who have implemented these standards vary from design to development. On the other hand, the ISO 14000 standards require achieving more than what the ISO 9000 does. Those businesses who have implemented the ISO 14000 need to satisfy their customers as well as satisfying external stakeholders such as local regulators in meeting environmental expectations.

Operational Benefits

- Efficiency, discipline and operational integration with ISO 9000
- Standards may allow businesses to obtain operational permits and authorizations more easily than before
- It may assist in developing and transferring technology within the company
- Fewer operating costs
- Safer working conditions including workplace will be provided and savings could be made as a result
- Changes in processes lead to improvement in products
- Since the environmental effects have been taken into account the standards allow businesses to produce safer goods for their customers

Environmental Benefits

- The standards reduce or eliminate both hazardous and non-hazardous wastes
- Since it cares for the environment most it prevents pollution and reduces wastage

Quiz

- What is ISO 9000 standard?
- What is ISO 14000 standard?
- What is the main difference between ISO 9000 and ISO 14000?
- What can you tell more about each standard?

Notes

- http://www.carlsonschool.umn.edu/assets/140554.pdf Page 393
- Lai & Wong, 2012, http://www.sciencedirect.com/science/article/pii/S0305048311001046
- Lai & Wong, 2012, http://www.sciencedirect.com/science/article/pii/S0305048311001046 Page 1663
- Rodrigue et al, 2001, p.2, http://people.hofstra.edu/jean-paul_rodrigue/cownloads/Green%20Logistics.pdf Page 2
- KLM, 2011, http://www.klm.com/csr/en/climate/footprint/biofuels/index.html
- Lai & Wong, 2012, http://www.sciencedirect.com/science/article/pii/S0305048311001046
- Viadiu, F.M., Fa, M.C. and Saizarbitoria, I.H. (2006), ISO 9000 and ISO 14000 standards: an international diffusion model, International journal of operations and production management, Vol. 26, No. 2. pp. 141-165.
- http://www.smacna.org/management/ISO914.htm
- Steer, A. (2013), Resource depletion, climate change and economic growth, Working paper 5, Global Citizen Foundation.
- United Nations Framework Convention on Climate Change (2008), Kyoto Protocol Reference Manual on Accounting of Emissions and Assigned Amount.

CASE STUDY

Efforts Toward Implementing Green SCM

CASE STUDY 1

General Motors Green Supply Chain Management

General Motors is one of the world's largest automotive companies with over 100 years of history. Its operations span over 120 countries worldwide producing ten brands (Chevrolet, Buick, GMC, Cadillac, Holden, Opel, Vauxhall, Wuling, Baojun, Jie Fang, UzDaewoo). With over 200,000 employees worldwide, GM has been the number one global automobile selling company for 77 consecutive years from 1931 to 2007. Due to its size and selling power, GM supply chain's environmental impacts can be significant to the global environment. GM's efforts and commitment to reduce negative environmental impacts are setting world precedent in suitability efforts. GM is famous for implementing green efforts throughout the supply chain, but below show 4 sectors-supplier selection, manufacturing, resource, and water management- in particular where GM is making a difference.

Supplier Selection

The modern business world requires competitiveness in almost every field and there is no exception in selecting suppliers. For businesses, both developing the existing suppliers and discovering the new suppliers are critically important.

Supplier selection refers to the process which firms identify, evaluate, and contract with suppliers. The supplier selection process deploys a tremendous amount of a firm's financial resources. In return, firms expect significant benefits from contracting with suppliers offering high value. Organizations may consider to select suppliers under a number of situations. It could be as a result of having problems with the current suppliers or simply because they are reaching the end of contract with the current suppliers. GM shows a good example of applying supplier selection to enforce environmental requirements.

GM is requiring their suppliers to be certified and conform to ISO 14001. ISO 14001 is an internationally recognized framework (set of criteria) companies can follow to establish an effective environmental management system. It assures a company is 'environmentally conscious' and its environmental impact is being measured and efforts toward improving it are in effect. ISO 14001 is mainly concerned with natural resources, waste handling and treatment, and energy consumption. By requiring GM's supplier base to comply with international standards, GM can ensure that their parts or products are eco-friendly and effectively reduce products' carbon footprint. Also in order to encourage supplier's environmental stewardship, GM gives out several awards to suppliers who demonstrate environment friendly practices. Environmental Excellence Award is handed out annually to "recognize a supplier that supports our (GM) environmental initiatives, exhibits transparency in its environmental performance and/or brings new technologies to us (GM) that improve environmental performance of our (GM) facilities or product". There are many other awards such as GM Overdrive awards and Supplier of the Year that encourages suppliers to join GM in their sustainability efforts. ISO 14001 is not just a requirement for suppliers but also for all GM owned or affiliated operations. In order to comply with international environmental standards while maximizing production, all GM owned and associated manufacturing and service facilities have implemented Environmental Management System (EMS) which is a combination of elements from ISO 14001 and elements that are specific to GM operations. According to GM's sustainability report, EMS is "an overarching management system designed to drive a continuous performance improvement cycle in line with legal requirements, site-specific objectives and targets, and corporate and sector polices and strategies". GM requires all operations across the world to implement a common EMS so environmental performances can be compared and best practices can be shared for improvement.

GM has always emphasized the importance of cooperating with its suppliers to maximize results. Best practice of incorporating suppliers to reduce their environmental impacts, increase productivity and generate saving is Shanghai General Motors (SGM) partnering up with World Environment Center (WEC) for "Greening the Supply Chain Initiative" project. The project's goal was to facilitate sustainable growth throughout SGM's national supply chain by cooperating with suppliers to reduce negative environmental impacts. This 50 to 50 joint venture targeted 125 suppliers to reduce water, waste, energy while improving supplier's competitive advantage. 125 suppliers invested $21 million USD over 498 projects. The economical and environmental results were very impressive. This supplier cooperation led to $19 million annual costs savings, avoided 55,400 tons of GHG emissions in 2009, reduced 9,300 tons of solid waste and 137,000 kiloliters of liquid waste annually, and reduced water usage by 1,070,700 tons. SGM also reported that the project led to reduced risk to human health and environment, stronger relationship with supplier and customers and supplier's increased ability to adapt to evolving government's requirements.

Reducing Energy Use and Emissions in Manufacturing Process

GM is one of the leading companies in the world that focuses both on reducing GHG reduction and increasing the use of renewable energy.

While many operations consume energy, manufacturing is the most carbon intensive activity and efforts to reduce GHG emissions and promote renewable energy proved to be significant. GM is committed to reducing energy and carbon intensity by 20% and doubling the use of renewable energy by 2020 in manufacturing facilities. In 2012, energy efficiency increased 2% compared to 2011 figures and carbon emission intensity decreased by 2%. This was due to energy saving initiatives and investments in renewable energy. Renewable energy efforts include utilizing landfill gases and installment of renewable energy facilities-3MW solar project in South Korea assembly plant which will lead to reduction in carbon emissions by 2,400 metric tons anuually. GM is the number one automobile company in the U.S. that utilizes solar power in manufacturing operations. 30MW solar power is installed in the U.S. alone and plans to double its capacity by 2015. GM promises to install an additional 125 MW capacity of renewable energy by 2020. Energy saving initiatives in 2012 include; implementation of advanced energy monitoring system in Thailand which allows control of real-time energy consumption, new lighting system in Talegaon (India), energy conservation projects in South Korea leading to $820,000 annual savings and LED lamps powered by solar panels in Ecuador. GM encourages employees to join the efforts towards saving energy. An employee can receive up to $20,000 when his or her idea leads to power saving measures. Also GM holds cross functional energy workshops to facilitate energy saving ideas.

U.S Environmental Protection Agency (EPA) has recognized GM's efforts towards greening their supply chain and awarded GM with the 2013 Energy Star Partner of the Year award. It is the highest acknowledgment for an energy efficient corporation. GM has a total of 54 facilities that meets EPA's Energy Star Change requirements. All plants on average, have reduced energy usage by 26% produces 35% less GHG emissions and energy compared to other similar buildings, and saved a total of $90 million energy costs. Graphs below show accomplishments of GM's efforts.

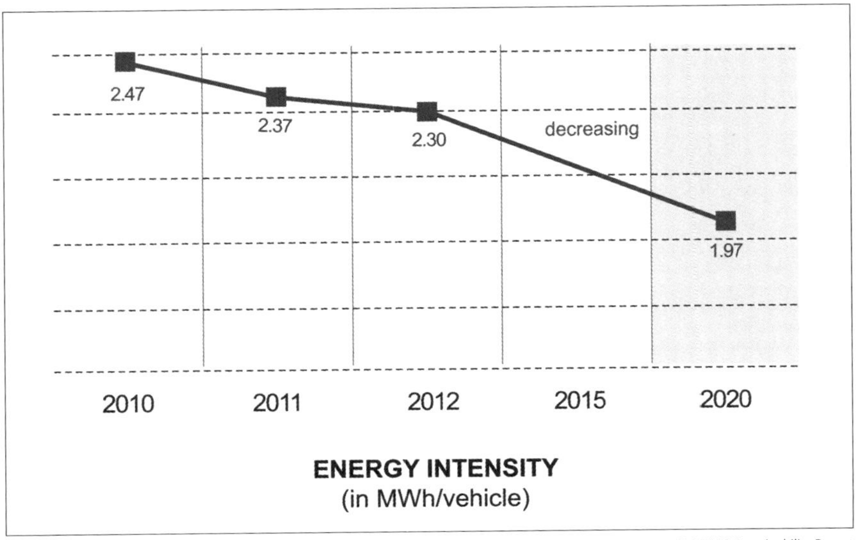

Source: GM 2012 Sustainability Report

Figure 1 Decrease in Energy Intensity

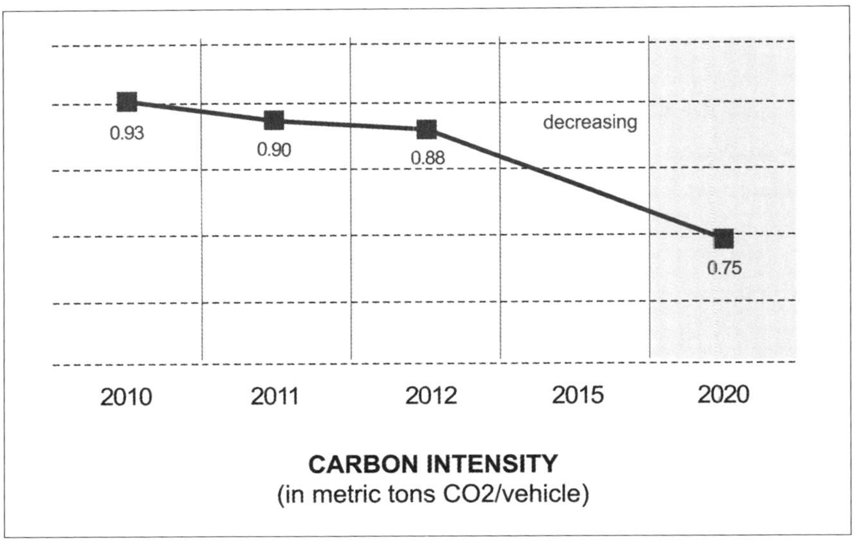

Source: GM 2012 Sustainability Report

Figure 2 Decrease in Carbon Intensity

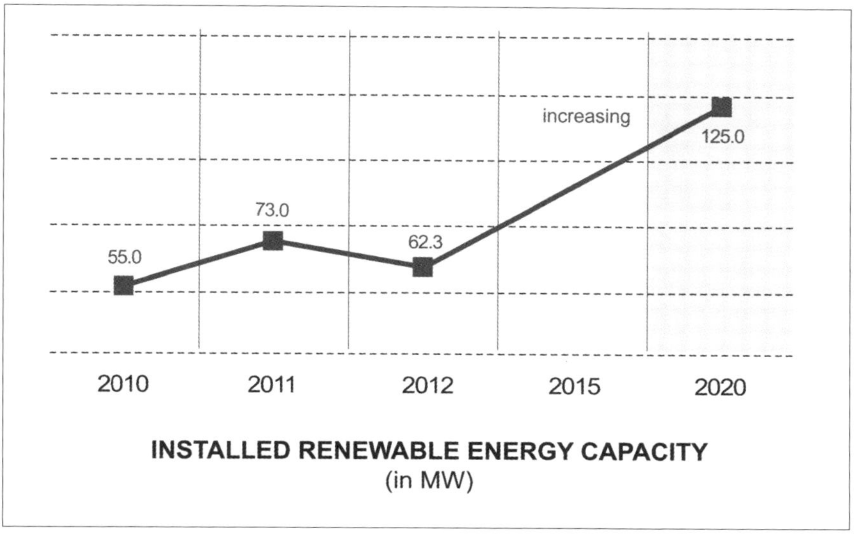

Source: GM 2012 Sustainability Report

Figure 3 Installed Renewable Energy Capacity

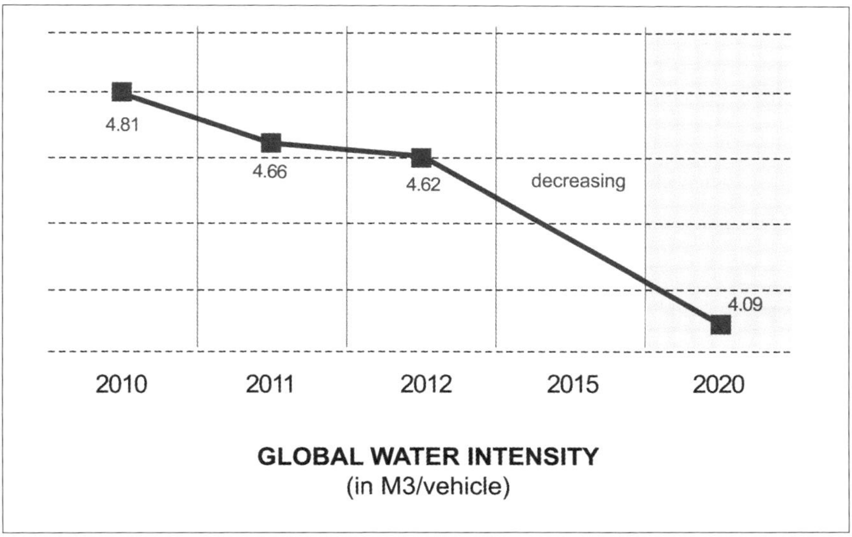

Source: GM 2012 Sustainability Report

Figure 4 Water Consumption per Vehicle Built

Water Management

Water scarcity affects 1.2 billion people as of today and has been named the number one risk by many reports. GM's manufacturing (paint shops and casting plants) accounts for 85% of water usage and GM is committed to reducing 15% (2010 baseline) of water usage by 2020. During 2012, water usage decreased by 4%. This was achieved by localizing water management policy in order to meet with local resource conditions and regulations and incorporating best practices into building designs. Water management is done at the individual facility level where local managers best equipped with local knowledge can make the most effective decisions. General tactics to minimize water withdrawals include water reuse from condensation or treated wastewater and harvesting rainwater. San Luis Potosi plant in Mexico is reusing 90% of wastewater after cleaning process. This effort results in saving approximately 264 gallons of water per vehicle. Also Drayton warehouse in Michigan transformed 6 acre gravel parking lot into wetland to store storm water.

Quiz

- Why is supplier selection important to an organization?
- What are the likely consequences of having the incorrect suppliers?
- What should be considered when discovering a new supplier?

Notes

- Practical Solutions for Economic and Environmental Vitality, http://www.pprc.org/pubs/grnchain/casestud.cfm (accessed on January 29th 2014)
- GM (2012), "GM 2012 Sustainability Report; Charging Ahead When Customers Drive Sustainability"
- GM (2011), "Sustainability in Motion; General Motors Sustainability Report"
- Terry F. Yosie (2010) "SGM-WEC Partnership in Greening the Supply Chain:2009-2010 Project Results", World Environment Center

CASE STUDY 2

Green Logistics (packaging) on Heineken

Applications of green logistics

The Dutch beer company, Heineken, is well-known for having built a strategic mission of being more eco-friendly and continuously focusing on reducing the environmental impact of their products. The company applied the green logistics management in their supply chain by identifying where potential improvements could be made. According to Heinekens' sustainability report, they focused on many elements to become green. It focused on inbound and outbound logistics, packaging and the logistics of their human resources.

Packaging

Heineken by developing new packaging methods for their products the production processes have become more environment friendly and at the same time the delivery of products have become more efficient as well. Although packaging is a way to express their brand name and value it was also a big part of their carbon footprint and part of polluting factors. In turn, Heineken renewed their packaging policy during the second half of 2012. This policy tried to maintain the quality and the brand value on packaging, but tried to lower the environmental costs that packaging brings with it. This included the whole lifecycle of the product, from production to recycling. As a member of the European Organization for Packaging and the Environment (EUROPEN), Heineken strives to meet the terms EUROPEN stands for: "Packaging exists to deliver products to consumers in perfect condition. Well-designed packaging meets the requirements of the product while minimizing economic and environmental impacts of both the product and its package." Good packaging uses only as much of the right kind of material as necessary to perform this task.

Saving material eases pressure on the environment because of less transport costs and less materials needed. But, this also leads to cost reduction, less material is one of the main measures that Heineken uses with their packaging. Product loss however increases when reducing packaging. "Beyond a certain point of reducing packaging the increase in product loss exceeds the savings from the use of less packaging material. Any reduction in packaging beyond that point is a false economy, since the total amount of waste in the system increases."

To accomplish improvement of packaging regarding the material, Heineken introduced a tool to review the recyclability and weight of the material used in the design process and already implemented this with up to 90% of the production of their product. Next to that, all people involved in the production process becomes trained/educated in these tools. To search for improvements, together with their suppliers of glass, can and other materials, Heineken uses "environmental scoring cards" to collect data on the performance and durability of the material. Together with research agencies they try to look into the chemical process in production of the packaging and try to determine factors that can undermine the recycling phase or chemicals that inflict the environment badly. All in all, in cooperation with their packaging suppliers Heineken tries to reduce materials used, use more recycled materials, try to monitor the improvements: weight of packaging, the amount of material recovery after recycling and average produced carbon per product. Recycling goes in cooperation with the consumer, to recover and recollect used products efficiently after use.

Heineken puts a lot of effort in being green in their distribution of their finished products. The transportation industry is crucial to Heineken when delivering the beer products to different destinations all over the world. Heineken was aware that this industry was polluting and came up with their green distribution program. It includes different ideas to reduce the CO_2 production of trucks used to deliver the beer. One initiative was an e-learning module for the logistics and distribution team. This module made the teams to become aware of how they could apply green logistics management in their daily activities for the firm. Furthermore, it came up with the idea of making an efficient framework such that logistical teams had a method to reduce CO_2 via analysing distance driven, fuel consumed and transport mode used. With this framework Heineken could calculate how much CO_2 they produced per product and how to be more efficient with their freights. Besides these efficient ideas, Heineken also replaced 34 trucks, responsible for distribution in the Netherlands, equipped with more efficient engines. It is also testing electric trucks to deliver the beer product in the areas around Amsterdam. The electricity needed for the trucks is planned to been generated by the distribution centre in Amsterdam where the company would like to use green energy gained from solar cells.

Moreover, Heinekens' production process includes the application of reverse logistics. Heineken sells most of its products in returnable packaging materials; this includes bottles, crates and barrels. The bottles of beer which are empty have to be delivered back together with the crates to the Heineken production plants. For this process, Heineken needs to use the transportation industry again. Besides the measures, Heineken came up with an idea to make the trucks more environment friendly. They need to know how often the trucks need to pick up empty crates with bottles at the local markets. To be more efficient with the use of the trucks and get information about the circulation of returnable crates and bottles in the market, Heineken invented the Chip 'n Crate. The company came up with a chip to be placed in every crate they produce to get information about the location of the crates. This invention gives Heineken all the information about the time a crate takes from production to the market and its return to production plants. With this information the company is able to apply their reverse logistics strategy in the most efficient way. Another advantage of using the system is that it is easier to identify broken crates because the chip cannot be read anymore. When broken crates are identified at the return at the production plant, Heineken sends them to the crate producer which recycles the crate. It is an example how information systems can be used to make support green logistics in the supply chain.

Before the beer is finally delivered to the customer, it has to be stored at local stores, restaurants and other catering industries. The beer is stored in small fridges. Heineken mostly owns all the fridges where the beer is stored in. Since Heineken is responsible for this form of warehousing it has tried to transform it as well to get it more environment friendly. Heineken replaced all the old fridges with new ones which use 15% less energy.

Non output related green logistics

Not only logistics in terms of the product are involved. Heineken also involves green logistics in commuting and business travel in the Netherlands. They try to realize this by using green energy-label cars and lease-cars to reduce CO_2 emission. The Head office in Amsterdam uses an electric taxi service and saves energy and reduces CO_2 emission with it as well.

Ultimately, since 2012 Heineken co-funds the 'Future Fuel Programme' in cooperation with KLM Airline Company. This programme helps to develop sustainable biofuel. This "bio-kerosene" is made of cooking oil which not harms the environment. Next to co-funding this, part of Heineken's business travel and staff flights are done by the bio-fuel programme.

Notes

- http://www.sustainabilityreport.heineken.com/improve/green-commerce/distribution.html
- http://download.springer.com/static/pdf/567/chp%253A10.1007%252F3-540-27251-8_4.pdf?auth66=1382447730_d7fe6395528a056d91cb0ff5e50a3687&ext=.pdf
- http://www.sustainabilityreport.heineken.com/improve/green-commerce/cooling.html
- http://www.sustainabilityreport.heineken.com/improve/green-commerce/packaging.html
- http://www.europen-packaging.eu/
- http://www.sustainabilityreport.heineken.com
- http://www.sustainabilityreport.heineken.com/improve/green-commerce/distribution.html

CASE STUDY 3

Corporation's Adaptation to Climate Change Related Natural Disasters: Embedding Resiliency in Supply Chain

In 2011 Japan was hit hard by earthquakes and tsunamis leaving major damages. The earthquake left Japan's infrastructure (building, roads, homes, factories) in the ruins. At least 46,027 buildings were destroyed and Fukushima nuclear power plant was among one of them. Damages to the nuclear power plant led to additional damages which will haunt Japan for decades to come. 15,828 deaths were officially confirmed while 3,760 people are still missing. 2011 Japan earthquake is recorded as the biggest natural disaster catastrophe in the world with an economic loss of $300 billion. Global corporations with production or manufacturing facilities in Japan were severely affected. Leading automakers such as Toyota, Honda, Nissan, Mitsubishi, Mazda, Subaru and Suzuki experienced economic loss due to disruptions in production and damages in inventory. The world largest automaker Toyota was hit the hardest and lost its world leader position. It took 6 months to fully recover to its normal operations and the delay of two models resulted in over 140,000 vehicle production loss and 30% fall in profits. Even within a decade, many other natural disasters which caused major social problems, economic loss, and disruptions to corporations easily come to mind; tropical cyclone in Myanmar in 2008, flood in the UK in 2007 which destroyed $8billion in economic value, US Hurricane Katrina in 2005 which resulted in over 1,000 death and $125 billion economic loss, European heat wave of 2003 with more than 35,000 fatalities and 2011 Thailand flood with 815 fatalities and $45.7 billion in damages.

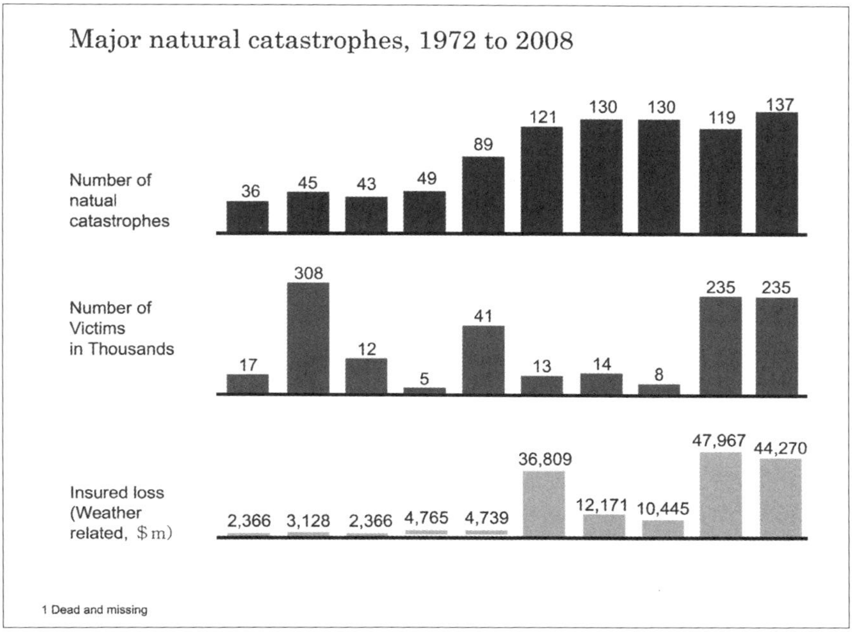

Source: ECA (2009)

Figure 1 Major Natural Catastrophes

Numerous literature shows natural disasters caused by climate change have increased in frequency and severity. According to ECA (2009), the number of natural disasters increased over the past decades and weather related natural disasters resulted in some 800,000 fatalities and over trillion dollars in economic loss over the past 50 years. World's economic loss due to weather disasters, just counting insured loss, is recorded to be about $10-50 billion a year.

Due to globalization, supply chains are becoming more complicated and wider linking different regions and players around the world. Even the smallest disruptions and complications will lead to a ripple effect. Problems will amplify and rapidly spread throughout the supply chain with major consequences effecting suppliers, producers, manufacturers, distributors and even customers. The pattern of increase in frequency and severity of natural disasters caused by climate change and the fact of increasing interconnectedness of supply chains are well acknowledged by leading global corporations.

Leading global corporations' awareness towards the importance of managing climate change risks is supported by Global Risk Survey 2012 conducted by World Economic Forum. Global Risk Survey 2012 identified 50 global risks across five categories; economic, environmental, geopolitical, societal, and technological risks. 469 experts in business, government and academic fields were asked to assess the likelihood and potential impact of each risk over the next decade. Global risk experts were mostly concerned about risks associated with severe income disparity, chronic fiscal imbalances, rising greenhouse gas emissions, cyber attacks, and water supply.

Environmental risk category includes risks from natural disasters to man-made disasters. Rising greenhouse gas emissions and failure of climate change adaptation, both closely related to climate change, were identified as risks with severe impact and a high likelihood of occurrence in the environmental risk catagory (figure 2). 'Failure of adapting to climate change' (second highest risk in the environmental risk category) is high in rank even among total risks and can be interpreted as being considered as one of the major concerns for corporations, governments, and academic experts.

Although climate change risks are less frequent than costs containment risk or most risks encountered by corporations, the severity and impact of a natural disaster caused by climate change risk are detrimental. Corporations can no longer afford to treat climate change related natural disasters as 'black swan' events that have negligible chance of happening and dismissible concerns that only affect 'other' corporations. Faced with increasing climate change risk, a framework for corporations to assess, manage, and adapt to climate change is in dire need. This chapter ex-

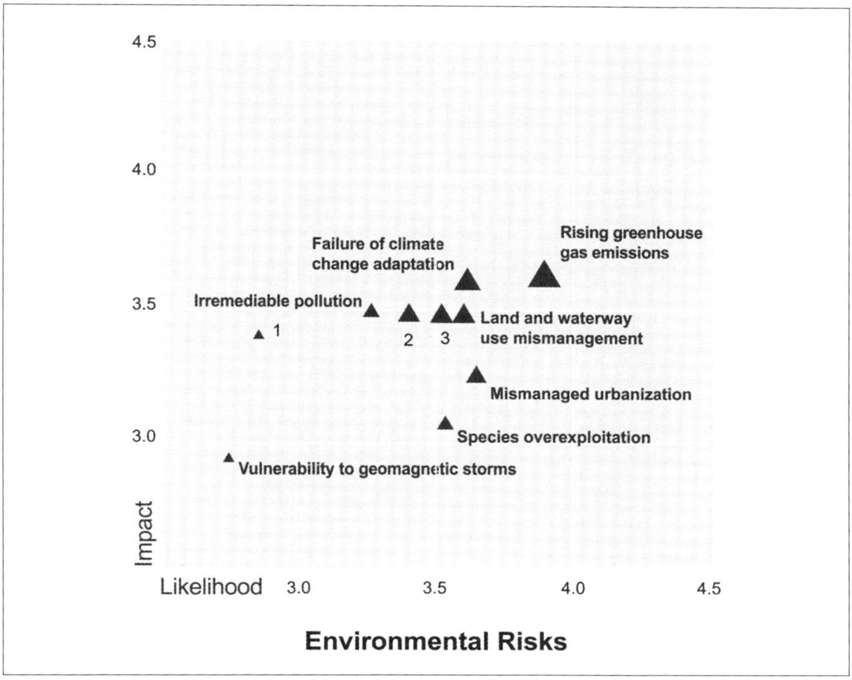

Source: World Economic Forum, 2012

Figure 2 Environmental Risks

plores best practices of adaptations to climate change related natural disasters and attempts to offer a comprehensive checklist of existing climate change related naturals disaster adaptation strategies. It starts by providing effects of climate change and how it impacts global corporation's operations and supply chain. Followed by how to manage climate change related natural disaster risks and building resiliency in the supply chain by implementing both mitigation and adaptation strategies is described. Adaptation process to climate change related naturals disaster and establishing 'climate change disruption proof' supply chain is offered.

Effects and impacts of climate change

Opponents of global warming argue any one natural disaster cannot be blamed on global warming (climate change) but many scientists predict that natural disasters will increase in frequency and intensity as global warming proceeds. Figure 3 illustrates a proportionate increase in natural disasters to rising global mean temperature.

There is no doubt of the existence of climate change and climate variation has been increasing in recent decades. In 2007, Intergovernmental Panel on Climate Change (IPCC) officially published that climate change will lead to adverse physical effects such as rise of sea level, temperature pattern variation, extreme weather events, etc.

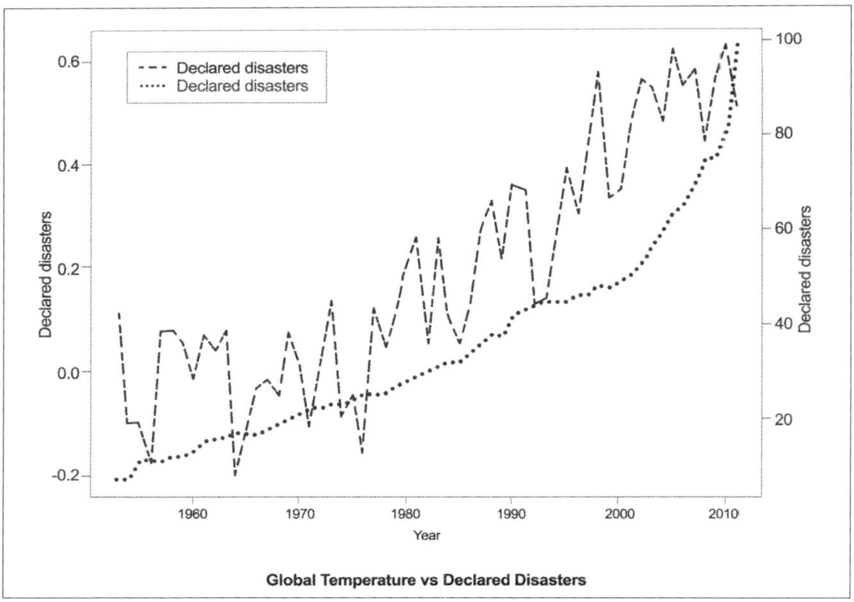

Source: created by Amstrup using data on disasters from the federal emergency management agency website in comparison with the global mean temperature anomaly

Figure 3 Comparison between declared natural disasters and global temperature

Adverse effects of climate change include:

Table 1 Climate change effects

Temperature increase • Average global warming is approximately 0.2°C per decade and expected to continue for the next two decades • Long term global warming is projected to be between 2°C to 4.5°C • Temperatures is expected to increase by 1.8—reaching 4 8C by the end of the century • Warming will result in fewer cold days and nights, and warmer and more frequent hot days and nights • Heat waves with increased frequency, intensity and duration will occur in the central European, western United States, East Asia, and South Korea region
Sea level rise • Due to thermal expansion and loss of land ice, sea levels will rise during the continuing decades • Sea level rise is estimated to rise 18 to 59 centimeters until the 21st century • Sea level rise will continue for many centuries even after greenhouse gas concentration are stabilized
Precipitation and humidity • There will be increase in wet days and precipitation in high latitudes and in subtropical areas, there will be increased dry spells • Northern Europe, Canada, northeast United States and Arctic will experience increased annual precipitation • Northern Asia and Tibetan Plateau is expecting increased winter precipitation
Extreme wind and rain storms and other events • Increase in intense tropical cyclone • Increased frequency of flash floods and large-area floods in many regions • Risk of drought in Australia, eastern New Zealand, and the Mediterranean will increase and central Europe and Central America will experience increased seasonal droughts • Increased wildfires in arid and semi-arid areas
Other related effects • Snow season length and snow depth will decrease for Europe and North America • Fewer cold days and nights

ource: IPCC, 2007

Additional to effects stated above in the table 1, the risk of species extinction will increase leading to loss of biodiversity. Catastrophic effects of climate change in longer terms, if mitigation efforts are not carried out to the fullest, include irreversible and eventual meltdown of the Greenland ice sheets, disruption of global ocean circulation system due to slowing or shutting down of Atlantic Gulf Stream and faster global warming from higher methane concentration in the atmosphere, which is caused by methane released from the ocean.

These changes will in turn affect human health, built environments, natural ecosystems, and impose tremendous stress on existing social, institutional, and legal arrangements. Climate change damages are global and do not discriminate where and who to affect. But poor developing countries will suffer the greatest since they lack the means to protect themselves.

Risks stemming from climate change

How does climate change effect business and its operations? Impacts of climate change for corporations include; limited availability of raw material and natural resources, supply chain and logistics system interruptions, higher maintenance cost, O&M cost, and product price, reduced production efficiency, varying asset values and property loss, market change, insurance premium increase, infrastructure damage, increased investment, and declining financial returns and growth. Also Current systems that business and governments rely on were built on past climate conditions before climate change and global warming became an issue. But now climate conditions have changed due to human generated adverse effects such as frequent natural disasters. Existing systems are not suitable to cope and manage the risk arising from frequent and intense natural disasters. Negative climate change impacts in the form of natural disasters in turn, become motivation and driving factors for climate change adaptation.

There are five driving factors for climate change related natural disaster adaptation and it may be anything that persuades business or governments to act. It can be any pressure, compelling information, key triggering external event, economic costs of inaction, and realizing opportunities or any other reasons. Adaptation is not caused by a single factor; instead it is a culmination of different factors that drive adaptation. It is true that driving factor is a combination of several reasons but adaptation only occurs when these reasons are perceived as risks. Climate change effects stated above (limited availability of raw material and natural resources, supply chain and logistics system interruptions, etc) all have the potential to become a risk factor to organizations, thus this risk is mitigated by adapting to climate change related natural disasters.

Organizations are in general, able to reduce their exposure to these disruptions by acquiring knowledge about them and implementing ad-

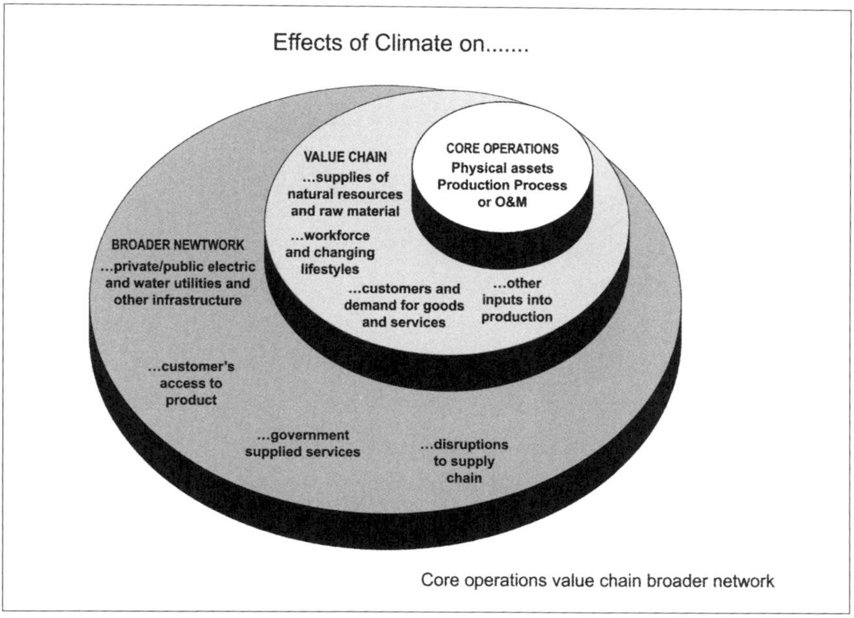

Source: Sussman and Freed, 2008

Figure 4 Risk Disk

equate adaptation measures. Also managing climate change related natural disaster risks can generate a competitive advantage. By proactively managing climate change related natural disaster risks, businesses can mitigate negative effects and at the same time turn potentially damaging uncertainties, risks, into advantages.

Physical risks of climate change that can damage businesses are classified into three categories. The concept of 'risk disk', figure 4, illustrates 3 types of physical climate change risk that business can encounter; core operation risk, value chain risk, and broader network risk.

Core operation risk is illustrated in the innermost circle and includes risk related to physical structure or assets, production process, and O&M. Climate change has direct impact on core operation risk. Extreme weather may directly damage physical structures or assets affecting asset values. Climate also directly influences the effectiveness or efficiency of production, costs of O & M, and quality of product. Value chain risk is listed in the middle and include natural resources and raw material supply, workforce and changing lifestyle, customers and demand for goods and services, and other inputs in production process. Climate change can influence the quality and quantity of products that goes into productions and raw materials supplied. Climate change has the risk of effecting workforce and the demand pattern. Broader supply and demand network risk is the outmost ring and displays risks that arise because of broader changes in the economy and infrastructure. Climate change (extreme weather conditions) can cause distribution to the supply chain which in turn influences customer's access to product. Publicly and privately owned utilities, services, and related infrastructure provide support to business operations and production processes, and to supply chains and distribution networks. Disruption to utilities, especially electricity generation, water supply, and sewerage can severely affect the supply chain.

The Importance of actively managing climate change risk and preparing for supply chain disruptions due to natural disasters are not only found in literature but practiced by leading global corporations as well. According to "The Smarter Supply Chain of the Future" by IBM in 2009, one practice that separates a 'top' global supply chain management corporation from the rest is 'managing disruption risks and disaster monitoring'. IBM asked 393 supply chain executives in 25 countries and 29 different industries to identify top 5 supply chain challenges that impact business operations. Supply chain visibility was ranked as the top challenge (70%) followed by risk management (60%), increasing customer demand (56%), cost containment (55%), and globalization (43%). Among the 393 respondents, 17 top global leaders where identified and responses from the 'top leader group' and 'remaining group' was compared. Supply chain risk management practices, ranked second in manager's challenges, include process controls in logistics and operations, compliance programs with suppliers/providers, risk management in supply chain planning, and event management to monitor disruptions. Results show 'top' global supply chain corporations actively managed disruptions risks while the rest showed little to no concern. Monitoring disruptive events and acting on disaster response simulation models was what differentiated 'top' global leaders from the rest making disruption (climate change) risk management a key component of effective and resilient supply chain.

It is suggested that only 25% of Fortune 500 companies can survive and is prepared for a $50 million-$100million loss per day when supply chain is disrupted by natural disasters. Also the time to recover period is two years in average when major supply chain failure occurs. But this is not always the case, some corporations bounce back fast with little to no damages. 9/11 caused major distribution disruptions around the world due to temporary border shutdowns and inspections. The normal lead time for garment businesses in that period was 90 days but Zara filled shelves with clothes within 5 days due to its agile supply chain. The difference is adapting to climate change related natural disasters. The following sections provide a checklist to businesses wishing to adapt to climate change related natural disasters. It will list strategies and frameworks that implement adaptation and best practices of adaptation. It is not a comprehensive framework since strategies or best practices are not applicable for every type of business due to the different nature of businesses. Also not all elements need to be applied in order for a corporation to be adapted to climate change. A corporation can satisfy only one or several recommendation and still be 'climate change ready'.

Mitigation vs Adaptation Strategies

In recent years, many organizations have set targets and mitigation strategies of measuring, controlling and reducing CO_2 and GHG and substantial research on green shipping has been done. These are all mitigation strategies for climate change which is inherently different from adaptation strategies. United Nations Framework Convention on Climate Change (UNFCCC), defines adaptation strategies to climate change as "the adjustment in natural or human systems in response to actual or expected climatic stimuli or their effects, which moderates harm or exploits beneficial opportunities". An adaptation strategy is the ability to adjust to climate change and moderate existing damages. Whereas IPCC defines mitigation strategy as "An anthropogenic intervention to reduce the source or enhance the sinks of greenhouse gases." Mitigation strategies are defined as "actions that reduce future exposure and its effect and impacts are long term (e.g. through regulations, location or technological shifts), while adaptation strategies on the contrary refers to the adjustments that population takes in response to current or predicted change." Mitigation strategies focus on cause and adaptation strategies focus on the effect of climate change. As different definitions illustrates, mitigation and adaptation can be differentiated by incentives and resulting benefits. Benefits of implementing mitigation strategies in business include, saving energy thus costs, improving environmental performance, developing new energy saving production process and gaining market advantage, etc. Benefits of implementing adaptation strategies include establishing a risk management system, saving costs due to pro-active risk preparation and measurements, gaining technological innovation which leads to competitive advantage, etc. Much effort is being made by governments and business to reduce emission and to meet Kyoto Protocol targets. Clearly, current existing literature and policy emphasizes mitigation strategies rather than adaptation strategies but only implementing mitigation strategy is not sufficient since it cannot correct the damage already done and substantial climate change is unavoidable. Also, it is evident that even if global emission reduction and mitigation efforts are carried out to the fullest, further climate change and its impacts will continue on for decades to come. In order for governments and business to be less effected by climate change, mitigation strategies (greenhouse gas reduction efforts) are not enough, thus the necessity of adaptation strategy. But implementing only adaptation strategy is also insufficient since most adaptation strategies are less effective; adaptation strategies focus on avoiding the short term negative consequences rather than eliminating global warming or climate change in the long run. Mitigation efforts mainly produce public benefits as reducing GHG emissions without having a direct benefit in doing so, adaptation mainly produces private benefits for private business. Also two strategies have different degrees of uncertainty, effectiveness and efficiency. The degree of uncertainty is higher for adaptation since climate change projections are hard to forecast as well as the magnitude of impact. Climate change continues to disrupt the supply chain (supply, production, distribution) with floods, earthquakes, hurricane, drought, tsunami, and other natural disasters. Climate related disruptions can decrease the quantity and quality of recourses, cause physical infrastructure damage, and affect the quality of products and services. Climate in the past will not be the same in the future, future climate will bring extreme weather related disasters. These weather related disasters can only be managed by implementing both mitigation and adaptation strategies.

UKTI indicates that most business acknowledges the threat of climate change but few have begun the process of building resilience in their supply chain. 90% of worldwide companies admit they have experienced climate related risks but only 30% are actively responding to climate risks. 5 types of adaptation to climate change:

- Reactive adaptation: measures which are taken after the fact, in response to climate change
- Anticipatory adaptation: takes place before climate change impacts are observed and is a deliberate measure in preparation of potential effects
- Autonomous adaptation: it is not a conscious response to climate change but spontaneous adaptation in the face of climate change
- Planned adaptation: this strategy requires conscious intervention. It stems from the awareness that climate has changed or about to change and human planning in necessary to return to its original state.
- Pro-active adaptation: building resilience by implementing both climate change mitigation and adaptation strategies which in turn produces financial benefits and strategic advantages.

Pro-active adaptation embeds resilience within the supply chain and copes with change not in terms of switching to alternative stable states but rather in terms of retaining essentially the same function, structure and therefore identity and gives options for new and creative responses. Pro-active adaptation is "climate resilience supply chain" and this can only be achieved by implementing both mitigation and adaptation strategies. Pro-active adaptation is a system wide-supply chain adaptation which addresses disruptions beyond the corporate boundaries, not limiting itself to the organization itself. Since supply chain resilience approach goes beyond corporate boundaries it can consider supplier's, production's, and distribution's climate risk as well. It has the ability to analyze vulnerability of climate for each link and identify hotspots for risks across the whole supply chain, asses risk for each link individually and account how different impacts can have a compound effect, identify opportunities for new markets, asses full economic benefit to costs ratio for the whole supply chain, and implement climate resilience strategies for partners as well.

Process of adaptation to climate change

There are four stages in accomplishing climate change related natural disaster adaptation, screen process, climate knowledge absorption, establishing climate related operational flexibility, and strategic climate integration.

① Risk and Impact Assessment, Screening Process: The purpose of screening process is to identify the existence of potential climate change related natural disaster risks for short and long term and if a more complete risk assessment is needed or not. During screening, it classifies risk into three categories: assess now, wait and study, and take no action. There are several things that must be checked in order to determine whether climate change is potentially important in decision making (e.g. identifying sensitivities, identifying the types of decisions susceptible to climate change, evaluating the magnitude of what is at risk, etc).

The following risk assessment model assesses where further in-detailed risk assessment is needed and where risk management might be appropriate. This process consists of three stages, question, illustrated in Figure 5. Question 1 is "is climate important to business risk?" This question leads to identifying parts of business that are sensitive to climate change and the possibility of being at risk. This stage requires gathering and projecting climate and weather information for all the location in value chain (suppliers, production, distribution, customer location). Accurately quantifying uncertainty of climate effects is not necessary in this screening

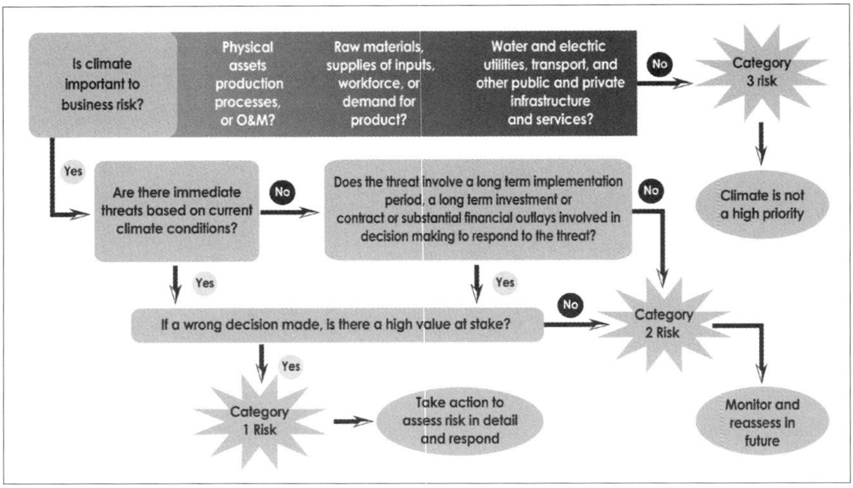

Source: Sussman & Freed, 2008

Figure 5 Screening for climate risk

process since accurate quantification is required in actual risk assessment. Applying general climate changes will be sufficient. Question 2 is "is there an immediate threat? Or are long-term assets, investments, or decisions being locked into place?" This question leads to the identification of the immediacy of potential treat. If potential risk imposes an immediate threat (e.g. deciding a long term contract with supplier which is located in climate risk hot zone) then the process continues on to question 3. Not all potential risks need immediate action and these risks can be set aside for further screening. But for risks that were determined to have immediacy in stage 2 continues on to question 3. Question 3 is "is a high value at stake if a wrong decision is made?" The last step is determining how much a wrong decision would cost. If the magnitude of costs due to wrong decision is large enough and requires additional research, this risk must be subjected to further risk assessment in detail and mitigation options. This risk would be categorized as risk 1, which is risk with potential significant climate risk that needs to be managed in the short term. It requires in-depth assessment and development of risk management strategies to adapt to climate change. Category 2 risks (risks that were set aside at the end of stage 2) have potential treats that needs to be monitored or reassessed over time. Category 3 risks (risks that are not hugely impacted by climate) are insignificant and no further action is necessary.

For operations or areas that climate is a concern, further risk assessment and mitigation-adaptation strategies need to be established. This can take the form of identifying alternative suppliers who can meet the required capacity or identifying lead time in the case of natural disaster. Cisco was one of the first companies to proactively manage climate change natural disasters by building resiliency into their supply chain. Cisco identified every "node" (suppliers, manufacturing partners, logistics centers and business partners responsible for other business operations) in the supply chain and made sure each node had alternate sourcing options, alternative production locations and risk buffers. Also Cisco went one step further by dispatching their risk management experts to each node to accurately assess its capacities and establish recovery plan in case of natural disasters. Thus, each node was responsible for reporting their "time to recover" when disaster strikes. Due to Cisco's proactive impact assessment, Cisco was able to identify potential exposure, see which nodes were affected and the magnitude of impact for the 2008 China earthquake. The earthquake affected many other corporations while Cisco experienced no customer or revenue impact.

② Information-monitoring system: Absorbing climate knowledge and establishing a free flow information-monitoring system is essential in climate change related natural disaster adaptation since without climate information, risks cannot be assessed properly. This process is internalizing information about changes of mean temperature, dynamics, intensity, sources, consequences and future developments of disruptions. Information systems have two purposes; (1) to determine the probability that existing and planned operation facilities and other areas of the supply chain will be affected; (2) to analyze the potential impacts on them.

Cisco has an excellent climate-related crisis monitoring system. Cisco has a contract with National Center for Crisis and Continuity Coordination (NC4) and this information system provides 24/7 round the clock monitoring of natural disaster disruptions in important locations of Cisco's supply chain. Utilizing NC4 program, Cisco has mapped all its critical nodes and set its own criteria for alarms. Monitoring system takes into account previous natural disaster history of the location and climate information. If climate related disruption occurs, an alert is sent to Cisco's risk management team stating for example, "earthquake occurred within 200 miles of Cisco location". Cisco's Supply Chain Risk Management Team utilizes this information and response to potential or immediate risks. Cisco's team performs an impact assessment which includes identifying which nodes are near the natural disaster region, what parts are produced in the affected region, what mitigation/adaptation strategies Cisco should engage in, how much revenue will be lost and what part of market will be affected. After Cisco's Supply Chain Risk Management Team decides on the immediate action plan, it is passed down to different cross function units to be executed. When the 2011 Japan earthquake hit, Cisco's crisis management system sent out an alarm and Cisco's supply chain incident manager was notified within 30 minutes. Within 12 hours, Supply Chain Risk Management team was consisted and business contingency plan was fully activated. The team completed a profile of every supplier sites affected which included the extensiveness of damage, future production capacity, emergency power generation capabilities, alternate sourcing options, time-to-recover, etc. Due to the information monitoring system and Cisco's proactive mitigation strategies, Cisco was able to avoid disruptions down the supply chain in spite of the fact that more than 100 of Cisco's suppliers were hit hard by the earthquake.

③ Climate-related Operational Flexibility: Operational flexibility is defined as the ability of a manufacturing system to quickly cope with changing environment or unstable external environment. Since there are many types of environmental instabilities, different types of operational flexibility is necessary and Busch identifies three types of climate-related operational flexibility: supply flexibility, routing and process flexibility and distribution flexibility. Supply flexibility describes the ability of an organization to provide a variety of inbound resource sourcing and warehousing. This flexibility is utilized when resource supply is slowed or disrupted by climate change related disruptions. Diversifying supply channels of resources and stocking inventory is a way to strengthen supply flexibility. Routing flexibility is responsible for continuing production in case of disruption in resource supply by routing production to other production site. And process flexibility is the ability to continue producing the same products by utilizing different production system or technology. Both routing and process flexibility has the purpose of continuing production even if resources are unavailable due to climate change related disruptions. Lastly, distribution flexibility is the ability to distribute products by utilizing other distribution channels. Also building operation flexibility can include building business contingency plans, practice emergency drills and using playbooks. Playbooks are frameworks that corporations can follow in case of an emergency. It provides detailed step by step action plans which can include risk assessment methods, climate change related natural disaster impact assessment, how to implement mitigation strategies and so on.

④ Strategic Climate Integration: Strategic climate integration refers to the organizational capability to address and incorporate climate change into the continuous, long-term innovation process. Continuous innovation can be defined as the "changing experiential base of organizational activities, routines, and goals [targeting the long-term optimization of] technologies, processes, specifications, inputs, and products". There are two types of strategic integrated climate change; improvements of existing processes and the development of new process configurations. Improvements involve incremental innovation and new process requires radical innovation. Both improvement and new strategic climate integration is crucial for long-term organizational adaptation to disruptions in the environment.

Notes

- Amado, Jean-Christophe., Adams, Peter., "Value Chain Climate Resilience: A Guide to Managing Climate Impacts in Companies and Communities", Partnership for Resilience and Environmental Preparedness (PREP), 2012.
- Beermann, Marina., "Linking Corporate Climate Adaptation Strategies with Resilience Thinking", Journal of Cleaner Production, Vol 19, pp 836-842, 2011.
- Bierbaum, Rosina., Smith, Joel.B., Lee, Authur., Blair, Maria., Carter, Lynne., Chapin, F. Stuard 3rd., Fleming, Paul., Ruffo, Susan., Stults, Missy., McNeeley, Shannon., Wasley, Emily., Verduzco, Laura., "A comprehensive review of climate adaptation in the United States: more than before, but less than needed", Mitig Adapt Strateg Glob Change, Vol. 18, pp 361-406, 2013.
- Biesbroek, G. Robbert., Swart, Rob.J., Carter, Timothy.R., Cowan, Caroline., Henrichs, Thomas., Mela, Hanna., Morecroft, Michael. D., Rey, Daniela., "Europe adapts to climate change: comparing national adaptation strategies", Global Environmental Change, Vol 20, pp. 440-450, 2010.
- Busch, Timo., "Organizational Adaptation to Disruptions in the natural Environment: The Case of Climate Change", Scandinavian Journal of Management, Vol 27, pp 389-404, 2011.
- Carbon Disclosure Project (CDP), "Carbon Disclosure Project Report 2007: Global FT500", Carbon Disclosure Project (CDP), 2007.
- Chegini, A., "Climate change and adaptation: Business impacts and adaptation", London: Risk Solutions, 2005.
- Day, G. S., "The capabilities of market-driven organizations", Journal of Marketing, Vol. 58, No.4, pp.37-52, 1994.
- Economics of Climate Adaptation, "Shaping Climate-Resilient Development; a Framework for Decision Making, Economics of Climate Adaptation", ClimateWorks Foundation, Global Environment Facility, European Commission, McKinsey & Company, The Rockefeller Foundation, Standard Chartered Bank, SwissRe, 2009.
- Firth, J., Colley, M., "The adaptation tipping point: Are UK businesses climate-proof?", Acclimatise and UKCIP, Oxford, 2006.
- Hendricks, Kevin.B., Singhal, Vinod.R., "An Empirical Analysis of the Effect of Supply Chain Disruptions on Long-Run Stock Price Performance and Equity Risk of the Firm", Production and Operation Management, Vol. 14, issue 1, pp.35-52, March 2005.

- IBM, "The Smarter Supply Chain of the Future: Global Chief Supply Chain Officer Study", IBM Corporation, 2009.
- Langley, C. J., Holcomb, M. C., "Creating logistics customer Value", Journal of Business Logistics, Vol. 13, No.1, pp.1-27, 1992.
- Metcalf, Gerry., Jenkinson, Kay., "A Changing Climate for Business: Business Planning for the Impacts of Climate Change", U.K. Climate Impacts Program (UKCIP), 2005.
- Meyer, L., "Synthesis Report of IPCC's Fourth Assessment: Key Findings", Global Roundtable on Climate Change, 2008.
- Mitroff, Ian.I., Allpaslan, Murat.C., "Preparing for Evil", Harvard Business Review, April 2003.
- Nelson, D.R., Adger, W.N., Brown, K., "Adaptation to environmental change: contributions of a resilience framework", Annual Review of Environment and Resources, Vol. 32, pp. 395-419, 2007.
- Niang-Diop, I., Bosch, H., "Adaptation Policy Frameworks for Climate Change: Developing Strategies, Policies and Measures", Cambridge University Press, Cambridge, pp.185-204, 2005.
- O'Connor, John., Steele, James.B., Scott, Kristina., "Supply Chain Risk Management at Cisco: Embedding End-to-End Resiliency into Supply Chain", ISM 2012 Award for Excellence in Supply Chain Management Submission, 2012.
- O'Connor, John., "Innovating Through Supply Chain Risk Management", 94th Annual International Supply Chan Management Conference, May 2009.
- Overbye, T., Dobson, I., Jewell, W., Kezunovic, M., Sen, P.K., Tylavsky, D., "The Electric Power Industry and Climate Change: Power Systems Research Possibilities", Power Systems Engineering Research Center Publication, 2007.
- Parry, M.L., Canziani, O.F., Palutikof, J.P., Linden, van der., Hanson, C.E., "Climate Change 2007b: Impacts, Adaptation and Vulnerability. Contribution of Working Group II to the Fourth Assessment Report of the Intergovernmental Panel on Climate Change", Intergovernmental Panel on Climate Change (IPCC), Cambridge University Press, 2007.
- Resilient Organisations, "Resilience Management: a Framework for Assessing and Improving the Resilience of Organisations", Resilient Organisations, 2007.
- Schwartz, P., "Investing in global security", Harvard Business Review, Vol. 85, No.10, pp.26-28, 2007.

- Sharma, Sanjay., Vredenburg, Harrie., "Proactive Corporate Enviromental Strategy and the Development of Competitively Valuable Organizational Capabilities", Strategic Management Journal, Vol. 19, pp.729-753, 1998.
- Sussman, F. G., Freed, R., "Adapting to climate change: A business approach", Pew Center on Global Climate Change, 2008.
- Solomon, S., Qin, Manning, M., Chen, Z., Marquis, M., Averyt, K.B., Tignor, M., "Climate Change 2007a: The Physical Basis. Contribution of Working Group I to the Fourth Assessment Report of the Intergovernmental Panel on Climate Change", Intergovernmental Panel on Climate Change (IPCC), Cambridge University Press, 2007.
- UKTI, "Adapting to an Uncertain Climate: A World of Commercial Opportunities." UK Trade and Investment and The Economist Intelligence Unit, 2011
- U.S. Resilience Project, "De-risking the Supply Chain: Cisco's Risk Intelligence and Analytic Tools", U.S. Resilience Project, August 2011.
- van Bergen, B., "Climate changes your business", KPMG, 2008.

CASE STUDY 4

Port of Rotterdam: Striving for the World's Most Sustainable Port.

Home to city Rotterdam, Netherland, Port of Rotterdam is the largest, oldest and busiest port in Europe. Port of Rotterdam is the heart of Netherland and Europe's economy with a market share of 37.5%, throughput of 440.5 million tonnes, investment of 263 million euros, 226.6 million euros in profit, 1,118 employees, and 5,971 hectares of port area as of 2013. Located in the second largest city in Netherlands, Port of Rotterdam's economic and social influence goes beyond port boundaries effecting Netherlands and parts of Europe. Direct Added value was 15.5 billion euro and indirect added value was 6.7 billion euro, together accounting for 3.3% of national GDP. Also Port of Rotterdam offers indirect employment to business, universities, and research institutes. Its position as a global hub attracts many global companies to establish headquarters at the port which is vital to Netherland's economy. Due to its advantageous location on the banks of river Maas, Port of Rotterdam's history dates back to the 14th century as a small fishing harbor. Owing to the enterprising sprit of Rotterdam people, small fish trade developed into large scale trades and ship preparation business. Since then, Port of Rotterdam has further developed into a major seaport. It enjoyed the position of world's busiest port for many decades but recent growth in Asian countries has led Port of Rotterdam to take a back seat. Economic power shift towards Asia has resulted in ports such as Singapore and Shanghai to become the world's largest and busiest ports and poses a major challenge to overcome for Port of Rotterdam. In order to overcome these limitations, Port of Rotterdam strategically sets itself as an industrial complex home to many mega corporations. Port vision 2030 assesses the present of Port of Rotterdam and sets out goals and aspirations for the future. High ranking officials offer what Port of Rotterdam will represent in the future.

"In 2030, Rotterdam is Europe's most important port and industrial complex. It is a strong combination of the Global Hub and Europe's Industrial Cluster, both leaders in efficiency and sustainability. Rotterdam is closely linked to other North West European industrial and logistics areas. Leading businesses make long-term investments in the most modern facilities. Close cooperation between businesses, government and knowledge institutions results in a high-quality labor market, living environment and accessibility. Our adaptive powers are unique. This makes the complex an important cornerstone for the welfare of the region, the Netherlands and Europe in 2030."

"In 2030, Rotterdam is the leading European hub for global and intra-European cargo flows. The Global Hub for containers, fuel and energy. Rotterdam forms an integrated network with the hinterland. Rotterdam is leading in sustainable and efficient chains."

Based on interviews of management and extensive research on Port of Rotterdam, it is clear that keywords used the most and emphasized are "industrial cluster", "energy port", "efficient and sustainable", and "global hub". Port of Rotterdam aims to become a global hub by establishing various industrial clusters such as energy port and petrochemical while implementing sustainable and efficient measures to reduce CO_2 footprint. It seems Port of Rotterdam is aiming too high but with its existing strong logistics network, nothing is impossible. Port of Rotterdam already acts as a logistics hub for various cargos such as crude oil, containers, mineral oil products, coal, and iron ore. Well over 50% of Northwest Europe's refineries are stored and supplied through Rotterdam and international and intra-Europe containers have long been passing through the port. Containers to or from Ireland, Scotland, Iceland, Northern Spain, Scandinavia, Poland, the Baltic States, Russia, Greece are transported by truck or rail and transshipped to vessels. Due to excellent port infrastructure and strong hinterland connections, 53% of world's mineral oil products are stored and transshipped at Rotterdam and supplies coal to 60% of Northwest Europe's coal-fired plants. Also the newly built and under construction LNG terminal, biomass powered plants, biomass energy plants, and CO_2 transport and storage infrastructure will contribute to Port of Rotterdam becoming a major global hub for LNG, biomass, and CO_2. Port of Rotterdam is aspiring to accomplish logistics (seaport) and industry (industrial complex) by taking advantage of already existing extensive, easily accessible, reliable, inexpensive, and efficient logistics network. With investments and implements already in process, the future seems bright.

Port of Rotterdam is highly conscious of sustainability and reducing ecological footprint. They seem to realize that in order for them to survive in the long run and distinguish themselves from other competitor ports is to be environmentally friendly and be superior in quality. Port of Rotterdam strives to be a 'sustainable' global hub & industrial cluster and this becomes apparent as specific strategies and action plans are further examined. Executives, experts, and government agencies of Rotterdam agree that CO_2 reduction is best served when increased efficiency, development of new innovative technology for CO_2 reduction, and converting from traditional fossil fuel to clean energy are implemented simultaneously creating synergy. Following sections will provide current and future efforts towards sustainability and CO_2 reduction efforts implemented by Port of Rotterdam and how Port of Rotterdam is striving to become a 'green port'.

CO_2 reduction efforts

Port of Rotterdam Authority joined forces with Municipality of Rotterdam, the port business community united in Deltalinqs and the DCMR

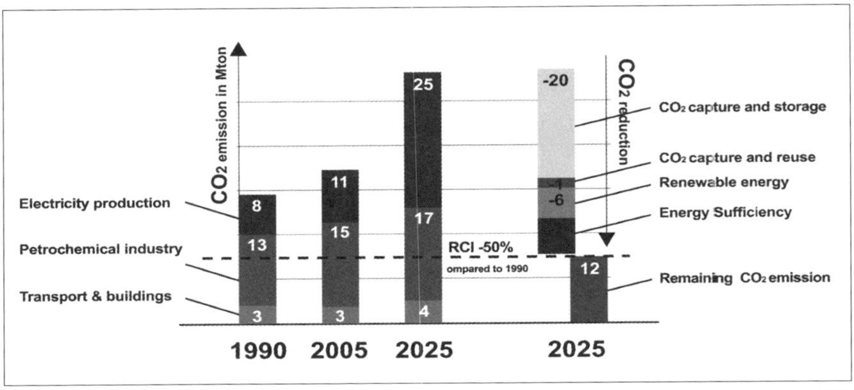

Source: port vision 2030

Figure. Target Co_2-reduction of Rotterdam climate initiative

Environmental Protection Agency Rijnmond to create Rotterdam Climate Initiative (RCI), which aims to reduce CO_2 emissions in the Rotterdam area by 50% until 2025 compared to 1990 and to reduce emission by 60% by 2030. This ambitious goal aligns with the target set by the EU, reducing 60% of CO_2 emission for transport sector in 2050 compared to 1990.

Port of Rotterdam executives, experts, and government agencies agree CO_2 reduction can be accomplished by increasing existing system's efficiency (energy efficiency), by investing in clean energy(renewable & biomass energy) and developing new technology that can bring about CO_2 reduction (CO_2 capture, storage, and reuse).

CO_2 Reduction by Increasing Efficiency

Almost every operation in the port uses energy and emits CO_2. The whole logistics system (transportation-inland and ocean shipping, handling, maintenance, storage), plants & facilities' operations, and sup-

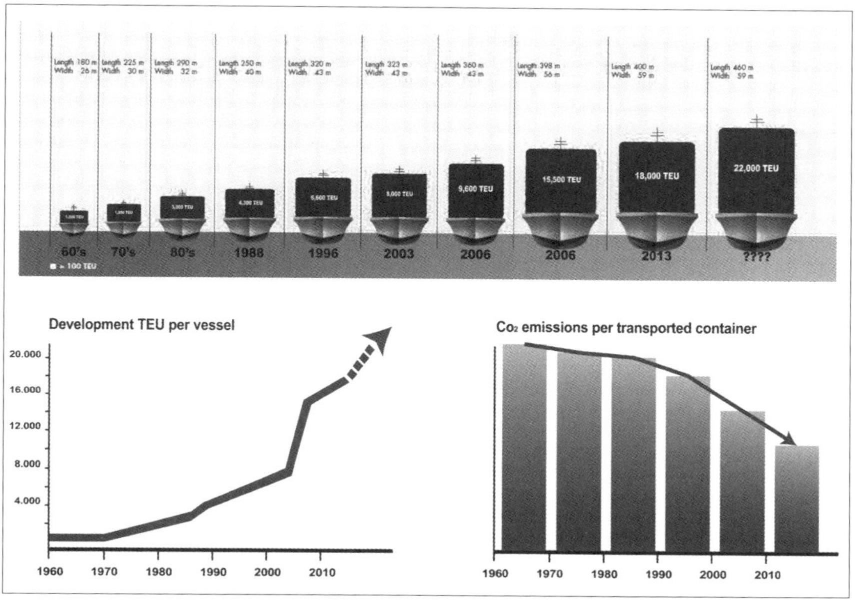

Source: port vision 2030

Figure. Development of container vessels over the years..

ply chain must be optimized and made efficient as much as possible to reduce CO_2 footprint. Increasing system efficiency leads to systems and facilities consuming less energy (fossil fuel) thus, producing less CO_2. In 2013, Port of Rotterdam reduced 6.5% of CO_2 compared to 2010 due to efforts such as utilizing efficient parts for facilities, improving vessel handling efficiency, optimizing logistics system and supply chain and other CO_2 cutting measures. Port of Rotterdam produced its first CO_2 footprint and started on reducing CO_2 in 2008. Port of Rotterdam announced their new motto 'new sailing, smarter use of fuel' and saved over 81,000 liters in 2008 alone.

Transport (ocean and inland shipping) is the core of a functioning port but is also the main source of CO_2 emission. Throughput has increased in the past (shown in figure above) and bound to increase in the future and as throughput increases, shipping and handling must become more efficient in order to reduce emissions. Figure above shows CO_2 emissions per transported container has declined over the years and this was obtained by Port of Rotterdam's efforts on centralizing shipping planning and information integration. Vessels frequently had to detour to other terminals or wait for a considerable amount of time at final destination terminal before being handled. But by improving ship handling and extensive information exchange between terminals, ship owners and other parties, lead time was minimized as well as costs and emissions. Also by sharing information with other ports and National Harbor master, vessels could optimize speed and traffic, estimate exact time of arrival, and clear space for other economic activity thus saving fuel consumption.

Port of Rotterdam is also optimizing logistics systems to cut redundant cargo flow which increases CO_2 emissions and costs. Port of Rotterdam is focusing on building an extensive network of inland hubs which will connect Port of Rotterdam to Europe's hinterland and also other surrounding ports. Before inland hubs, cargos were handled at sea terminals with limited space. At inland intermodal hubs such as Venlo and Duisburg, cargo will be transshipped and transported to their next destination. This is much more efficient in terms of cost, emission and time since it frees sea terminal space for other activities. Also hinterland transport system is specially built for rapid change between transportation modes. Several additional efforts to reduce CO_2 include using cleaner fuels such as LNG for ocean shipping and inland shipping. Port of Rotterdam also attempts to reduce CO_2 emissions at the source: more stringent emission standards for transportation, optimizing supply chain to reduce traffic by information integration, utilizing vapor-return system for loading and unloading of liquid cargo, allowing only cleanest trucks, and employing electric rail locomotives. Also cleaner engines must be used for vessels and trucks. Since 2000, it was mandatory for trucks to use EURO III engine but Port of Rotterdam is improving the standards by mandating trucks to use a EURO VI engine staring from 2014 which emits 95% less pollution. Industrial complex's infrastructure also plays a role in reducing CO_2 emissions. Plants and facilities are connected via extensive pipeline network for the purpose of exchanging heat and steam which leads to reduction in energy costs and CO_2 emissions.

CO_2 Reduction: Energy Port

Energy is a must in today's modern life. Economic and social growth of developing countries and improving living standards around the world will lead to world population growth and increased demand for raw and natural resources. But there are finite amount of raw materials such as fossil energy resources, water and minerals. Input price increase and political issues are already arising from the scarcity of resources. This calls for development of new energy sources and reducing, reusing and recycling of natural resources; becoming sustainable for long term survival and competitive advantage. Port of Rotterdam realizes the serious nature and focuses on building an energy port that is large enough to supply its customers on port with energy and also the Netherlands and Northwest Europe region. In the past, large volumes of coal and crude oil were transported and processed on port into fuel or electricity. But Port of Rotterdam is aiming to increase processing and supply of clean and renewable energy while still holding its advantageous position of supplying coal and oil. Energy capacity nearly doubled to 4,000 MW and with new power plants under construction, capacity increased to 7,000 MW in 2013 and will increase to 9,000 MW by 2030.

"In 2030, Rotterdam's industrial and energy complex functions as an integrated cluster with Antwerp, making it the largest, most modern and sustainable petrochemical and energy complex in Europe. This complex competes on a global scale, thanks to its major cluster advantages, integrated supply chains and energy efficiency. The transition to sustainable energy generation and bio-based chemicals is in full swing."

As mentioned in the interview above, Port of Rotterdam strives to become a major energy port in Europe in 2030 by offering reliable, affordable and sustainable energy and it is well on course. Its' extensive and efficient logistics system which guarantees the flow of energy raw material into and out of the port, abundant cooling water, innovative technology, and high energy demand by petrochemical industry cluster all contribute to the making of major energy port. But becoming just a major energy port in Netherlands and Northwest Europe is not sufficient. Port of Rotterdam also aspires to become the world's most sustainable seaport by 2030 and in order to do so; there must be an increase in sustainable energy and cleaner use of fossil fuels.

Cleaner use of fossil energy includes increased energy generation with natural gas (which is still fossil based but much cleaner than oil or coal) and use of coal while capturing, storing and reusing CO_2. And increasing sustainable energy includes developing generation with non-fossil fuel such as biomass and renewable energy (wind and solar). Without developing sustainable and renewable energy such as biomass, solar and wind,

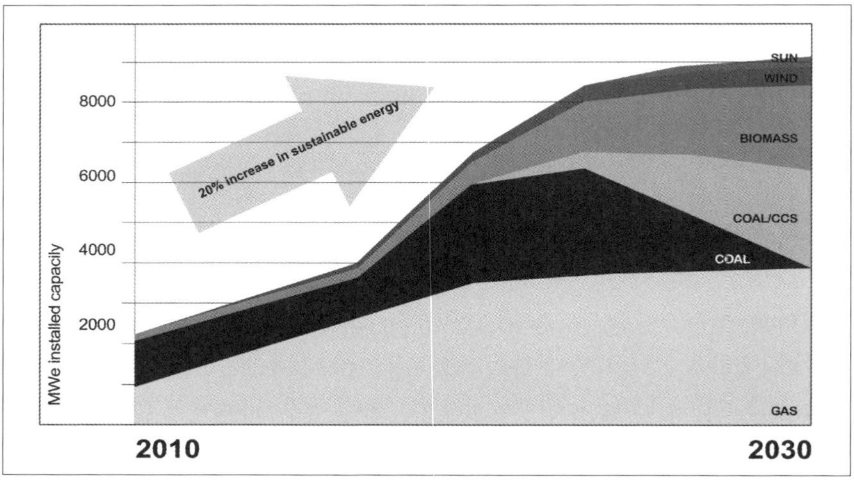

Source: port vision 2030

Figure. Energy Composition

Port of Rotterdam's energy port cannot be viable in the long run and exposed to energy security risk. As shown in the figure, Port of Rotterdam aims to increase sustainable energy generation from 10% to 30% by 2030. In 2030, energy generated will consist of 40% natural gas and 30% carbon neutral coal.

"In the future, Rotterdam will probably be the first location to cost-competitively generate wind energy, without the need for subsidies" says Wolbert Allaart, Head of Renewables at Nuon.

Its location and surrounding environmental circumstances (heavy and consistent wind) makes Port of Rotterdam ideal for wind power generation. Port of Rotterdam currently has a wind capacity of 150 MW but in order to realize these goals, Port of Rotterdam is aiming to double win capacity to 300 MW within several years by building new turbines at seven different locations including Maasvlakte 2. Goal is to increase wind capacity to at least 1400 MW by 2020. Maasvlakte 2 will become the location where new sustainable energy generation and carbon capture and storage is centralized with 108 MW of wind capacity and 400 hectares of roof space available for solar energy generation. Port of Rotterdam has a total of 3,500 hectares of ample roof space to establish a large scale solar power generation system. Port of Rotterdam will increase the use of biomass energy generation by converting fully coal-fired power plants to biomass and coal co-firing power plants.

CO_2 Reduction: New Technology (Carbon Capture and Storage)

Reduction of CO_2 via increasing efficiency and generating clean and renewable energy can only do so much. Developing new technology to reduce CO_2 such as Carbon Capture and Storage (CCS) is essential. Port of Rotterdam is striving to become a global CO_2 hub and become completely climate proof by 2025.

"Without CCS it's almost impossible to meet the climate targets. Of all the places in the world, Rotterdam is the best positioned to realize carbon capture and storage. It's already a hub for energy, for gas pipelines to the North Sea and for technology. So if Rotterdam can't do it..."

Carbon capture and storage (CCS) technology is capturing at least a quarter of CO_2 emitted from fossil-fired plants and transporting them by pipelines to empty gas fields for permanent storage and/or to be used in enhanced oil recovery. Technology behind CCS seems simple but complex in reality. When industrial or power plants are fired they emit CO_2. Part of the CO_2 is captured and moved to a capture installation. CO_2 is cleaned for sulfur dioxide, nitrogen and dust particles and injected into an absorption column in order to separate other remaining flue gases. Flue gases other than CO_2 is sent back and released to the atmosphere via chimney. Highly concentrated CO_2 is then channeled to a compressor and transported via pipeline to empty gas reservoirs 3.5 km under the sea bed of North Sea. Total capacity of reservoirs is about 35 million tones. By sealing the reservoir after maximum capacity is reached, Port of Rotterdam can emit CO_2 using fossil fuels but reduce CO_2 emissions by permanently storing them under water; a way of cleaner use of fossil fuels. CCS project is spearheaded by the Rotterdam Storage and Capture Demonstration Project (ROAD) established by E.ON and GDF Suez. CCS project consists of three phases; first phase is construction of pipelines that connects multiple plants to Maasvlakteh and has capacity to transport 3 million tones of CO_2 per year; second phase is building offshore pipelines from Maasvlakte to empty gas reservoirs in the North Sea with a capacity of 5 million tones of CO_2 per year; and third phase is to build a CO_2 shipping terminal at Maasvlakte for sea vessel CO_2 transportation. By using sea vessels, CO_2 can be transported to neighboring industrial clusters and ports in the Northwest Europe. By investing in CO_2 infrastructure, Port of Rotterdam will eventually have a capacity of twenty million tonnes in 2025. Captured CO_2 can be used in three ways; transported to empty gas fields underwater for permanent storage, recycled to generate energy or sold to greenhouses to facilitate crop growth. Port of Rotterdam has sufficient amount of CO_2 to capture since it is home to a large number of industrial and power plants that emit massive levels of CO_2 and it has the necessary infrastructure (pipeline network) that connects multiple CO_2 emitting plants throughout the port area and North Sea gas fields.

"Because of the concentration of business activities here in Rotterdam, it is possible to invest in a CO_2 infrastructure as well. Without sufficient mass, you cannot reach this point. Right from the very start, we have linked the construction of two new coal and biomass-fired power plants to the development of a parallel infrastructure for CCS" says Van Asshe from Port of Rotterdam Authority.

New plants built at Maasvlakte such as Electrabel's and E.ON's coal and biomass-fired power plant will have CO_2 capture installation and connected with pipelines to empty gas fields in North Sea. E.ON's power plant will capture a 1.1 million tonnes in a 5 year period reducing CO_2 emission into the atmosphere.

Port of Rotterdam is also considered a CO_2 hub sine it has been supplying CO_2 to neighboring greenports. Greenport is a cluster of greenhouses dedicated to cultivation and development of knowledge in the horticulture sector.

OCAP established in 2005 by Linde Gas and VolkerWessels constructed pipelines to transport CO_2 from the port to greenports. CO_2 emitted from Shell oil refinery and Abengoa bio-ethanol plant are captured, transported and used to facilitate growth in greenhouses. Approximately 0.3 tonnes of CO_2 is sold but this figure is expected to increase to 1 million in the very near future. Also plant waste produced from greenports is transported to the port for biomass fuel.

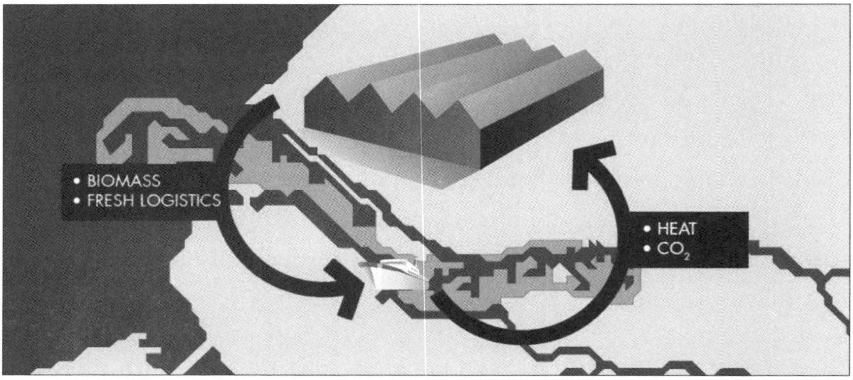

Source: Port Vision 2030

Figure. Exchange between Port of Rotterdam and Greenports.

Also Port of Rotterdam is wishing to use captured CO_2 to generate renewable energy. Starting from 2010, ANTECY is developing a technology that would transform CO_2 and solar power into renewable fuel and it is expected to be commercially available within 5 years.

Regardless of the type of business or industry, an organization needs to be sustainable in order to distinguish itself from competitors and survive in the long run. Businesses usually achieve sustainability by either reducing CO_2 emission or developing alternate sources of energy to traditional fossil fuels. Port of Rotterdam is aspiring to do both with development of renewable energy such as biomass, solar and wind energy and cutting back on CO_2 emissions through innovative technology (CCS) and emission cutting measures (increasing efficiency). Port of Rotterdam will have to prove the economical viability of these efforts but with immense investments and due diligent research, Port of Rotterdam is on the verge of becoming a benchmark for 'greening ports'.

Notes

- A. Castelein, R. Paul, P. Smits, "Port of Rotterdam Abridged Annual Report 2013; Investing in the Future", Port of Rotterdam Authority, Feb 2014
- Port of Rotterdam Authority, "Port Vision 2030; Port Compass", Port of Rotterdam Authority, Dec 2011
- Bosch, Hollen, Volberda, Baaij, "The Strategic Value of the Port of Rotterdam for the International Competitiveness of the Netherlands", Rotterdam School of Management, Erasmus University Rotterdam, May 2011
- Port of Rotterdam Authority, "Port Vision 2030; Port Compass", Port of Rotterdam Authority, Dec 2011
- Port of Rotterdam Authority, "Port Vision 2030; Port Compass", Port of Rotterdam Authority, Dec 2011
- Port of Rotterdam Authority, "Port Vision 2030; Port Compass", Port of Rotterdam Authority, Dec 2011
- Port of Rotterdam Authority, "Rotterdam Energy Port", Energy Port Magazine, June 2010
- Port of Rotterdam Authority, "Sustainability Report 2008", Port of Rotterdam, Feb 2009
- Port of Rotterdam Authority, "Port Vision 2030; Port Compass", Port of Rotterdam Authority, Dec 2011
- Port of Rotterdam Authority, "Rotterdam Energy Port", Energy Port Magazine, June 2010
- Port of Rotterdam Authority, "Port Vision 2030; Port Compass", Port of Rotterdam Authority, Dec 2011
- Port of Rotterdam Authority, "Port Vision 2030; Port Compass", Port of Rotterdam Authority, Dec 2011
- Port of Rotterdam Authority, "Rotterdam Energy Port", Energy Port Magazine, June 2010
- Port of Rotterdam Authority, "Rotterdam Energy Port: Europe's Sustainable Powerhouse", Port of Rotterdam Authority, 2011
- Port of Rotterdam Authority, "Port Vision 2030; Port Compass", Port of Rotterdam Authority, Dec 2011
- ROAD homepage retrieved from http://road2020.nl/en/, accessed July 3, 2014
- Rotterdam Climate Initiative, "Development CO2 Hub in Rotterdam", Rotterdam

Climate Initiative, May 2012.

- Port of Rotterdam Authority, "Sustainability Report 2008", Port of Rotterdam, Feb 2009
- Port of Rotterdam Authority, "Rotterdam Energy Port", Energy Port Magazine, June 2010
- Rotterdam Climate Initiative, "Port of Rotterdam CO2 Hub: Crucial Stepping Stone towards Sustainable Economic Growth", Rotterdam Climate Initiative, July 2012.
- Port of Rotterdam homepage, retrieved from http://www.portofrotterdam.com/en/News/perspectives/Pages/turning-co2-fuel.aspx, accessed on July 3rd, 2014

APPENDIX I

EXTRACTIONS - INCOTERMS ® 2010 ENTRY INTO FORCE FROM 1ST JANUARY 2011 ICC

Introduction

The Incoterms® rules explain a set of three-letter trade terms reflecting business-to-business practice in contracts for the sale of goods. The Incoterms rules describe mainly the tasks, costs and risks involved in the delivery of goods from sellers to buyers.

INCOTERMS® 2010 QUICK REFERENCE CHART

	Rules for any mode or modes of transport							Rules for sea and inland waterway transport			
	EXW	FCA	CPT	CIP	DAT	DAP	DDP	FAS	FOB	CFR	CIF
	Ex Works	Free Carrier	Carriage Paid To	Carriage & Insurance Paid To	Delivered at Terminal	Delivered at Place	Delivered Duty Paid	Free Alongside Ship	Free on Board	Cost & Freight	Cost, Insurance & Freight
SERVICES	Who Pays	Who Pays	Who Pays	Who Pays	Who Pays	Who Pays	Who Pays	Who Pays	Who Pays	Who Pays	Who Pays
Export Packing	Seller	Seller	Seller	Seller	Seller	Seller	Seller	Seller	Seller	Seller	Seller
Marking & Labeling	Seller	Seller	Seller	Seller	Seller	Seller	Seller	Seller	Seller	Seller	Seller
Block and Brace	1	1	1	1	1	1	1	1	1	1	1
Export Clearance (License, EEI/AES)	Buyer	Seller	Seller	Seller	Seller	Seller	Seller	Seller	Seller	Seller	Seller
Freight Forwarder Documentation Fees	Buyer	Buyer	Seller	Seller	Seller	Seller	Seller	Buyer	Buyer	Seller	Seller
Inland Freight to Main Carrier	Buyer	2	Seller	Seller	Seller	Seller	Seller	Seller	Seller	Seller	Seller
Origin Terminal Charges	Buyer	Buyer	Seller	Seller	Seller	Seller	Seller	Buyer	Seller	Seller	Seller
Vessel Loading Charges	Buyer	Buyer	Seller	Seller	Seller	Seller	Seller	Buyer	Seller	Seller	Seller
Ocean Freight / Air Freight	Buyer	Buyer	Seller	Seller	Seller	Seller	Seller	Buyer	Buyer	Seller	Seller
Nominate Export Forwarder	Buyer	Buyer	Seller	Seller	Seller	Seller	Seller	Buyer	Buyer	Seller	Seller
Marine Insurance	3	3	3	Seller	3	3	3	3	3	3	Seller
Unload Main Carrier Charges	Buyer	Buyer	4	4	Seller	Seller	Seller	Buyer	Buyer	4	4
Destination Terminal Charges	Buyer	Buyer	4	4	4	Seller	Seller	Buyer	Buyer	4	4
Nominate On-Carrier	Buyer	Buyer	5	5	5	5	Seller	Buyer	Buyer	Buyer	Buyer
Security Information Requirements	Buyer	Buyer	Buyer	Buyer	Buyer	Buyer	Buyer	Buyer	Buyer	Buyer	Buyer
Customs Broker Clearance Fees	Buyer	Buyer	Buyer	Buyer	Buyer	Buyer	Seller	Buyer	Buyer	Buyer	Buyer
Duty, Customs Fees, Taxes	Buyer	Buyer	Buyer	Buyer	Buyer	Buyer	Seller	Buyer	Buyer	Buyer	Buyer
Delivery to Buyer Destination	Buyer	Buyer	5	5	5	5	Seller	Buyer	Buyer	Buyer	Buyer
Delivering Carrier Unloading	Buyer	Buyer	Buyer	Buyer	Buyer	Buyer	Buyer	Buyer	Buyer	Buyer	Buyer

Notes:
1 – Incoterms® 2010 do not deal with the parties' obligations for stowage within a container and therefore, where relevant, the parties should deal with this in the sales contract.
2 – FCA Seller's Facility – Buyer pays inland freight; other FCA qualifiers. Seller arranges and loads pre-carriage carrier and pays inland freight to the "F" delivery place
3 – Incoterms® 2010 does not obligate the buyer nor must the seller to insure the goods, therefore this issue be addressed elsewhere in the sales contract.
4 – Charges paid by Buyer or Seller depending on contract of carriage.
5 – Charges paid by Seller if through Bill of Lading or door-to-door rate to Buyer's destination

INCOTERMS® IS A REGISTERED TRADEMARK OF THE INTERNATIONAL CHAMBER OF COMMERCE. THIS DOCUMENT IS NOT INTENDED AS LEGAL ADVICE BUT IS BEING PROVIDED FOR REFERENCE PURPOSES ONLY. USERS SHOULD SEEK SPECIFIC GUIDANCE FROM INCOTERMS® 2010 AVAILABLE THROUGH THE INTERNATIONAL CHAMBER OF COMMERCE AT WWW.ICCBOOKS.COM

Source: International Chamber of Commerce

Explanation of terms used in the Incoterms 2010 rules

As in the Incoterms rules, the seller's and buyer's obligations are presented in mirror fashion, reflecting under column A the seller's obligations and under column B the buyer's obligations. These obligations can be carried out personally by the seller or the buyer or sometimes, subject to terms in the contract or the applicable law, through intermediaries such as carriers, freight forwarders or other persons nominated by the seller or the buyer for a specific purpose. The text of the Incoterms 2010 rules is meant to be self-explanatory. However, in order to assist users the following text sets out guidance as to the sense in which selected terms are used throughout the document.

Carrier: For the purposes of the Incoterms 2010 rules, the carrier is the party with whom carriage is contracted.

Customs Formalities: These are requirements to be met in order to comply with any applicable customs regulations and may include documentary, security, information or physical inspection obligations.

Delivery: This concept has multiple meanings in trade law and practice, but in the Incoterms 2010 rules, it is used to indicate where the risk of loss of or damage to the goods passes from the seller to the buyer.

Delivery document: This phrase is now used as the heading to article A8. It means a document used to prove that delivery has occurred. For many of the Incoterms 2010 rules, the delivery document is a transport document or corresponding electronic record. However, with EXW, FCA, FAS and FOB, the delivery document may simply be a receipt. A delivery document may also have other functions, for example as part of the mechanism for payment.

Electronic record or procedure: A set of information constituted of one or more electronic messages and, where applicable, being functionally equivalent with the corresponding paper document.

Packaging: this word is used for different purposes:

1. The packaging of the goods to comply with any requirements under the contract of sale.
2. The packaging of the goods so that they are fit for transportation.
3. The stowage of the packaged goods within a container or other means of transport.

In the Incoterms 2010 rules, packaging means both the first and second of the above. The Incoterms 2010 rules do not deal with the parties' obligations for stowage within a container and therefore, where relevant, the parties should deal with this in the sale contract.

RULES FOR ANY MODE OR MODES OF TRANSPORT

EXW
EX WORKS
EXW (insert named place of delivery) Incoterms® 2010

GUIDANCE NOTE

The rule may be used irrespective of the mode of transport selected and may also be used where more than one mode of transport is employed. It is suitable for domestic trade, while FCA is usually more appropriate for international trade.

"Ex works" means that the seller delivers when it places the goods at the disposal of the buyer at the seller's premises or another named place (i.e. works, factory, warehouse, etc.). The seller does not need to load the goods on any collecting vehicle, nor does it need to clear the goods for export, where such clearance is applicable.

The parties are well advised to specify as clearly as possible the point within the named place of delivery, as the costs and risks to that point are for the account of the seller. The buyer bears all costs and risks involved in taking the goods from the agreed point, if any, at the named place of delivery.

EXW represents the minimum obligation for the seller. The rule should be used with care as:

a) The seller has no obligation to the buyer to load the goods, even though in practice the seller may be in a better position to do so. If the sell does load the goods, it does so at the buyer's risks and expense. In cases where the seller is in a better position to load the goods, FCA, which obliges the seller to do so at its own risk and expense, is usually more appropriate.

b) A buyer who buys from a seller on an EXW basis for export needs to be aware that the seller has an obligation to provide only such assistance as the buyer may require to effect that export: the seller is not bound to organize the export clearance. Buyers are therefore well advised not to use EXW if they cannot directly or indirectly obtain export clearance.

c) The buyer has limited obligations to provide to the seller any information regarding the export of the goods. However, the seller may need this information for, e.g., taxation or reporting purposes.

FCA
Free Carrier
FCA (insert named place of delivery) Incoterms® 2010

GUIDANCE NOTE

The rule may be used irrespective of the mode of transport selected and may also be used where more than one mode of transport is employed.

"Free Carrier" means that the seller delivers the goods to carrier or another person nominated by the buyer at the seller's premises or another named place. The parties are well advised to specify as clearly as possible the point within the named place of delivery, as the risk passes to the buyer at that point.

If the parties intend to deliver the goods at the seller's premises, they should identify the address of those premises as the named place of delivery. If, on the other hand, the parties intend the goods to be delivered at another place, they must identify a different specific place of delivery.

FCA requires the seller to clear the goods for export, where applicable. However, the seller has no obligation to clear the goods for import, pay any import duty or carry out any import customs formalities.

CPT
CARRIAGE PAID TO
CPT (insert named place of destination) Incoterms® 2010

GUIDANCE NOTE

This rule may be used irrespective of the mode of transport selected and may also be used where more than one mode of transport is employed.

"Carriage Paid To" means that the seller delivers the goods to the carrier or another person nominated by the seller at an agreed place (if any such place is agreed between the parties) and that the seller must contract for and pay the costs of carriage necessary to bring the goods to the named place of destination.

When CPT, CIP, CFR or CIF are used, the seller fulfils its obligation to deliver when it hands the goods over to the carrier and not when the goods reach the place of destination.

This rule has two critical points, because risk passes and costs are transferred at different places. The parties are well advised to identify as precisely as possible in the contract both the place of delivery, where the risk passes to the buyer, and the named place of destination to which the seller must contract for the carriage. If several carriers are used for the carriage to the agreed destination and the parties do not agree on a specific point of delivery, the default position is that risk passes when the goods have been delivered to the first carrier at a point entirely of the seller's choosing and over which the buyer has no control. Should the parties wish the risk to pass at a later stage (e.g., at an ocean port or airport), they need to specify this in their contract of sale.

The parties are also well advised to identify as precisely as possible the point within the agreed place of destination, as the costs to that point are for the account of the seller. The seller is advised to procure contracts of carriage that match this choice precisely. If the seller incurs costs under its contract of carriage related to unloading at the named place of destination, the seller is not entitled to recover such costs from the buyer unless otherwise agreed between the parties.

CPT requires the seller to clear the goods for export, where applicable. However, the seller has no obligation to clear the goods for import, pay any import duty or carry out any import customs formalities.

CIP

CARRIAGE TO INSURANCE PAID TO

CIP (insert named place of destination) Incoterms® 2010

GUIDANCE NOTE

This rule may be used irrespective of the mode of transport selected and may also be used where more than one mode of transport is employed.

"Carriage and Insurance Paid to" means that the seller delivers the goods to the carrier or another person nominated by the seller at an agreed place (if any such place is agreed between the parties) and that the seller must contract for and pay the costs of carriage necessary to bring the goods to the named place of destination.

The seller also contracts for insurance cover against the buyer's risk of loss of or damage to the goods during the carriage. The buyer should note that under CIP the seller is required to obtain insurance only on minimum cover. Should the buyer wish to have more insurance protection, it will need either to agree as much expressly with the seller or to make its own extra insurance arrangements.

When CPT, CIP, CFR or CIF are used, the seller fulfils its obligation to deliver when it hands the goods over to the carrier and not when the goods reach the place of destination.

This rule has two critical points, because risk passes and costs are transferred at different places. The parties are well advised to identify as precisely as possible in the contract both the place of delivery, where the risk passes to the buyer, and the named place of destination to which the seller must contract for carriage. If several carriers are used for the carriage to the agreed destination and the parties do not agree on a specific point of delivery, the default position is that risk passes when the goods have been delivered to the first carrier at a point entirely of the seller's choosing and over which the buyer has no control. Should the parties wish the risk to pass at a later stage (e.g., at an ocean port or an airport), they need to specify this in their contract of sale.

The parties are also well advised to identify as precisely as possible the point within the agreed place of destination, as the costs to that point are for the account of the seller. The seller is advised to procure contracts of carriage that match this choice precisely. If the seller incurs costs under its contract of carriage related to unloading at the named place of destination, the seller is not entitled to recover such costs from the buyer unless otherwise agreed between the parties.

CIP requires the seller to clear the goods for export, where applicable. However, the seller has no obligation to clear the goods for import, pay any import duty or carry out any import customs formalities.

DAT
DELIEVERED AT TERMINAL
DAT (insert named terminal at port or place of destination) Incoterms® 2010

GUIDANCE NOTE

This rule may be used irrespective of the mode of transport selected and may also be used where more than one mode of transport is employed.

"Delivered at Terminal" means that the seller delivers when the goods, once unloaded from the arriving means of transport, are placed at the disposal of the buyer at a named terminal at the named port or place of destination. "Terminal" includes any place, whether covered or not, such as a quay, warehouse, container yard or road, rail or air cargo terminal. The seller bears all risks involved in bringing the goods to and unloading them at the terminal at the named port or place of destination.

The parties are well advised to specify as clearly as possible the terminal and, if possible, a specific point within the terminal at the agreed port or place of destination, as the risks to that point are for the account of the seller. The seller is advised to procure a contract of carriage that matches this choice precisely.

Moreover, if the parties intend the seller to bear the risks and costs involved in transporting and handling the goods from the terminal to another place, then the DAP or DDP rules should be used.

DAT requires the seller to clear the goods for export, where applicable.

However, the seller has no obligation to clear the goods for import, pay any import duty or carry out any import customs formalities.

DAP
DELIVERED AT PLACE
DAP (insert named terminal at port or place of destination) Incoterms® 2010

GUIDANCE NOTE

This rule may be used irrespective of the mode of transport selected and may also be used where more than one mode of transport is employed.

"Delivered at Place" means that the seller delivers when the goods are placed at the disposal of the buyer on the arriving means of transport ready for unloading at the named place of destination. The seller bears all risks involved in bringing the goods to the named place.

The parties are well advised to specify as clearly as possible the point within the agreed place of destination, as the risks to that point are for the account of the seller. The seller is advised to procure contracts of carriage that match this choice precisely. If the seller incurs costs under its contract of carriage related to unloading at the place of destination, the seller is not entitled to recover such costs from the buyer unless otherwise agreed between the parties.

DAP requires the seller to clear the goods for export, where applicable. However, the seller has no obligation to clear the goods for import, pay any import duty or carry out any import customs formalities. If the parties wish the seller to clear the goods for import, pay any import duty and carry out any import customs formalities, the DDP term should be used.

DDP

DELIVERED DUTY PAID

DDP (insert named terminal at port or place of destination) Incoterms® 2010

GUIDANCE NOTE

This rule may be used irrespective of the mode of transport selected and may also be used where more than one mode of transport is employed.

"Delivered Duty Paid" means that the seller delivers the goods when the goods are placed at the disposal of the buyer, cleared for import on the arriving means of transport ready for unloading at the named place of destination. The seller bears all the costs and risks involved in bringing the goods to the place of destination and has an obligation to clear the goods not only for export but also for import, to pay any duty for both export and import and to carry out all customs formalities.

DDP represents the maximum obligation for the seller.

The parties are well advised to specify as clearly as possible the point within the agreed place of destination, as the costs and risks to that point are for the account of the seller. The seller is advised to procure contracts of carriage that match this choice precisely. If the seller incurs costs under its contract of carriage related to unloading at the place of destination, the seller is not entitled to recover such costs from the buyer unless otherwise agreed between the parties.

The parties are well advised not to use DDP if the seller is unable directly or indirectly to obtain import clearance.

If the parties wish the buyer to bear all risks and costs of import clearance, the DAP rule should be used.

Any VAT or other taxes payable upon import are for the seller's account unless expressly agreed otherwise in the sales contract.

RULES FOR SEA AND INLAND WATERWAY TRANSPORT

FREE ALONGSIDE SHIP

FAS (insert named port of shipment) Incoterms® 2010

GUIDANCE NOTE

This rule is to be used only for sea or inland waterway transport.

"Free Alongside Ship" means that the seller delivers when the goods are placed alongside the vessel (e.g., on a quay or a barge) nominated by the buyer at the named port of shipment. The risk of loss of or damage to the goods passes when the goods are alongside the ship, and the buyer bears all costs from that moment onwards.

The parties are well advised to specify as clearly as possible the loading point at the named port of shipment, as the costs and risks to that point are for the account of the seller and these costs and associated handling charges may vary according to the practice of the port.

The seller is required either to deliver the goods alongside the ship or to procure goods already so delivered for shipment. The reference to "procure" here caters for multiple sales down a chain ('string sales'), particularly common in the commodity trades.

Where the goods are in containers, it is typical for the seller to hand the goods over to the carrier at a terminal and not alongside the vessel. In such situations, the FAS rule would be inappropriate, and the FCA rule should be used.

FAS requires the seller to clear the goods for export, where applicable. However, the seller has no obligation to clear the goods for import, pay any import duty or carry out any import customs formalities.

FOB

FREE ON BOARD

FOB (insert named port of shipment) Incoterms® 2010

GUIDANCE NOTE

This rule is to be used only for sea or inland waterway transport.

"Free on Board" means that the seller delivers the goods on board the vessel nominated by the buyer at the named port of shipment or procures the goods already so delivered. The risk of loss of or damage to the goods passes when the goods are on board the vessel, and the buyer bears all costs from that moment onwards.

The seller is required either to deliver the goods on board the vessel or to procure goods already so delivered for shipment. The reference to "procure" here caters for multiple sales down a chain ('string sales'), particularly common in the commodity trades.

FOB may not be appropriate where goods are handed over to the carrier before they are on board the vessel, for example goods in containers, which are typically delivered at a terminal. In such situations, the FCA rule should be used.

FOB requires the seller to clear the goods for export, where applicable. However, the seller has no obligation to clear the goods for import, pay any import duty or carry out any import customs formalities.

A. THE SELLER'S OBLIGATIONS

A1. General provision of the seller

The seller must provide the goods and the commercial invoice in conformity with the contract of sale and any other evidence of conformity that may be required by the contract.

Any document referred to in A1-A10 may be an equivalent electronic record or procedure if agreed between the parties or cusotmary.

A2. Licences, authorisations, security clearance and other formalities

Where applicable, the seller must obtain, at its own risk and expense, any export licence or other official authorization and carry out all customs formalities necessary for the export of the goods.

A3. Contracts of carriage and insurance

a) Contract of carriage

The seller has no obligation to the buyer to make a contract of carriage. However, if requested by the buyer or if it is commercial practice and the buyer does not give an instruction to the contrary in due time, the seller may contract for carriage on usual terms at the buyer's risk and expense. In either case, the seller may decline to make the contract of carriage and, if it does, shall promptly notify the buyer.

b) Contract of insurance

The seller has no obligation to the buyer to make a contract of insurance. However, the seller must provide the buyer, at the buyer's request, risk, and expense (if any), with information that the buyer needs for obtaining insurance.

A4. Delivery

The seller must deliver the goods either by placing them on board the vessel nominated by the buyer at the loading point, if any, indicated by the buyer at the named port of shipment or by procuring the goods so delivered. In either case, the seller must deliver the goods on the agreed date or within the agreed period and in the manner customary at the port.

If no specific loading point has been indicated by the buyer, the seller may select the point within the named port of shipment that best suits its purpose.

A5. Transfer of risks

The seller bears all risks of loss of or damage to the goods until they have been delivered in accordance with A4 with the exception of loss or damage in the circumstances described in B5.

A6. Allocation of costs

The seller must pay

a) all costs relating to the goods until they have been delivered in accordance with A4, other than those payable by the buyer as envisaged in B6; and
b) where applicable, the costs of customs formalities necessary for export, as well as all duties, taxes and other charges payable upon export.

A7. Notices to the buyer

The seller must, at the buyer's risk and expense, give the buyer sufficient notice either that the goods have been delivered in accordance with A4 or that the vessel has failed to take the goods within the time agreed.

A8. Delivery document

The seller must provide the buyer, at the seller's expense, with the usual proof that the goods have been delivered in accordance with A4.

Unless such proof is a transport document, the seller must provide assistance to the buyer, at the buyer's request, risk and expense, in obtaining a transport document.

A9. Checking –packing–marking

The seller must pay the costs of those checking operations (such as checking quality, measuring, weighing, counting) that are necessary for the purpose of delivering the goods in accordance with A4, as well as the costs of any pre-shipment inspection mandated by the authority of the country of export.

The seller must, at its own expense, package the goods, unless it is usual for the particular trade to transport the type of goods sold unpackaged. The seller may package the goods in the manner appropriate for their transport, unless the buyer has notified the seller of specific packaging requirements before the contract of sale is concluded. Packaging is to be marked appropriately.

A10. Assistance with information and related costs

The seller must, where applicable, in a timely manner, provide to or render assistance in obtaining for the buyer, at the buyer's request, risk and expense, any documents and information, including security-related information, that the buyer needs for the import of the goods and/or for their transport to the final destination.

The seller must reimburse the buyer for all costs and charges incurred by the buyer in providing or rendering assistance in obtaining documents and information as envisaged in B10.

B. THE BUYER'S OBLIGATIONS

B1. General provision of the buyer

The buyer must pay the price of the goods as provided in the contract of sale.

Any document referred to in B1-B10 may be an equivalent electronic record or procedure if agreed between the parties or cusotmary.

B2. Licences, authorisations, security clearance and other formalities.

Where applicable, it is up to the buyer to obtain, at its own risk and expense, any import licence or other official authorization and carry out all customs formalities for the import of the goods and for their transport through any country.

B3. Contracts of carriage and insurance

a) Contract of carriage

The buyer must contract, at its own expense for the carriage of the goods from the named port of shipment, except where the contract of carriage is made by theseller as provided for in A3 a).

b) Contract of insurance The buyer has no obligation to the seller to make a contract of insurance.

B4. Taking delivery

The buyer must take delivery of the goods when they have been delivered as envisaged in A4.

B5. Transfer of risks

The buyer bears all risks of loss of or damage to the goods from the time they have been delivered as envisaged in A4.

If

a) the buyer fails to notify the nomination of a vessel in accordance with B7; or
b) the vessel nominated by the buyer fails to arrive on time to enable the seller to comply with A4, is unable to take the goods, or closes for cargo earlier than the time notified in accordance with B7; then, the buyer bears all risks of loss of or damage to the goods:

(i) from the agreed date, or in the absence of an agreed date,
(ii) from the date notified by the seller under A7 within the agreed period, or, if no such date has been notified,
(iii) from the expiry date of any agreed period for delivery, provided that the goods have been clearly identified as the contract goods.

B6. Allocation of costs

The buyer must pay

a) all costs relating to the goods from the time they have been delivered as envisaged in A4, except, where applicable, the costs of customs formalities necessary for export, as well as all duties, taxes and other charges payable upon export as referred to in A6 b);
b) any additional costs incurred, either because:

(i) the buyer has failed to give appropriate notice in accordance with B7, or

(ii) the vessel nominated by the buyer fails to arrive on time, is unable to take the goods, or closes for cargo earlier than the time notified in accordance with B7, provided that the goods have been clearly identified as the contract goods; and

c) where applicable, all duties, taxes and other charges, as well as the costs of carrying out customs formalities payable upon import of the goods and the costs for their transport through any country.

B7. Notice to the seller

The buyer must give the seller sufficient notice of the vessel name, loading point and, where necessary, the selected delivery time within the agreed period.

B8. Proof of delivery

The buyer must accept the proof of delivery provided as envisaged in A8.

A9. Inspection of goods

The buyer must pay the costs of any mandatory pre-shipment inspection, except when such inspection is mandated by the authorities of the country of export.

B10. Assistance with information and related costs

The buyer must, in a timely manner, advise the seller of any security information requirements so that the seller may comply with A10.

The buyer must reimburse the seller for all costs and charges incurred by the seller in providing or rendering assistance in obtaining documents and information as envisaged in A10.

The buyer must, where applicable, in a timely manner, provide to or render assistance in obtaining for the seller, at the seller's request, risk and expense, any documents and information, including security-related information, that the seller needs for the transport and export of the goods and for their transport through any country.

CFR

COST AND FREIGHT

CFR (insert named port of shipment) Incoterms® 2010

GUIDANCE NOTE

This rule is to be used only for sea or inland waterway transport.

"Cost and Freight" means that the seller delivers the goods on board the vessel or procures the goods already so delivered. The risk of loss of or damage to the goods passes when the goods are on board the vessel. The seller must contract for and pay the costs and freight necessary to bring the goods to the named port of destination.

When CPT, CIP, CFR or CIF are used, the seller fulfils its obligation to deliver when it hands the goods over to the carrier in the manner specified in the chosen rule and not when the goods reach the place of destination.

This rule has two critical points, because risk passes and costs are transferred at different places. While the contract will always specify a destination port, it might not specify the port of shipment, which is where risk passes to the buyer. If the shipment port is of particular interest to the buyer, the parties are well advised to identify it as precisely as possible in the contract.

The parties are well advised to identify as precisely as possible the point at the agreed port of destination, as the costs to that point are for the account of the seller. The seller is advised to procure contracts of carriage that match this choice precisely. If the seller incurs costs under its contract of carriage related to unloading at the specified point at the port of destination, the seller is not entitled to recover such costs from the buyer unless otherwise agreed between the parties.

The seller is required either to deliver the goods on board the vessel or to procure goods already so delivered for shipment to the destination. In addition, the seller is required either to make a contract of carriage or to procure such a contract. The reference to "procure" here caters for multiple sales down a chain ('string sales'), particularly common in the commodity trades.

CFR may not be appropriate where goods are handed over to the carrier before they are on board the vessel, for example goods in containers, which are typically delivered at a terminal. In such circumstances, the CPT rule should be used.

CFR requires the seller to clear the goods for export, where applicable. However, the seller has no obligation to clear the goods for import, pay any import duty or carry out any import customs formalities.

CIF
COST INSURNACE AND FREIGHT
CIF (insert named port of shipment) Incoterms® 2010

GUIDANCE NOTE

This rule is to be used only for sea or inland waterway transport.

"Cost, Insurance and Freight" means that the seller delivers the goods on board the vessel or procures the goods already so delivered. The risk of loss of or damage to the goods passes when the goods are on board the vessel.

The seller must contract for and pay the costs and freight necessary to bring the goods to the named port of destination.

The seller also contracts for insurance cover against the buyer's risk of loss of or damage to the goods during the carriage. The buyer should note that under CIF the seller is required to obtain insurance only on minimum cover.

Should the buyer wish to have more insurance protection, it will need either to agree as much expressly with the seller or to make its own extra insurance arrangements.

When CPT, CIP, CFR, or CIF are used, the seller fulfils its obligation to deliver when it hands the goods over to the carrier in the manner specified in the chosen rule and not when the goods reach the place of destination.

This rule has two critical points, because risk passes and costs are transferred at different places. While the contract will always specify a destination port, it might not specify the port of shipment, which is where risk passes to the buyer. If the shipment port is of particular interest to the buyer, the parties are well advised to identify it as precisely as possible in the contract.

The parties are well advised to identify as precisely as possible the point at the agreed port of destination, as the costs to that point are for the account of the seller. The seller is advised to procure contracts of carriage that match this choice precisely. If the seller incurs costs under its contract of carriage related to unloading at the specified point at the port of destination, the seller is not entitled to recover such costs from the buyer unless otherwise agreed between the parties.

The seller is required either to deliver the goods on board the vessel or to procure goods already so delivered for shipment to the destination. In addition the seller is required either to make a contract of carriage or to procure such a contract. The reference to "procure" here caters for multiple sales down a chain ('string sales'), particularly common in the commodity trades.

CIF may not be appropriate where goods are handed over to the carrier before they are on board the vessel, for example goods in containers, which are typically delivered at a terminal. In such circumstances, the CIP rule should be used.

CIF requires the seller to clear the goods for export, where applicable. However, the seller has no obligation to clear the goods for import, pay any import duty or carry out any import customs formalities.

A. THE SELLER'S OBLIGATIONS

A1. General provision of the seller

The seller must provide the goods and the commercial invoice in conformity with the contract of sale and any other evidence of conformity that may be required by the contract.

Any document referred to in A1-A10 may be an equivalent electronic record or procedure if agreed between the parties or cusotmary.

A2. Licences, authorisations, security clearance and other formalities

Where applicable, the seller must obtain, at its own risk and expense, any export licence or other official authorization and carry out all customs formalities necessary for the export of the goods.

A3. Contracts of carriage and insurance

a) Contract of carriage

The seller must contract or procure a contract for the carriage of the goods from the agreed point of delivery, if any, at the place of delivery to the named port of destination or, if agreed, any point at that port. The contract of carriage must be made on usual terms at the seller's expense and provide for carriage by the usual route in a vessel of the type normally used for the transport of the type of goods sold.

b) Contract of insurance

The seller must obtain, at its own expense, cargo insurance complying at least with the minimum cover provided by Clauses (C) of the Institute Cargo Clauses (LMA/IUA) or any similar clauses. The insurance shall be contracted with underwriters or an insurance company of good repute and entitle the buyer, or any other person having an insurable interest in the goods, to claim directly from the insurer.

When required by the buyer, the seller shall, subject to the buyer providing any necessary information requested by the seller, provide at the buyer's expense any additional cover, if procurable, such as cover as provided by Clauses (A) or (B) of the Institute Cargo Clauses (LMA/IUA) or any similar clauses and/or cover complying with the Institute War Clauses and/or Institute Strikes Clauses (LMA/IUA) or any similar clauses.

The insurance shall cover, at a minimum, the price provided in the contract plus 10% (i.e., 110%) and shall be in the currency of the contract.

The insurance shall cover the goods from the point of delivery set out in A4 and A5 to at least the named port of destination. The seller must provide the buyer with the insurance policy or other evidence of insurance cover. Moreover, the seller must provide the buyer, at the buyer's request, risk, and expense (if any), with information that the buyer needs to procure any additional insurance.

A4. Delivery

The seller must deliver the goods either by placing them on board the vessel or by procuring the goods so delivered. In either case, the seller must deliver the goods on the agreed date or within the agreed period and in the manner customary at the port.

A5. Transfer of risks

The seller bears all risks of loss of or damage to the goods until they have been delivered in accordance with A4, with the exception of loss or damage in the circumstances described in B5.

A6. Allocation of costs

The seller must pay

a) all costs relating to the goods until they have been delivered in accordance with A4, other than those payable by the buyer as envisaged in B6;
b) the freight and all other costs resulting from A3 a), including the costs of loading the goods on board and any charges for unloading at the agreed port of discharge that were for the seller's account under the contract of carriage;
c) the costs of insurance resulting from A3 b); and
d) where applicable, the costs of customs formalities necessary for export, as well as all duties, taxes and other charges payable upon export, and the costs for their transport through any country that were for the seller's account under the contract of carriage.

A7. Notices to the buyer

The seller must give the buyer any notice needed in order to allow the buyer to take measures that are normally necessary to enable the buyer to take the goods.

A8. Delivery document

The seller must, at its own expense provide the buyer without delay with the usual transport document for the agreed port of destination.

This transport document must cover the contract goods, be dated within the period agreed for shipment, enable the buyer to claim the goods from the carrier at the port of destination and, unless otherwise agreed, enable the buyer to sell the goods in transit by the transfer of the document to a subsequent buyer or by notification to the carrier.

When such a transport document is issued in negotiable form and in several originals, a full set of originals must be presented to the buyer.

A9. Checking –packing–marking

The seller must pay the costs of those checking operations (such as checking quality, measuring, weighing, counting) that are necessary for the purpose of delivering the goods in accordance with A4, as well as the costs of any pre-shipment inspection mandated by the authority of the country of export.

The seller must, at its own expense, package the goods, unless it is usual for the particular trade to transport the type of goods sold unpackaged. The seller may package the goods in the manner appropriate for their transport, unless the buyer has notified the seller of specific packaging requirements before the contract of sale is concluded. Packaging is to be marked appropriately.

A10. Assistance with information and related costs

The seller must, where applicable, in a timely manner, provide to or render assistance in obtaining for the buyer, at the buyer's request, risk and expense, any documents and information, including security-related information, that the buyer needs for the import of the goods and/or for their transport to the final destination.

The seller must reimburse the buyer for all costs and charges incurred by the buyer in providing or rendering assistance in obtaining documents and information as envisaged in B10.

B. THE BUYER'S OBLIGATIONS

B1. General provision of the buyer

The buyer must pay the price of the goods as provided in the contract of sale.

Any document referred to in B1-B10 may be an equivalent electronic record or procedure if agreed between the parties or cusotmary.

B2. Licences, authorisations, security clearance and other formalities

Where applicable, it is up to the buyer to obtain, at its own risk and expense, any import licence or other official authorization and carry out all customs formalities for the import of the goods and for their transport through any country.

B3. Contracts of carriage and insurance

a) Contract of carriage

The buyer has no obligation to the seller to make a contract of carriage.

b) Contract of insurance

The buyer has no obligation to the seller to make a contract of insurance. However, the buyer must provide the seller, upon request, with any information necessary for the seller to procure any additional insurance requested by the buyer as envisaged in A3 b).

B4. Taking delivery

The buyer must take delivery of the goods when they have been delivered as envisaged in A4 and receive them from the carrier at the named port of destination.

B5. Transfer of risks

The buyer bears all risks of loss of or damage to the goods from the time they have been delivered as envisaged in A4.

If the buyer fails to give notice in accordance with B7, then it bears all risks of loss of or damage to the goods from the agreed date or the expiry date of the agreed period for shipment, provided that the goods have been clearly identified as the contract goods.

B6. Allocation of costs

The buyer must, subject to the provisions of A3 a), pay

a) all costs relating to the goods from the time they have been delivered as envisaged in A4, except, where applicable, the costs of customs formalities necessary for export, as well as all duties, taxes and other charges payable upon export as referred to in A6 d);
b) all costs and charges relating to the goods while in transit until their arrival at the port of destination, unless such costs and charges were for the seller's account under the contract of carriage;
c) unloading costs including lighterage and wharfage charges, unless such costs and charges were for the seller's account under the contract of carriage;
d) any additional costs incurred if it fails to give notice in accordance with B7, from the agreed date or the expiry date of the agreed period for shipment, provided that the goods have been clearly identified as the contract goods;
e) where applicable, all duties, taxes and other charges, as well as the costs of carrying out customs formalities payable upon import of the goods and the costs for their transport through any country, unless included within the cost of the contract of carriage; and
f) the costs of any additional insurance procured at the buyer's request under A3 b) and B3 b).

B7. Notices to the seller

The buyer must, whenever it is entitled to determine the time for shipping the goods and/or the point of receiving the goods within the named port of destination, give the seller sufficient notice thereof.

B8. Proof of delivery

The buyer must accept the transport document provided as envisaged in A8 if it is in conformity with the contract.

B9. Inspection of goods

The buyer must pay the costs of any mandatory pre-shipment inspection, except when such inspection is mandated by the authorities of the country of export.

B10. Assistance with information and related costs

The buyer must, in a timely manner, advise the seller of any security information requirements so that the seller may comply with A10.

The buyer must reimburse the seller for all costs and charges incurred by the seller in providing or rendering assistance in obtaining documents and information as envisaged in A10.

The buyer must, where applicable, in a timely manner, provide to or render assistance in obtaining for the seller, at the seller's request, risk and expense, any documents and information, including security-related information, that the seller needs for the transport and export of the goods and for their transport through any country.

APPENDIX II

REVISED INCOTERMS 2010

Revised Incoterms 2010

Incoterms have provided a set of rules that the global trade community can use for the interpretation of shipping terms. The ICC has consistently attempted to update Incoterms in a way that keeps pace with the evolution of business practices. The ICC recently published the new listing of terms, which hints at some of the significant changes ahead in the new publication.

The International Chamber of Commerce has formulated and published Incoterms, which are known officially as 'international commercial terms'. The rules are periodically revised and changes were made in 1953, 1967, 1976, 1980, 1990, 2000 and 2010. The Incoterms are intended to reflect current international practices with respect to the matters covered by them, hence the periodical revision of the Incoterms.

The Background and Revision Methodology of Incoterms 2010

The ICC has reflected the changes to trade practices in the world economic environment into the Incoterms rules every decade. Incoterms 2010 became effective on January 1, 2011. The background of the revision is as follows. First, the Incoterms rules were limited to international trade in the past. Since the expansion of customs free zones, frontier-passing procedures have become meaningless. As a result, it has been permitted to apply Incoterms 2010 to both domestic and international trades. Second, in consideration of changes in the trade environment in which the use of electronic communication has skyrocketed, it was stipulated that electronic messages were as binding as paper documents. Third, since the September 11 terrorist attacks, logistics security has been strengthened around the globe, and safety on international cargo trade has become more important. As a result, it has been stipulated that contractual parties should be cooperative in securing the safety of their goods as a part of trade terms. Fourth, according to trade practices, it has been interpreted that the risk of goods shifted from the seller to the buyer when they pass the ship's rail at the port of shipment under FOB, CFR and CIF Incoterms. Due to changes in the international transport environment, however, 'a ship's rail' has become meaningless. Instead, the risk of goods shifted at the time of shipment of the goods, which alters the previous reasoning which insisted that risk is shifted when goods pass through the virtual line.

The Presentation and Characteristics of Incoterms 2010

In order to induce traders to use Incoterms correctly, the ICC publication No. 715 E on the front cover indicates: "ICC rules for the use of domestic and international trade terms." It is important to highlight the word "domestic", since Incoterms is a short expression for international commercial terms, which seems to indicate that their use is only restricted to international contracts of sale. However, by referring to Incoterms in any contract of sale, they become incorporated as part of the contract in the same manner as other terms. The inclusion of the word "domestic" is intended to promote the general use of Incoterms and particularly in countries such as the United States where the transport of the goods from seller to buyer may cover much longer distances than between parties in neighboring countries. The main changes in Incoterms 2010 from the 2000 version are as follows. Firstly, the Incoterms were divided into multimodal transport and sea and inland water transport terms. As a result, 13 trade terms were pared down to 11 terms in Incoterms 2000. In particular, the DAF, DES, DEQ and DDU terms were substituted with DAT and DAP. Delivered At Terminal (DAT) means that the seller hands over the goods which were unloaded at the named port or place of destination to the buyer without customs clearance for the importation. Delivered At Place (DAP) means that the seller hands over the goods which are ready for unloading to the buyer at the named place of destination without customs clearance for importation. The difference between DAT and DAP is that the terms of the delivery of goods are decided depending on whether or not the goods are unloaded from the carrier's means of transport. Secondly, the Incoterms rules have been applied to international trades. Due to the emergence of Regional Trade Agreements (RTA) such as in the EU, however, a national frontier has become less important. In addition, some traders have used Incoterms in domestic deals. In the U.S., in particular, the clauses on shipment and delivery terms were deleted in the revision of the Uniform Commercial Code (UCC) 2004 to apply the Incoterms rules to domestic transactions. Considering these changes, Incoterms 2010 can be applied to domestic transactions as well as to international trades. Thirdly, in Incoterms 2010, obligation rules associated with contractual parties' security were added because of the increase in terror threats and loss of property. In A10/B10, in particular, it was stipulated that contractual parties should help each other through confirmation of security information by strengthening the 'chain of custody.' For example, a party which submits confiscated drugs as a proof shall be responsible for keeping it until it is actually submitted. Security rules have been stricter on the acquisition, transfer, handling and disposition of the documents associated with this kind of case.

Under CPT, CIP, CFR, CIF, DAT and DDP terms, the seller is liable to deliver the goods to the place of destination. The seller pays all freight. Because transportation charges include the seller's sales price in general, however, it is the buyer who ultimately pays the bill. Generally, transportation charges include the handling charge of goods at a port or container terminal. Therefore, the carrier or terminal company tends to charge the buyer for the bill. Because the buyer would often pay the same service twice, Incoterms 2000 clarified the charge-related rules in A6/B6.

In Incoterms 2010, trade terms are classified by transport method. The terms which could be used regardless of the transport method include EXW, FCA, CPT, CIP, DAT, DAP and DDP while the terms which are available for sea and inland waterway transportations only are FAS, FOB, CFR and CIF.

Notes

- McCue, D.(2009). "Taking Supply Chain Security to the Next Level," *World Trade* Vol. 100, (August), pp. 28-33.
- ICC, (2010), "Incoterms® 2010" ICC Publication No. 715.
- Frank Reynolds(2011), "Revised Incoterms 2010 Take Effect", *MANAGING CREDIT, RECEIVABLES & COLLECTIONS*.
- Paul Casuccio(2012), "International Trade Other Related Subject: Sale of goods", *Global Trade and Customs Journal*. Vol 7 No 2, pp. 71.
- ICC (2010), "ICC rules for the use of domestic and international trade terms", (http://www.iccwbo.org/incoterms)
- Frank Reynolds (2010), "Incoterms 2010, With Focus on Security, Will Be More User-Friendly," *Managing Credit, Receivable & Collections* (www.ioma.com/credit).
- Sarathy, R. (2006), "Security and the Global Supply Chain," *Transportation Journal*, Vol. 45, No. 4, pp. 28-51.

Greening Global Logistics

발 행 일 | 2014년 9월 30일 초판 발행
저　　자 | Pak Myong-Sop, Hwang Seok-Joon,
Shin Soo-Yong, Kim In Sun, Justin Hiraga
발 행 인 | 홍진기
발 행 처 | 아카데미프레스
주　　소 | 413-756 경기도 파주시 문발동 출판정보산업단지 507-9
전　　화 | 031-947-7389
팩　　스 | 031-947-7698
웹사이트 | www.academypress.co.kr
이 메 일 | info@academypress.co.kr
등 록 일 | 2003. 6. 18 제406-2011-000131호
ISBN | 978-89-97544-53-0 93320

값 18,000원

* 저자와의 합의하에 인지첨부는 생략합니다.
* 잘못된 책은 바꾸어 드립니다.